A Concise History of Latin American Culture

Other Writings by
PEDRO HENRÍQUEZ UREÑA

Seis ensayos in busca de nuestra expresión (Buenos Aires, 1928; new edition, 1952, with introductory essays by Alfonso Reyes and Ezequiel Martínez Estrada).

La cultura y las letras coloniales en Santo Domingo (Buenos Aires, 1936).

Literary Currents in Hispanic America (Cambridge, Mass., 1945).

Historia de la cultura en la América Hispánica (Mexico, 1947; second edition, 1949; third edition, 1955).

Antología. A selection of prose writings, with a prologue and notes by Max Henríquez Ureña (Ciudad Trujillo, 1950).

Plenitud de América. Selected essays (Buenos Aires, 1952).

Obra crítica. Critical essays, with a prologue by Jorge Luis Borges and a complete chronological bibliography by Emma Susana Speratti Piñero (Mexico, 1960). Frontispiece portrait.

A
Concise
History
of
Latin
American
Culture

Pedro Henríquez Ureña

Translated and with a
Supplementary Chapter by
GILBERT CHASE

FREDERICK A. PRAEGER, *Publishers*
New York • Washington • London

Frederick A. Praeger, Publishers
111 Fourth Avenue, New York, N.Y. 10003, U.S.A.
77-79 Charlotte Street, London W.1, England

Published in the United States of America in 1966
by Frederick A. Praeger, Inc., Publishers

First published in Mexico in 1947 by Fondo de Cultura Económica
under the title *Historia de la cultura en la América Hispánica*

Second printing, 1967

Library of Congress Catalog Card Number: 65-18079

Printed in the United States of America

Translator's Preface

This translation is the result of the need for a text to use with a new course, "The Cultural Heritage of Latin America," that I began to teach at Tulane University in the fall of 1961. There was no book in English that would suit my purpose. A concise survey of the historical development of Hispanic American culture from a humanistic point of view, neither overemphasizing nor neglecting political, economic, and social factors, was needed. My intention, furthermore, was to let my students study the culture of Latin America from the viewpoint of Latin American writers, for it seemed to me that this viewpoint, this self-interpretation, was a significant aspect of the cultural patterns that "outsiders" would be trying to understand. Given the need, then, for the work of a Latin American and a humanist on the cultural history of Hispanic America, the writer to whom one would most naturally turn was Pedro Henríquez Ureña, whose admirable *Literary Currents in Hispanic America* had firmly established his reputation in North American academic circles. I had known and used the *Historia de la cultura en la América hispánica* ever since its publication, in Mexico, in 1947; it was clearly the book I now needed—concise, comprehensive, authoritative, humanistic. The author had no opportunity to revise and polish this work before his death; hence it is not among his most finished productions. Nevertheless, its merits outweigh any shortcomings arising from the circumstances of its posthumous publication.

It seemed evident, however, that a supplementary chapter,

bringing the book up to date, would be necessary; also, a completely new bibliography, of titles in English, was needed. It was in preparing the supplementary chapter, passing from the role of translator to that of co-author (in however small a measure), that I came to appreciate fully the amazing achievement of Henríquez Ureña in compressing within so small a compass so many different phases of culture. Not only were literature, music (even popular music!), and the fine arts included, but also science, education, the periodical press, political backgrounds, constitutional changes, and population statistics.

Since Henríquez Ureña was not a social scientist, he did not attempt in this book to define what he meant by the term "culture," but obviously it was for him a widely inclusive concept. Elsewhere, and notably in an essay on culture and the humanities (1914), he did indicate, without defining it, what culture meant to him as a humanist. The humanities were for him the heart of culture, because they revealed the secrets of human perfection and provided both a stimulus and a model for achieving perfection through education. "Education, understood in the ample human sense attributed to it by the Greeks," he said, "is the only salvation of nations."

Pedro Henríquez Ureña was born in Santo Domingo in 1884 and died in Argentina in 1946. He was brought up in a household where music, arts, and letters were both honored and loved. His mother was the celebrated poetess Salomé Ureña de Henríquez, and his father was a noted educator who became Foreign Minister and later President of the Dominican Republic. In 1901, his father brought him to the United States to learn English and enjoy the cultural advantages of New York, which he did to the fullest, frequenting lectures, concerts, art galleries, libraries, and operas. He left New York in 1904 to go to Cuba, then to Mexico, where he lived until 1914. From 1914 to 1921, he was in the United States again, first as correspondent for the *Heraldo de Cuba* and after 1916 as Instructor (later Assistant Professor) at the University of Minnesota, where he also obtained his Ph.D. with a dissertation (written in Spanish) on "La versificación irregular en la poesía castellana" (Irregular Versification in Spanish Poetry).* In 1921, he went back to Mexico, and soon afterward to Argentina, where he lived for the rest of his life, teaching at the universities of Buenos Aires and La Plata. But there was to be one more North American episode in his career: he was invited to deliver the Charles Eliot Norton Lectures at Harvard University for the academic year 1940–41. The subject he chose was "In Search of Expression: Literary and Artistic Creation in Hispanic America," taking as his point of departure the *Seis ensayos en busca de nuestra expresión* (Six Essays in Search of Our Expression), which had been published in Buenos Aires in 1928. The lectures resulted in a new book, written in English and published by the Harvard University Press in 1945 as *Literary Currents in Hispanic America* (translated into Spanish by Joaquín Díez-Canedo and published in Mexico in 1949).

In the *Historia de la cultura en la América hispánica,* Henríquez Ureña used the term "Hispanic America" to designate all of the Spanish- and Portuguese-speaking nations of the New World. He thereby excluded Haiti, which is French-speaking, as well as the British West Indies and the Guianas. For the English version of this book, the more familiar term "Latin America" has been adopted, with the understanding that it does not include the French- or English-speaking groups within that area. In calling the translation *A Concise History of Latin American Culture,* I also had in mind its nature as a compendium or manual rather than as a complete history of the subject. For Henríquez Ureña, Chapter 8, covering the period 1920–45, was "The Present Moment"; that chapter now becomes "The Immediate Past." The supplementary chapter I have added becomes "The Approximate Present," since no book can capture the actual present. I have found it advisable to make a few changes in the text, notably in the last paragraph of Chapter 1, and in parts of Chapter 8, mainly in the section

---

* *See* Alfredo A. Roggiano, *Pedro Henríquez Ureña en los Estados Unidos* ("State University of Iowa Studies in Spanish Language and Literature," No. 12 [Mexico, 1961]).

on music, but as a matter of policy, I have preferred not to make changes or revisions in the text. The original bibliography has not been included because it was largely in Spanish, and one assumes that readers of this translation do not read Spanish. A new bibliography has been prepared, entirely in English; although it is not as extensive as the original, it may at least be more useful to the present reader.

Henríquez Ureña was one of the leading intellectuals of Latin America, a scholar of remarkable achievements in his special field of philology. But he was by no means a narrow specialist, for he wrote illuminatingly and with exceptional knowledge on many subjects: music, painting, architecture, theater, dance, philosophy, sociology, history, and every branch of literature from Greek tragedy to the contemporary novel.*

In addition to his technical studies in philology and prosody, he wrote poetry, essays, newspaper articles, fiction, drama, criticism, and literary and cultural history. The words that he wrote of the great Argentine educator and statesman Domingo Faustino Sarmiento could be applied to himself: "The inflexible hand selects; the ample spirit is open to all the winds." On whatever subject he wrote, he was not only acute and lucid but also just and temperate, casting the light of reason and truth on all that he touched. In this respect, the model is provided by the first of the *Seis ensayos en busca de nuestra expresión,* titled "The Discontent and the Promise," in which he dispassionately discusses all aspects of "originality versus imitation" in Latin American literature and concludes that there is no single road to salvation. The partisans of "Europeanization" have some justification on their side, as have the partisans of "Americanization." In the end, it is the honesty and quality of the work that count: "My guiding thought has been that there is only one secret to the achievement of our expression: to work at it deeply, striving to make it pure,

* *See Homenaje a Pedro Henríquez Ureña* (Ciudad Trujillo, 1946). Four commemorative addresses delivered at the University of Santo Domingo on June 29, 1946. The frontispiece is an excellent portrait of P. H. U. as a young man.

going down to the very roots of the things that we want to say; refining, defining, with a desire for perfection."

"Maestro de América"—America's teacher—his friend Jorge Luis Borges called him; and, defining and refining the thought, he added: "A teacher is one who shows us by example a way of dealing with things, a generic style of confronting the incessant and varied universe." Pedro Henríquez Ureña was at home in all the mansions of the incessant and varied universe of the spirit. May this book bring his presence once more among our universities—the exemplary teacher, the profound scholar, the lucid writer, the serene mediator, the complete humanist.

GILBERT CHASE

Sabine Farm
Chapel Hill
June, 1966

Contents

Introduction

HISPANIC AMERICA, which is usually designated by the name of Latin America, today comprises nineteen nations. Brazil, the largest in size, is Portuguese-speaking. Eighteen are Spanish-speaking: Uruguay, Paraguay, Argentina, Chile, Bolivia, Peru, Ecuador, Colombia, Venezuela, Panama, Costa Rica, Nicaragua, Honduras, El Salvador, Guatemala, Mexico, Cuba, and Santo Domingo. To these independent nations must be added the Commonwealth of Puerto Rico, where Spanish culture, together with the language, is kept alive.

In the first half of the nineteenth century, we would have had to include also the Southwest of the United States, which was part of the Spanish empire until 1821 and afterward became part of an independent Mexico. After 1848, it lost contact with Hispanic culture (something that did not happen in Puerto Rico), but in the state of New Mexico, and in parts of Colorado, Arizona, and Texas, the Spanish language is still spoken alongside English. Since 1910 the vitality of Spanish, which had begun to decline here, has been renewed by the constant coming and going of Mexican nationals.

In the Caribbean, there are many islands, large and small, that belonged to Spain and passed into the hands of other nations—France, England, Holland, Denmark—during the seventeenth and eighteenth centuries. They retain very few traces of Spanish culture. Only in the Dutch possessions of Curaçao, Aruba, and Bonaire is there a linguistic vestige, in the form of the creole dialect called *papiamento*. This dialect, the only

[3]

one up to now that has sprung from the Spanish language in all its long history, owes its birth to the circumstance that these islands interrupted their communications with the rest of the territories governed by Spain when Holland took possession of them in 1634.

Thus Spanish has remained the standard language throughout Spanish America, and the same is true with respect to Portuguese in Brazil. This does not mean that there are no differences between these languages as they are used on the Iberian Peninsula and in the Western Hemisphere, but they are like the differences between English as it is spoken in England and as it is spoken in the United States. The example that most nearly resembles the use of English in the United States is that of Portuguese in Brazil, for political unity has brought about a relative linguistic uniformity within its borders.* The Spanish language, spread over extremely vast territories with little intercommunication, offers less uniformity. It can be said that until 1936, Madrid was the cultural and unifying center of the Spanish language in America; at the present time, this cultural direction is divided between Mexico City and Buenos Aires, the two principal publishing centers of Latin America.

There is no single Hispanic American language. The only trait common to all of Spanish America is the pronunciation "s" instead of the Castilian "th" for z and c, but this trait is also found in the Canary Islands, in a large part of Andalusia, and in the speech of many Catalans, Valencians, and Basques when they speak Spanish. The use of "y" instead of "ll" is not equally characteristic, although it is believed to be so by many. The "ll" survives in extensive regions of Colombia, Ecuador, Peru, Chile, and Argentina; on the other hand, the "y" in place of "ll" abounds in Spain, and not only in Andalusia but

---

* In the matter of spelling, however, the Portuguese language in Brazil is in a state of some confusion due to a number of orthographic changes in the 1930's and 1940's. The Brazilian writer Rubens Barba de Morais is quoted as having said: "We now have three ways of spelling—the old way, the latest way, and one's own personal way." This will explain the inconsistencies that may be found in the present translation, although an effort has been made to follow current "official" usage wherever possible.—TRANS.

also in a large part of Castile, including the common speech of Madrid. In the Americas there are five zones, not always very clearly delimited, with five ways of speaking Spanish: (1) Mexico and Central America (Guatemala, El Salvador, Honduras, Nicaragua, Costa Rica, Panama); (2) the area of the Caribbean, which comprises the Antilles, the greater part of Venezuela, and the Atlantic coast of Colombia; (3) the Andean region, comprising part of Venezuela, the greater part of Colombia, Peru, Ecuador, Bolivia, and northwestern Argentina; (4) Chile; and (5) the Río de la Plata region, comprising the greater part of Argentina, and Uruguay and Paraguay. Each one of these zones, in turn, offers regional differences within itself, as is natural. Moreover, there are many indigenous peoples who keep their own languages and who have not learned Spanish. In Mexico, for example, a little more than 1 million persons, out of a total population of more than 35 million, do not speak Spanish. But every Spanish-speaking native of the Americas, whether he comes from Mexico or from Ecuador or from Paraguay, has no difficulty in understanding or being understood by any native of Castile, of Leon, of Extremadura, or of Andalusia.

The
Indigenous
Cultures

THIRTY YEARS AGO, in discussing Latin American civilization, it would have been considered unnecessary to mention the indigenous cultures. Today, with the development and diffusion of sociological and historical studies, and of ethnology and archaeology in particular, we think differently. Although the structure of our civilization and its basic orientation come from Europe, a good many of the materials with which it has been built are autochthonous.

At the time of the Discovery, a very broad range of cultures existed in the Western Hemisphere, from the most rudimentary, such as that of the Ona Indians of southern Patagonia, to the highly complex ones of Mexico and Peru. Moreover, high cultures had existed earlier, of which only ruins remained: in Yucatán, in Guatemala, along the coast of Peru, and in the region of Tiahuanaco, near Lake Titicaca.

The variety among the indigenous peoples was enormous. Hundreds of languages were spoken. According to the classification of the French ethnologist Paul Rivet, there were 123 families. Some of these families, such as the Araucanian of Chile, comprised only one language, others included dozens: for example, the Uto-Aztec or Shoshone-Aztec, which embraced twenty-five groups in Mexico, the United States of America, and Central America; the Chibcha family in Central and South America, with sixteen types. Other large groupings include the Maya or Maya-Quiché family, in Mexico and Central America; the Arawak and the Carib, in the Antilles and South America; and the Tupí-Guaraní of southern Brazil and Paraguay.

Of these languages, those that gave the largest contingent of words to the Europeans, especially to the Spanish, were the Taino of the Greater Antilles, a language of the Arawak family; the Náhuatl, the language of the Aztecs; the Quechua of Peru; the Tupí-Guaraní; and, to a lesser extent, the Carib languages of the Antilles. Among the more familiar words the Spanish, and later English, languages derived from the Taino are *batata* or *patata, caníbal, canoa, hamaca, huracán, iguana, maíz, papaya, tabaco.* From the Náhuatl come *cacao, coyote, chicle, chile, chocolate, petate, tomate.* From the Quechua, *alpaca, cóndor, guano, llama, mate, pampa, puma, vicuña.* From the Tupí-Guaraní, *jaguar, maraca, petunia, tapioca, tapir, tucán.* A few words, notably *piragua,* come from the Carib family.

In addition to their language differences, these groups differed in even more essential respects. There were warlike peoples, such as the Caribs of the Lesser Antilles and the northern part of South America (among the more primitive tribes) and the Aztecs of Mexico (among those with a more advanced civilization); and there were peacefully inclined peoples—though not ignorant of the arts of war—such as the Tainos of the Greater Antilles and the Bahamas, whose culture was elementary, and the Quechuas of Peru, whose civilization bears the name of its rulers, the Incas.

Among the peoples who had attained to moderately advanced cultures but who did not, however, constitute civilizations with large cities and complex political structures are the Tainos, the Araucanians, the Aymaras (in the region that is now Bolivia), the Omaguacas and the Diaguitas (including the Calchiquis) of northeastern Argentina, the Guaranís of Brazil and Paraguay, and the Guetares of Costa Rica. The most advanced were the Chibchas, who occupied the *mesetas,* or tablelands, of Bogotá and Tunja, in Colombia. At the time of the Spanish Conquest, they appear to have been on the point of organizing a sort of empire. They were remarkable for their work in metals, ceramics, and textiles, but little remains of their architecture, which was mostly of wood. According to some archaeologists, the Quimbayas, famous for their miniature sculptures in embossed gold, were Chibchas; according to others, they, like the Tainos, were Arawaks. Among these tribes, the most important activities were agriculture, weaving, pottery, and building. Construction was generally in wood or adobe, occasionally in stone.

Neither among the more primitive tribes nor among the peoples with superior cultures was the domestication of animals very advanced. The Tainos, for example, had domesticated none—which is explained by the fact that in the Antilles there are very few mammals or fowl that might be of some use. In Mexico, the turkey had been domesticated, and in large sections of the Andean region the llama and the alpaca were domesticated and used as beasts of burden. Their woolly skins and their meat were also put to use. The guanaco and the vicuña, ruminants of the same family as the llama and the alpaca, remained wild, but the Indians utilized their flesh and their wool. The dog and the guinea pig were domesticated in various places. Some tribes raised tortoises (for food), bees (for honey), and parrots (for amusement). The horse, which had existed in both North and South America, became extinct before the beginning of the advanced cultures. In all the coastal areas, fishing was practiced, and in Peru, fish were brought from the sea to the highland capital of Cuzco for the delectation of the Incas. The coastal people were skillful in making boats, as witness the canoes of the Tainos and the piraguas of the Caribs, while the inland Aztecs and the Aymaras built boats to navigate the lakes and canals.

The cultivation of plants reached a truly remarkable development. It is well known that the cultivation of a plant requires, at times, the prolonged efforts of man in order to render it useful as food or medicine, or as material for construction, or for textiles or dyes, or even ornamentation. The Americas have given the civilized world many of its most important plants: cacao (from which cocoa and chocolate are made), maize (Indian corn), the potato and sweet potato, the yuca or manioc, the tomato, the avocado, the peanut, the guava, the papaya, the pineapple, the sapota and the sapotilla (which, besides being luscious fruit, also produce the chicle from which chewing gum is made), the trees from which rubber is extracted, tobacco, cacti, American agave or aloe (from which fiber for rope is made), yerba maté or maté (from which a drink is made by infusion), the quina or cinchona tree (from which quinine is extracted), ipecacuana (a medicinal root), jalapa (another medicinal plant), the guayacan or lignum vitae tree, sarsaparilla, coca, vanilla, logwood (*palo de campeche,* used for dyes), brazilwood, mahogany, jacaranda or palisander, and species of beans, gourds, red peppers, palms, pines, and cotton plants.

High cultures were developed in three regions of the New World: (1) in the central and southern parts of Mexico now occupied by the states of Oaxaca, Veracruz, Puebla, Tlaxcala, Hidalgo, Morelos, Mexico, and the Federal District; (2) in the territory now occupied by the states of Yucatán, Campeche, Tabasco, and Chiapas; in the region that is now the republics of Guatemala, Honduras, and El Salvador; and in British Honduras; (3) in the territory that is now the republics of Peru, Ecuador, and Bolivia.

It is difficult to determine how many civilizations there were in Mexico and to what periods they belong. They probably originated in the first centuries of the Christian era, after the so-called archaic cultures, and it is estimated that they reached their apogee between the seventh and the fifteenth centuries. Of the great cultures, the oldest in the central part of Mexico are the Teotihuacán (probably fourth to ninth centuries) and the Toltec, about which, until recently, there was little but conjecture. Its center, Tula, was founded in the eighth century and was destroyed in the eleventh or twelfth.

Among later cultures, the most important were the Totonac,

in Veracruz and Puebla, and the Zapotec and Mixtec, in Oaxaca. They are characterized by monuments in the form of truncated pyramids, used for purposes of worship and usually topped by a temple. The most notable are the pyramids of the Sun and the Moon in Teotihuacán, a short distance from Mexico City. The Pyramid of the Sun is not as high as the famous pyramids of Egypt, but has a larger volume. Other interesting monuments are found in Tula, Cholula, El Tajín, Tenayuca, Calixtlahuaca, and Tepoztlán. There are also important ruins in Mochicalco, Mitla, and Monte Albán, including tombs with an extraordinary wealth of jewels. The art of sculpture had been developed to a high level, comparable to any of the other great cultures of the world. Some of the masterpieces are, in the words of the English art critic Roger Fry, "strangely similar to the best works of the civilizations of the Old World."

The civilization of the Mayas and the Quichés, which flourished from the fourth to the fifteenth centuries, in the Yucatán Peninsula and in Central America, has left large constructions in stone—a multitude of pyramids, temples, and palaces adorned with remarkable sculptures, as at Tikal, Copán, Yaxchilán, Palenque, Piedras Negras, Quiriguá, Tulum, Sayil, Uxmal, Chichén Itzá. These "cities"—believed to have been religious centers rather than cities proper, as their population was dispersed about the vicinity—were not all contemporaneous. According to Indian tradition, some were abandoned as others were built. Still others were destroyed by war. When the Spaniards arrived, the principal sites had been in ruins for some time; after the Conquest, a few were preserved, but the last of them, Tayasal, was destroyed in 1697.

The Mayas and the Quichés had extensive and precise astronomical knowledge, which was not surpassed by Europe until the sixteenth century. They also had a grasp of advanced mathematical concepts. At the beginning of the Christian era, five centuries ahead of the Hindus, they utilized the zero and the principle of position, which enormously facilitate mathematical calculation. They had writing, which had begun as a system of ideographs, in the manner of the ancient Egyptian hieroglyphs, and had made some advances toward a phonetic method, the conventional representation of the basic sounds of speech, as in the European languages. They were, moreover, in the habit of preserving their religious and historical traditions in writing, and when they learned the Latin alphabet from the Spaniards, they used it to write in their own languages. Several of their most important works were preserved in this manner: the *Popol Vuh* (or *Popol Buj*), the Quiché book on the origins of the world and of man; the *Rabinal Achí,* a Quiché drama of war (the Mayas and the Quichés, like the Aztecs of Mexico and the Quechuas of Peru, had a form of drama of a ritualistic type, as all theater was in its origins); the *Annals of the Cakchiqueles,* a tribe of Guatemala; the magic books of *Chilam Balam,* of Yucatecan origin; and many other works.

In the Andean region were to be found the civilizations of Tiahuanaco, at least two of which are known to have existed successively. Important ruins remain of edifices made of enormous stones. From the way they face, it has been inferred that their builders had some knowledge of astronomy. On the coast of Peru, the principal civilizations were the Chimu, in the north, and the Nazca, in the south. The Chimus, who had at least one large city (Chan-Chan), are remembered today for their ceramics, especially the portrait vases of unexcelled realism. The Nazcas built truncated pyramids and made pottery of high artistic value, as well as skillfully colored textiles.

The two civilizations that were flourishing in the sixteenth century, at the time of the Conquest, were the Mexican and the Peruvian. To these two great political entities, the Spaniards gave the name of "empire." The legitimacy of this term has been much disputed, particularly with respect to the Aztecs. However, it is not inexact if employed in the sense in which one says "the British Empire" or "the Athenian empire."

The Aztecs, a warlike people, had established themselves in the thirteenth century or earlier, in the valley of Anáhuac, where Mexico City is now located, and had succeeded, after a long struggle, in becoming the principal political power of the region. At the beginning of the sixteenth century, there existed in the valley of Anáhuac a confederation consisting of the Aztecs of Tenochtitlán (the present Mexico City, which is said to have been founded in 1325, and which had grown into a lacustrine metropolis with streets bordered by navigable canals and joined by wooden bridges); the Acolhuas of Tezcoco; and the Tecpanecas of Tlacopán (called Tacuba by the Spaniards). The direction of military operations was entrusted to the Aztecs. The military chieftain (*tlacatecuhtli*), whom the Spaniards called "emperor," exercised functions similar to those originally accruing to the *imperator* in Rome. He was not king, yet he held office for life; and the office was elective, not hereditary. The civil power was in the hands of another chieftain (*cihuacóhuatl*), and both the civil authorities and the military appear to have depended ultimately on the council (*tlatocan*) of representatives of the regional groups (*calpulis*), derived from local clans. The confederation dominated a large portion of the territory now occupied by the Republic of Mexico, and extended as far as Central America. The subjugated territories did not constitute provinces, but were simply tributaries. Some centers, such as Tlaxcala, were never subdued; it was with the aid of Tlaxcala that Hernán Cortés succeeded in conquering Mexico City.

Religion dominated the life of the Aztecs, and their rulers had sacerdotal functions. The characteristic ritual of their religion—human sacrifice—is mythological in origin. Strange as this ritual may seem to modern man, it was common in primitive epochs among ancient peoples, including the forerunners of European civilization, the Greeks, the Germans, and the Celts. The gods, according to Aztec belief, had sacrificed themselves in order to create man; man, therefore, should sacrifice himself in order that the gods might be nourished. The chief deity of the Aztec mythology, Huitzilopochtli, is the Sun, who each day is born, does battle, and dies. "As the god that he is," wrote the Mexican archaeologist Alfonso Caso, "he disdains the gross food of mankind and can be nourished only on life itself, on the magic substance found in the blood of man." War, among the Aztecs, was conducted principally in order to obtain victims for human sacrifices. Aztec mythology also included gods of a more benign nature, such as Quetzal-cóatl the civilizer (the plumed serpent, symbol of the planet Venus), who taught mankind the sciences and arts and crafts. Their religion was polytheistic, but a philosophical school that had been in existence for a long time had reduced the multitude of gods to a single divinity who combined both masculine and feminine attributes.

From the social and political points of view, the Mexican confederation has been described as a theocratic, militaristic democracy. In the beginning, the land had been common property. Everyone worked, in agriculture or in a craft, for his sustenance and for that of the community, and all males performed military service. Each head of a family was assigned a lifetime interest in a parcel of land, which reverted to the community upon his death or if he failed to cultivate it for a period of two years. Abandonment of the land and refusal to marry, as well as many crimes, were punished by a kind of slavery, in which the offenders were forced to labor for others. At first, social classes, in the European sense, did not exist, but the priests and the military and civil leaders received honors and riches and they were not obliged to work on their lands. In the last years of the empire, this system began to change, and an aristocracy with private property started to develop.

The commerce of the Aztecs was very active. The market of Tenochtitlán was always busy, with thousands of people moving about the marketplace, according to the descriptions by Cortés and the soldier-chronicler Bernal Díaz del Castillo. Goods were sold by number and measure, but not by weight. (In Peru, however, it was customary to sell by weight.)

The Aztecs had a wide knowledge of astronomy, which they had inherited from previous cultures, but they were less advanced in this science than the Mayas and Quichés. As evidence of their knowledge, we have the Aztec Calendar, a monumental stonework that until 1964 was housed in the National Museum of Anthropology and History in Mexico City. They had hieroglyphic writing, which was splendidly drawn and colored. Several codices have been preserved, some antedating the Spanish Conquest, some of a later date. But the art of reading them has been lost, and they have been deciphered only in part. The Aztecs manufactured paper, as did the Mayas, from the fibers of wild fig trees.

The Aztec civilization inherited its architecture, with the characteristic pyramid, from earlier Mexican cultures. Examples are found in Cuernavaca and in Tepoztlán. On the monument at Tepoztlán, the date 1502 is inscribed in hieroglyphs. There was, as well, the enormous pyramid in Mexico City, which was destroyed by the Spaniards. It stood in the main square, where the Government Palace and the Cathedral now stand. The Aztecs also inherited the arts of sculpture and painting, and excelled in gold and silver work, ceramics, textiles, stone carving, and ornamental featherwork. They mined and worked with gold, silver, copper, and tin, as well as manufacturing bronze. They built many roads, bridges, and aqueducts. Their culture included ritual dances and games, drama (devoted principally to Quetzalcóatl), and epic and lyric poetry. Among the songs that have been preserved, a number are worthy of special mention, particularly those attributed or referring to Netzahualcóyotl, fifteenth-century king of Tezcoco, in central Mexico. The Aztecs also composed prose narratives, and several of these have come down to us in adaptations, for example, those contained in the *Codex Ramirez* and in the *Historia general de las Indias de Nueva España* (General History of the Indies of New Spain), compiled by Friar Diego Durán. Education was rigorously organized: studies in higher education consisted of religion, astronomy, history, law, medicine, and music. In the common schools, the only subjects taught were religion and the art of warfare. In addition, the Aztecs kept live animals in their houses, in gardens, and in pools. They also had botanical gardens and nurseries.

The nation comprising the Quechua-speaking peoples—

ruled by the Incas—merits the name of "empire" in the Roman sense. From its capital, Cuzco—founded in the thirteenth century and "built at the greatest height above sea level of all imperial capitals," as the Argentine archaeologist Fernando Márquez Miranda wrote—the Incas succeeded in ruling over a vast territory, extending into the Andean highlands and along both slopes of the cordillera, from Quito (conquered in 1487) in the north, to northern Chile and Argentina in the south. The southern boundaries of the empire are not known with certainty, but even in areas where military control was not effective, cultural influence did, in any case, penetrate. Thus, the Quechua language is still spoken in the province of Santiago del Estero, in Argentina.

The religion of the Incas centered around the cult of the Sun, ancestor of the monarchs. He was surrounded by a pantheon of lesser gods. In addition, there were purely spiritual divinities, without a form that could be represented, such as Pachacámac, who animated the world and its creatures. The Incas had both priestly and military functions. The monarchy was hereditary: the reigning Inca chose a successor from among his sons, according to merit. There was, moreover, a kind of consultative council, whose advice was evidently necessary in order to make laws.

Inca society was not organized along the lines of a democracy, as the Aztec society is said to have been, at least in its early stages, but was rigorously divided into classes, each having its distinctive dress and insignia. The upper classes included the monarch, the numerous descendants of the Incas (who were polygamous), and the provincial governors *(curacas)* and their families. On rare occasions, the Inca would elevate a man of merit to the privileged classes. The members of the upper classes received a special education; no one could belong to them in full right until he had undergone a severe examination and submitted to the ordeal of initiation.

The common people had to perform agricultural labor or work in crafts. As with the Aztecs, the land was distributed among the heads of families (allotments were made annually), together with the rights to the supply of water needed for irrigation. Idleness was not tolerated, and no one was allowed to go hungry or without clothing. The proletariat had the obligation of cultivating, by turns, the lands belonging to the Sun and the Inca, and those set aside for assistance to the needy—the aged, widows, children, and the disabled in general. In the granaries and storehouses they kept food, textiles, arms, and all kinds of raw and finished materials, which were used to meet the needs of the army and, in emergencies, of the populace. Commerce existed on a small scale; it was permissible to sell any surplus individual production. Houses and household goods were private property.

In order to govern this vast empire with such an economic system, it was essential to keep a detailed census of the population and its needs; the Incas carried statistics to a degree of precision that even today is unequaled in official practice in any civilized country. They retained the division of the inhabitants into the landholding communities (*ayllus*) that had been established before the organization of the empire.

The Incas regarded themselves as civilizers: they imposed their culture on the peoples they subdued, and tried to assimilate them completely. The capital of the empire was linked to the rest of the territory by means of roads and bridges, which facilitated rapid communication. In sixteenth-century Europe, there were no comparable roads, nor had any such existed previously except under the Roman Empire. Pedro Cieza de León, the illustrious historian of the conquest of Peru, says that "the road built by the Romans that passed through Spain was in no way comparable to this [the great road of the Incas]." Their bridges, made of wood or of osier, were remarkable.

Like the Mayas and the Quichés, and like the Aztecs, the Quechuas had a fully developed literature, transmitted by oral tradition.* Specimens of their lyric poetry have been preserved, including poems attributed to the Inca Pachacútec. Only fragments have been preserved from their drama, which was of

* The first written specimens date from the period of the Spanish Conquest.—TRANS.

great importance in their lives. They had no writing, but they transmitted messages and kept accounts by means of different-colored strings in which knots were made *(kipus)*. Government orders and official notices were transmitted through *kipus* carried by relays of trained runners *(chasquis)*, who were relieved at posts situated approximately three miles apart. *Kipus* were also used by the Incas for their complex statistics.

Ancient Peruvian architecture had many varied forms, ranging from the simple individual dwelling to the splendid temples of Machu Picchu and the mighty fortress of Sacsahuamán near Cuzco. The Peruvian buildings were not, however, as elaborate or as richly decorated as many of the ancient structures of Mexico and Central America. Today the most impressive vestiges of pre-Hispanic architecture in Peru are to be seen at Chan-Chan, Paramonga, La Centinela (all in the northern coastal region), and in addition to Sacsahuamán and Machu Picchu, at Tiahuanaco, Cuzco, Ollantaitambo, and Pisac in the highland region of the south. For its natural setting, nothing can equal Machu Picchu. In the words of Pál Kelemen: "In the daring and majesty of its isolation, it is a perfect expression of the austere and orderly mountain folk who created and maintained it."

{ 2 }

Discovery
and
Colonization

THE DATE 1492 divides the history of Spain into two parts. In that year the Catholic Monarchs, Isabella of Castile and León (1451–1504) and Ferdinand of Aragón (1452–1516)—who achieved the political unification of the nation—reconquered the city of Granada, the last stronghold of the Moors, who had occupied the Iberian Peninsula for nearly eight centuries, since 711. They also expelled the Jews, thereby eliminating the last vestige of the religious tolerance that until around 1400 had characterized the Middle Ages in Spain. Later, in 1609, the Moors who had remained in Spain and retained their Moham-medan faith were likewise expelled. Thus ended the ties with Oriental culture, which had attained such a brilliant flowering in Spain among both the Arabs and the Jews in literature, philosophy, and science, and among the Arabs in architecture and the industrial arts, as well. And, in 1492, Columbus (called Cristóbal Colón by the Spaniards), sailing on behalf of Castile and León, discovered the New World.

The Middle Ages had lasted longer in Spain than in Italy, but in the fifteenth century the influence of that other great Mediterranean peninsula began to penetrate the Spanish world. The Renaissance may be said to have begun in Spain with the ascension of the Catholic Monarchs, in 1474, but here the

Renaissance did not involve a complete break with the Middle Ages. While in France medieval literature was forgotten when the Renaissance forms were adopted, in Spain the national ballad, called the *romance,* was never abandoned; it survives to the present day as traditional folk poetry sung by the common people of Spain and America, and also by the Jews in the Balkans and in North Africa who still use the Spanish language. At the same time, it persists as a poetic form cultivated by leading poets of our day, such as Leopoldo Lugones and Federico García Lorca, Fernández Moreno, and Rafael Alberti.

The reign of the Catholic Monarchs was followed by that of Charles V (V of Germany and I of Spain), who ruled from 1516 to 1556. With the advent of Charles V, Spain became the first power of Europe. In the early years of his reign, there was varied and free intellectual activity; in religious matters, there were heated discussions provoked by Erasmus; in politics, Francisco de Vitoria and his disciples were establishing the fundamental principles of law, including the self-determination of nations; in philosophy, Juan Luis Vives was challenging the scholastics; in science, inquiry was directed especially toward mathematics, physics, and biology. Advances in linguistics, too, were made around this time. In 1492, Antonio de Nebrija published his Spanish grammar, the first grammar of a modern language written in Europe, and in 1493, his first dictionary appeared. Juan de Valdés wrote his *Diálogo de la lengua* around 1535. Other achievements of the period were registered in literature, for the Golden Age was beginning; and in art, this was a time of great architecture, and Berruguete flourished in sculpture. Before the close of Charles's reign, however, freedom of discussion about religious doctrines had ended; in fact, it was the Council of Trent (1545–63), dominated by Spaniards, that formulated the restriction.

Under Charles's successor, Philip II, who ruled from 1556 to 1598, philosophy became theology and scholasticism (but a scholasticism considerably altered, from that of Vitoria to that of Suárez in the seventeenth century). Research in the pure sciences was abandoned, and work was carried on only in the descriptive or applied sciences, such as geography, botany, and mineralogy. Literature flourished, along with the graphic arts, which were carried to new heights by El Greco. In music, Tomás Luis de Victoria, one of the world's greatest composers, competed with the Italian Palestrina.

During the seventeenth century, under Philip III (1598–1621) and Philip IV (1621–65), Spain maintained the splendor of its literature and its art. With Cervantes, Lope de Vega, Tirso de Molina, Calderón de la Barca, Quevedo, Góngora, and Gracián, this was truly the Golden Age of the drama and the novel. In painting, Velázquez, Ribera, Zurbarán, and Murillo were producing glorious works. But the economic life of the nation faltered, through lack of good administration, and in the political sphere, Spain surrendered to France under Louis XIV after the battle of Rocroi (1643). In the reign of Charles II (1665–1700), the nation suffered a general decline; even the population decreased.

In the eighteenth century, the situation improved, chiefly during the reign of Charles III (1759–88), who adopted many of the ideas of the Enlightenment. But Spain never again regained its former splendor.

The history of Portugal is very similar to that of Spain, whose destiny it shared in ancient and medieval days, until the establishment of the kingdom in the twelfth century. At that time, too, the Moors were driven out of the whole territory, from Lisbon to the extreme south. The kingdom of Portugal was united to Spain in 1580, but recovered its independence in 1640.

From the fourteenth century onward, the Portuguese displayed great skill as navigators, and in the fifteenth century, they explored the coasts of Africa and the nearby islands. Vasco da Gama rounded the Cape of Good Hope and reached India in 1498; Pedro Alvares Cabral discovered Brazil in 1500. In 1519, Magellan (Magalhães in Portuguese) undertook, in the name of King Charles of Spain, the first voyage of circumnavigation of the globe, which, after his death in 1521, was completed by his companion the Spaniard Sebastián Elcano, in 1522. The Portuguese empire in the sixteenth century was second only to the Spanish in extent. It comprised Brazil, the coastal areas of Africa, India, and Indochina, and a number of islands in the Atlantic and Indian oceans.

The history of Portuguese culture is linked to that of its neighbor on the Iberian Peninsula. Their literatures display mutual influences; for example, in the twelfth and thirteenth centuries, it was common for the Castilians to write lyrics in Portuguese; in the sixteenth and seventeenth centuries, the Portuguese wrote a great deal in Spanish, both in verse and in prose. Camoëns, the great national poet of Portugal, sang the deeds of Vasco da Gama in his epic poem *Os Lusiadas* (The Lusiads; 1572). The distinctive features of Portuguese architecture were carried to remote colonies in India and Africa, in the Azores and in Madeira, and from north to south in Brazil.

After the discovery of the New World in 1492, a first attempt at colonization was made, a year later, when Columbus established himself, with about 1,500 men, on the island which he called Española and which the Italian Chronicler Pietro Martire d'Anghiera afterward latinized to Hispaniola. Soon European-type cities were founded, beginning in 1494 with Isabela, which was soon afterward abandoned. The second city founded, and the oldest still in existence, was Santo Domingo, established by Bartholomew Columbus (brother of the discoverer) in 1496. Subsequently, the city gave its name to the whole island. By 1505, Hispaniola had seventeen towns of European type, not counting isolated fortresses.

Although many expeditions were undertaken from Hispaniola, no towns or cities were founded anywhere else for fifteen years. Not until 1508 was colonization of the other three islands of the Greater Antilles begun. Puerto Rico, colonized in 1508, was the first, followed by Jamaica in 1509, and Cuba in 1511. The northern coasts of South America (that is, territory now forming part of Venezuela and Colombia) and parts of Central America were also settled at this time. Then came the conquest of Mexico (1519–21), where the Spaniards established themselves at once, and of Guatemala (1524). This was followed by the conquest of the Incan empire (1531–33), consisting of territories that now form part of Peru, Ecuador, and Bolivia. The conquest of the region of the Río de la Plata (now occupied by Argentina, Uruguay, and Paraguay) began in 1534, while the campaign to win Chile began a year later. The conquest of Yucatán was not achieved until 1539–42.

In Brazil, after the visit of Alvares Cabral, the Portuguese made their first attempt at a settlement in 1503. For many years, America was of slight interest to the Portuguese; the explorers and the Crown devoted their attention principally to India. Finally, in 1530, the King dispatched an expedition, led by Martim Affonso de Sousa, which around 1532 founded the first settlement, São Vicente. In 1534, the country was divided into captaincies.

The territories conquered by Spain were at first governed from the city of Santo Domingo, in Hispaniola, where Diego Columbus, the son of the discoverer, exercised the functions of viceroy from 1509 until 1526. After his death, the Spanish Crown abolished the Viceroyalty-General of the Indies and divided its American possessions into separate jurisdictions, the most important of which were the two new viceroyalties: that of New Spain, with its capital at Mexico City, and that of Peru, with its capital at Lima, established in 1543. In the eighteenth century, two more viceroyalties were created: that of Santa Fe de Bogotá in 1739, and that of Buenos Aires in 1776. Between 1508 and 1565, the Spaniards founded a great number of cities.* Some important centers were founded much later, such as Montevideo in 1722. Neither Mexico City nor

* The principal cities were: San Juan de Puerto Rico, 1508; Santiago de Cuba, 1514; La Habana (Havana), 1515; Veracruz (Mexico), 1519; Panama, 1519; Guatemala, 1524; León (Nicaragua), 1524; Granada (Nicaragua), 1524; Puebla de los Angeles, 1531; Cartagena de Indias, 1533; Guadalajara, 1533; Quito, 1534; Lima, 1535; Guayaquil, 1535; Buenos Aires, 1536 (it was abandoned and then re-established in 1580); Asunción (Paraguay), 1537; Santa Fe de Bogotá, 1538; Charcas, or Chuquisaca (now called Sucre), 1539; Santiago de Chile, 1541; Valladolid de Michoacán (today named Morelia), 1541; Mérida de Yucatán, 1542; Potosí, 1545; La Paz, 1549; Caracas, 1562 (abandoned soon afterward and re-established in 1567); San Agustín (Saint Augustine, Florida, the oldest city founded by Europeans in the territory now occupied by the United States), 1565.

Cuzco was founded by the Spaniards: the conquerors simply occupied the Indian capitals and gradually replaced the native constructions with edifices of European style. In Cuzco, part of the ancient construction sometimes served as a foundation for the new.

In Brazil, the Portuguese founded, after São Vicente, the city of Olinda (*c.* 1534), near the site of the present city of Recife, in Pernambuco; and, in 1549, São Salvador da Bahia, destined to be the capital of the colony. In 1554, the Jesuits established the College of São Paulo, around which the city of São Paulo was formed; and in 1567, Rio de Janeiro was founded, on a site which the Portuguese seized from the French, who had been established there since 1555. In 1717, the colony was designated a viceroyalty, with São Salvador da Bahia as the capital; but in 1763, Rio de Janeiro became the capital.

When the Spanish and the Portuguese settled in America, they brought with them the culture of Europe: religion, social organization, judicial system, arts, sciences, agriculture, the breeding of domestic animals, industries, commerce, dress, amusements, and customs in general. They tried to transmit their culture to the natives, in greater or lesser measure, but this could not be carried out systematically, as had been done by Rome with its European conquests: the colossal extent of the territory prevented it. Large centers of native population remained beyond reach of the new culture, some because they offered strong resistance to it, as did the Araucanians in Chile and the Apaches in Mexico; others because of their location in areas difficult to penetrate. As a consequence, there are today more than two million Indians who speak neither Spanish nor Portuguese. A much larger proportion of the population speaks a native tongue in addition to Spanish or Portuguese; for example, in the bilingual cities of Cuzco, Asunción, and Mérida (Yucatán), Spanish is spoken as well as, respectively, Quechua, Guaraní, and Maya. Even in Argentina, where few pure Indians remain, bilingual regions exist, such as Santiago del Estero (Quechua), and Corrientes and Misiones (Guaraní).

Hundreds of languages survive, ranging from those spoken by more than half a million people, such as Náhuatl (the language of the Aztecs), Quechua, Aymara, and Guaraní, to those that are spoken only by very small groups, such as Tehuelche in Patagonia, Otomaco in Venezuela, Paya in Honduras, and Huari and Karayá in Brazil. The Spanish and Portuguese languages have taken hundreds of words from these native tongues; some, like *cacao* and *tabaco,* have spread all over the world; others are used only in limited areas. It is interesting to note, furthermore, that the Spanish and Portuguese missionaries, after learning indigenous languages, which were important for catechizing the natives, spread their use beyond the areas where they were originally spoken; such was the case with Náhuatl in Mexico, and with Quechua and Guaraní in South America.

The culture that the Spanish and the Portuguese implanted in the New World could not, of course, wholly retain its original character. The mere transplantation obliged the Europeans to modify it, perhaps unconsciously, in order to adapt it to a new land and to new conditions of life, exactly as occurred in the British colonies of North America that gave rise to the United States. Moreover, the Indian cultures exercised a deep influence on the Europeans. True, the Conquest deprived these cultures of their religion, their art, their science (where any existed), and their writing (in the case of the Aztecs and the Mayas); but many local traditions survived in daily and domestic life. A fusion of European and indigenous elements took place which persists to the present day.

The diet is partly European, partly native. From the Old World, the conquerors and the colonizers brought wheat, rice, coffee, oranges, apples, pears, peaches, figs, sugar cane, and many other plants; they brought the horse, the cow, the hog, the sheep, the chicken; from Africa, they imported the banana tree, the yam, and the guinea hen. From the natives, they adopted Indian corn (maize), which is still not used as food for humans in many European countries; the potato; the sweet potato; the cacao seed; the yuca; the tomato; the peanut; and the enormous variety of tropical fruits, from the pineapple to the guava; the turkey; the wild partridge. Along with these, the Europeans also took over the culinary methods of the Indians. Thus, alongside bread made from flour in the European manner, we find the *tortilla de maíz*, a pancake made of mashed Indian corn, in Mexico, Central America, and parts of Colombia; and the cassava bread, made from the yuca plant, in the Antilles. In many countries, the basic rural diet of vegetables retains its indigenous character. In Mexico, for example, there is a prevalence of maize, beans, chili or *ají* (red pepper), cacao, and maguey (from which the beverage called *pulque* is extracted), in addition to the foreign staples, rice and coffee. In the Antilles, in spite of the fact that there are no longer any pure-bred Indians, we find maize, beans, *ají,* cacao, yuca, and sweet potatoes, together with yams, rice, and coffee. In Peru, the staples are maize, yuca or manioc (there called *mandioca*), the potato (in numerous varieties), and the *ulloco,* an edible tuberous plant similar to the potato. In Brazil, there are *mandioca* and maize. "*Mandioca,*" wrote the Brazilian sociologist Gilberto Freyre, "is the basic food of the [rural] Brazilian, and the technique of its preparation remains almost identical with that of the Indians." In agriculture, along with European techniques, we find such indigenous practices as the cultivation of slopes by means of terraces with retaining walls (called *pircas*) and the fertilization of the soil with guano.

In the cities, the grandiose indigenous architecture disappeared; but in the midst of houses, palaces, fortresses, and churches built in the styles of the Mediterranean, the more modest types of native dwellings were retained. Thy are known by different names in different places: *choza, rancho, bohío* (in the Antilles), and *jacal* (in Mexico). Today these humble dwellings are banished from the cities, where at times they have been replaced by inferior constructions of galvanized iron, commonly called zinc; but the native dwellings survive still in the villages and in the countryside. Among the indigenous construction materials employed by Europeans are many kinds of stone, for example, the dark red *tezontle* and the light gray *chiluca* of Mexico, and many woods, such as jacaranda and mahogany, used today more commonly for furniture than for houses.

The native crafts that have survived include weaving, especially of ponchos and serapes, of footwear (sandals), mats, hammocks, and baskets; also pottery, and gold and silver work, which retain all their extraordinary variety, blending the native tradition with the European.

The fusion of European and native elements extends to the fine arts—architecture, sculpture, painting. The Indians, supervised by European craftsmen, introduced characteristic details that give a distinctive aspect to their works. The process has been studied in detail, particularly in architecture. The Spanish poet and art critic José Moreno Villa gave the name *tequitqui* to these forms of art. *Tequitqui* means "vassal" in Náhuatl, and is analogous to Mudejar (from the Arabic), the name given to the art of the Moslems who lived among the Christians in Spain.

This fusion appears also in the drama. When the missionaries organized dramatic representations as an aid to the instruction of the Indians in Christian doctrine, they combined the meager resources of the medieval European theater with those of the indigenous drama. This is told us, for instance, by Father Motolinía, who probably directed the presentation of some religious plays at Tlaxcala in 1538. Moreover, the plays were frequently written in the native languages, whether in California in the north or in Argentina and Paraguay in the south. The indigenous drama survived, although precariously, among the Indians, and in turn was influenced by European forms. In the eighteenth century, this combination produced a remarkable work, the drama *Ollantay,* which is written in Quechua, in three acts and in verse after the manner of Lope and Calderón. Its theme antedates the Conquest and carries numerous reminiscences of pre-Hispanic character. (*Ollantay,* incidentally, has been translated into Spanish, French, German, English, Czech, and even Latin.) Especially in Yucatán and Paraguay, the indigenous drama in the native language endures to the present day.

{ 3 }

The
Colonial
Culture

No sooner had they conquered a city, or founded one, than the Spanish and Portuguese established there the political, religious, and educational institutions of Europe. Political life had two fundamental forms: the government representing the Crown, and the autonomous municipalities. Religious life began with the construction of churches, followed shortly by monasteries. The first of these was that of the Franciscans in the city of Santo Domingo, founded in 1502; next, in the same city, came the Dominicans (1510) and the Mercedarians (1514). Convents for the female orders were established somewhat later. The first diocese was created by the Vatican in 1504.

The religious orders played a very important role in colonial life: in addition to spreading Christianity, they defended the Indians against exploitation by the *encomenderos,* who held them as serfs (in this defense, the Dominican order was especially outstanding), and, at least in the beginning, they organized and guided teaching. The Catholic Church consecrated as saints, beatified, or venerable, among others, Archbishop Toribio Alfonso de Mogrovejo (1538–1606), Bishop Juan de Palafox (1600–1659), Friar Francisco Solano (1549–1610), Friar Luis Beltrán (1523–81), Father Pedro Claver (1580–1654), defender of the slaves, Sister Rosa de Lima (1586–1617), the Mexican Friar Felipe de Jesús (1573–97), martyr to the faith crucified in Japan, and the Peruvian mulatto Friar Martín de Porres (1569–1639), who taught agriculture and established the first orphanage in Lima.*

Teaching in schools began as early as 1505, at the school founded by Friar Hernán Suárez in the Franciscan monastery in the city of Santo Domingo; later, in addition to the schools run by the orders, independent institutions of learning were established. Schooling was available both for children of Spaniards and for natives; in 1513, the Spanish Crown provided for the teaching of Latin to selected Indians in the Antilles. The schools for Indians were especially important in Peru and Mexico. In Mexico City, in 1523, the Flemish Friar Pedro de Gante founded the College of San Francisco, where the curriculum included religion, Latin, music, painting, sculpture, and crafts. In 1536, the Imperial College of Santa Cruz, for Indian chiefs, was established in the town of Tlaltelolco, today a district within the capital city. Its curriculum included the teaching of native medicine, from which the Europeans very wisely wished to learn, and did.

Although schools and colleges were established, naturally, in the cities, there was no attempt to extend intellectual learning to all the people. In sixteenth-century Europe, general compulsory education had not yet been introduced, and it was not to be expected that the Europeans would impose it in America. In the villages, the only instruction was religious, with some occasional training in European arts and crafts. There were two famous examples of the latter. One was the experiment conducted by Bishop Vasco de Quiroga, who, under the inspiration of Sir Thomas More's *Utopia* (published shortly before, in 1516), established a number of villages in the region of Michoacán, in Mexico, each with its own distinctive craft, a system that has not entirely disappeared even to this day. The other was that carried out by the Jesuits, through their missions in Paraguay and northeastern Argentina, where they

* Martín de Porres was canonized by the Catholic Church in 1962.—
TRANS.

established a kind of collectivist society, prescribing rules for conduct, work, art, and recreation among the Guaraní Indians. This organization lasted from the end of the sixteenth century until the year 1767, when the Jesuits were expelled from all the Spanish dominions.

After colleges had become established and had begun to expand, they looked to the day when they would become universities. Less than half a century after the Discovery, in 1538, the college established by the Dominicans in Santo Domingo was authorized to call itself the University of Santo Tomás de Aquino. In 1540, the creation of another university, Santiago de la Paz, was authorized, also in Santo Domingo, elevating to this higher rank the college established many years before by Bishop Sebastián Ramírez de Fuenleal. Funds for the purpose were donated by the wealthy colonizer Hernando de Gorjón. In 1551, the Spanish Crown decided to set up universities in the capitals of the two viceroyalties then in existence: in Mexico City and in Lima. They were opened in 1553. The University of San Marcos in Lima is today the oldest in America that has not experienced any significant interruptions since its founding. The two universities in Santo Domingo and the one in Mexico City did suffer considerable disruptions. After these four, other universities were also founded. With the exceptions of those in Mexico City and Lima, these were colleges that received authorization to assume the rank of university and to confer the degree of doctor (even the university in Lima was, from 1553 to 1574, merely a college of the Dominican monks). The authorization was subject to rescission, and in point of fact was rescinded on various occasions.

The universities were patterned on medieval models, with four faculties: arts (which conferred the degrees of bachelor and master), law, theology, and medicine; but not every university had all four faculties. The specific models generally followed were the universities of Salamanca and Alcalá de Henares in Spain. The obligatory language for all subjects, except medicine, was Latin. In colonies with a large Indian population, such as Mexico, Guatemala, and Peru, the universities offered courses in the native languages for theology students who would have to teach and preach among the Indians.

Including all the institutions that enjoyed or had assumed the prerogatives of universities (if only for a few years), there was a total of twenty-six.* But there were never that many functioning simultaneously, because at various times their privileges were revoked. The most important universities were: Santo Tomás de Aquino in Santo Domingo, to which for three hundred years students went from Cuba, Puerto Rico, and Venezuela; the University of Mexico City, which graduated more than 1,400 doctors; San Marcos in Lima; San Carlos Borromeo in Guatemala City, founded in 1676 with a legacy from Pedro Crespo Suárez; San Jerónimo in Havana, established in 1728; Santa Rosa in Caracas, established in 1725; the Dominican university in Bogotá, founded in the seventeenth century; the Jesuit University of San Gregorio Magno (St. Gregory the Great), in Quito, founded in 1620; another Jesuit university, San Francisco Javier, in Charcas, founded in 1624; and San Ignacio de Loyola, in Córdoba, also founded by the Jesuits, in the seventeenth century.

There were, in addition, a sizable number of theological seminaries, which at times were more advanced than the universities in introducing modern philosophical doctrines. During the final phase of the colonial era, various other kinds of educational institutions were founded, such as the School of Mining in Mexico (1792), whose faculty included the Spaniards Fausto de Elhúyar (1757–1833), discoverer of tungsten, and Andrés del Río (1765–1849), discoverer of vanadium, and the Mexican Antonio de León y Gama (1735–1802), an eminent as-

* There were two in Hispaniola (both in the city of Santo Domingo); one in Cuba (in Havana); three in Mexico (one in the capital, one in Guadalajara, and one in Mérida); one in Guatemala (in the capital); one in Nicaragua (in León); one in Panama (in the capital); two in New Granada, the present Republic of Colombia (both in Bogotá); two in Venezuela (one in Caracas and one in Mérida); four in Ecuador (all in Quito); four in Peru (one in Lima, two in Cuzco, one in Huamanga); one in Alto Perú, now Bolivia (in Charcas); two in Chile (both in Santiago); and two in Argentina (both in Córdoba).

tronomer. Contemporary with the School of Mining are the Academy of Fine Arts of Mexico (1783), the Academy of Fine Arts of Guatemala (1797), and similar academies elsewhere. In fact, teaching in the arts had been established since the earliest times, as has been mentioned. In the sixteenth century, there were special centers, such as the College of San Andrés, founded in Quito in 1553, to train architects, sculptors, and painters. The first public libraries were established in the eighteenth century, as were the Botanical Garden of Mexico City (1788), the Museum of Natural History and Botanical Garden of Guatemala City (1796), the Astronomical Observatory of Bogotá, and the Naval School of Buenos Aires, founded in 1799 by Manuel Belgrano (1770–1820). According to Alexander von Humboldt, writing at the beginning of the nineteenth century, "no other city of the New World, including the United States, had scientific esablishments so large and so solid as those of the Mexican capital." At that time, Mexico City had the largest population of any city in the Americas: 112,926 inhabitants, compared with 96,000 for New York. Potosí, in Alto Perú, had reached 114,000 in the seventeenth century, but its population dwindled when the neighboring mines were exhausted. According to Humboldt, moreover, there was not to be found anywhere in Europe a specialized botanical library comparable to the library of the team of researchers working under the direction of Mutis and Caldas in Bogotá.

In Brazil, there were also colleges of general studies and theological seminaries. The college of the Jesuits in Bahia ranked with the University of Evora in Portugal until 1759, the year in which the Jesuits were banished from all the territories governed by the Portuguese Crown. No university was established in Brazil; the Brazilians who wished to obtain professional degrees in medicine or law had to go to Europe, as a rule to the University of Coimbra in Portugal. In 1784, the Bureau of Natural History Studies was set up in Rio de Janeiro. Later, after the Portuguese court fled to Brazil in 1808, during the Napoleonic Wars, new cultural institutions were established in the capital.

The educated people of Hispanic America were very fond of reading. In Brazil, for instance, books compensated for the lack of universities. One cannot detect a substantial difference in cultural levels between the overseas subjects of the Portuguese Crown and those of the Spanish Crown—except in the two great centers of learning, Lima and Mexico City. The lists of works shipped from Europe to booksellers in the colonies comprise the greatest conceivable variety of titles and subjects. And the quantities were extraordinary. In 1785, a single shipment received at Callao, the port of Lima, totaled 37,612 volumes. During the eighteenth century, many books of a modern character were in circulation: the French *Encyclopédie,* the works of Bacon, Descartes, Copernicus, Gassendi, Boyle, Leibnitz, Locke, Condillac, Buffon, Voltaire, Montesquieu, Rousseau, Lavoisier, and Laplace. They continued to circulate even after they had come to be regarded as dangerous and reading them was prohibited. Along with Latin, which was the basis for all teaching in the urban schools, Italian was much read. In the sixteenth century, knowledge of that language was a common adornment of every cultivated Spanish- or Portuguese-speaking person. In the eighteenth century, French became fashionable, and later, English.

Printing made its appearance, like the universities, less than half a century after the Discovery. By 1535, it existed in Mexico City. The oldest Mexican book that has been preserved dates from 1539. In 1583, a printing press was established in Lima.

In 1640, two years after its appearance in the British colonies in North America, printing was introduced in Puebla, second in population (after Mexico City) of the cities of the Viceroyalty of New Spain; in Guatemala City, it was established in 1641 (and re-established in 1660); in the Jesuit missions of Paraguay and Argentina, presses were set up with type made by the Guaraní Indians under Jesuit supervision shortly before 1700; and, according to the United States bibliographer Isaiah Thomas, in Santo Domingo also during the seventeenth century (there is definite proof that printing existed on the island in the following century). Many more cities received printing presses as the eighteenth century wore on,* and in the years preceding the movement for independence, printing presses were installed in Montevideo (1807), Caracas, San Juan de Puerto Rico (1808), and Guayaquil, Ecuador (1810).

In Brazil, the first printing press was established in 1706, but it was shut down by the government and none replaced it until 1808, when the King of Portugal transferred his court to Brazil. In Mexico City during the eighteenth century, as many as six presses were in operation simultaneously; one of them (the Eguiara) had Greek and Hebrew type. Lima also had six printing presses, and in Puebla, there were three. The number of works printed in Mexico during the colonial period (up to 1821) totaled nearly 12,000; in Lima, 4,000.

The first newspapers appeared in the seventeenth century. Before 1600, broadsides containing news from Europe were printed in the capitals of the two viceroyalties. The first *Gaceta de México* appeared in 1667, but issues were published at very irregular intervals. In the eighteenth century, an effort was made to publish it regularly, with only sporadic success. Its two brief periods of regular publication were January to June, 1722, under the direction of Father Juan Ignacio de Castorena (1668–1733), and from 1728 to 1739, under the direction of Juan Francisco Sahagún de Arévalo. It was succeeded by the *Mercurio de México,* 1740–42. Finally, the last *Gaceta de México,* edited by the soldier-poet Manuel Antonio Valdés (1742–1814), was issued from January, 1784, to December, 1809. It was replaced in January, 1810, by the *Gaceta del Gobierno de México,* an official government publication (the previous gazettes had been privately run), which lasted until the end of Spanish rule in Mexico (September, 1821).

Guatemala City had its gazette from 1729 to 1731. A periodi-

---

* Havana (1707); Oaxaca, Mexico (1720); Colombia (around 1738; suspended in 1742; re-established in 1777); Ecuador (Ambato, 1754; transferred to Quito, 1760); Argentina (Córdoba, 1764; transferred to Buenos Aires, 1780); Cartagena de Indias (1776); Santiago de Chile (1780); Guadalajara de México (1793); Veracruz (1794); and Santiago de Cuba (1796).

cal of the same name appeared there in 1794, edited by the jurist Jacobo de Villaurrutia (1757–1833), a native of Santo Domingo; it was in existence until 1816. In Peru, publication of the *Gaceta de Lima* began in 1743 and lasted until 1767. It reappeared from 1793 to 1795, and again from 1798 to 1804 and from 1810 to 1821. Various other cities had regularly established newspapers before the end of the colonial regime: in Havana (1764), Bogotá (1785), Buenos Aires (1801), Veracruz (1805), Santiago de Cuba (1805), Montevideo (1807), San Juan de Puerto Rico (1808), Guadalajara de México (1809), and Santo Domingo (1821).

The first daily newsaper in Spanish America was the *Diario Erudito, Económico y Comercial* of Lima, appearing from October, 1790, to September, 1793, under the editorship of the Spaniard Jaime Bausate y Mesa. The second was the *Diario de México,* founded by Villaurrutia (editor of the *Gaceta de Guatemala*) with the assistance of the Mexican historian Carlos María de Bustamante (1774–1848); it lasted until 1817.

The periodicals devoted to literature and the sciences are also noteworthy. The principal ones were: the four published in Mexico between 1768 and 1795 by Father José Antonio Alzate (1729–90), who was particularly interested in physics, astronomy, and the biological sciences; the *Mercurio Volante* (1772), edited by the Mexican physician and mathematician José Ignacio Bartolache (1739–90); the *Mercurio Peruano,* of Lima, from 1791 to 1795, whose chief editor was the physicist and naturalist José Hipólito Unanue (1755–1833); the *Papel Periódico,* of Havana, from 1790 to 1804; *Primicias de la Cultura de Quito* (1791), edited by Francisco Eugenio de Santa Cruz Espejo (1747–95), a physician of encyclopedic knowledge; the *Semanario de la Nueva Granada,* of Bogotá, from 1808 to 1811, edited by the erudite physicist and naturalist Francisco José de Caldas (1771–1816).

The science the Europeans brought to the New World was that of the Renaissance, in which remnants of antiquity and of the Middle Ages were blended with knowledge derived from new experiments. The discovery of America was in itself one of the causes of the scientific revival. In America, particularly, the Europeans were obliged to modify and to widen their concepts of astronomy, physical geography, zoology, and botany. In metallurgy, which acquired major importance at this time, technical innovations were made in America; for example, new methods of processing silver ore. After the sixteenth century, there was little scientific activity until the end of the following century, when truly modern scientific and philosophical concepts—represented by the theories of Copernicus, Galileo, and Descartes—began to arrive from Europe.

In the eighteenth century, there was extraordinary interest in science; in all the countries of America, men emerged who were dedicated to this study and who read everything that was published in Europe and made valuable contributions to the development of modern science. Notable among the contributions are the astronomical and geographical observations made by Joaquín Velázquez de Cárdenas y León (1732–86) and Antonio de León y Gama (1735–1802) in Mexico; the experiments in physics of Caldas; and the classification and description of plants and animals made by the Mexican José Mariano Mociño (*c.* 1750–1821).

During the final phase of the colonial regime, many European men of science, from the Frenchman La Condamine to the German Alexander von Humboldt, came to America, and their presence led to fruitful new studies. Also deserving of mention are the important expeditions for scientific investigation financed by the Spanish Crown. The archaeology of the indigenous cultures of America had its beginnings at this time, its principal monument being the *Historia antigua de México* by Father Francisco Javier Clavijero (1731–87). Another noteworthy work of the times is the *Diccionario geográfico-histórico de las Indias Occidentales o América* (Geographical-historical Dictionary of the West Indies, or America), in six volumes (Madrid, 1786–89), compiled by the Ecuadorian Antonio de Alcedo (1735–1812), which was translated into English (London, 1812–15).

Among the conquistadors, the explorers, the government officials, and the ecclesiastics charged with the Christianization of America, there were many who undertook to describe these new lands and to relate the events that occurred there, beginning with Columbus' letters and the journals of his voyages. At times, the conquistador is a poet, as in the case of Alonso de Ercilla (1533–94), who, in his epic poem *La Araucana,* narrated the struggle between the Spaniards and the Indians of Chile. Later, in the sixteenth and seventeenth centuries, a large number of Spanish and Portuguese writers resided in America. The most eminent were Mateo Alemán, whose *Guzmán de Alfarache* was the first Spanish picaresque novel; the dramatist Tirso de Molina, creator of Don Juan; and the Portuguese historian Francisco Manuel de Melo.

After the mid-sixteenth century, native Americans began to emerge as writers, and by the end of the century, there were hundreds of them. Some were the offspring of Europeans living in the New World; others were Indian, or of mixed Indian and European descent (mestizo). The most notable of the mestizos was the Inca Garcilaso de la Vega (1539–1616), one of the finest historians in the Spanish language. His work *Comentarios reales* (Royal Commentaries) gives an admirable picture of the Inca civilization and a dramatic account of the conquest of Peru and of the ensuing quarrels among the conquistadors. Other distinguished historians were the Mexican Indians Hernando Alvarado Tezozómoc (*c.* 1520–1600) and Fernando de Alba Ixtlilxóchitl (*c.* 1568–1648). Among the mestizos were the historian Lucas Fernández de Piedrahita (1624–88) of New Granada, and Juan de Espinosa Medrano of Cuzco (*c.* 1640–82), a playwright and a fine literary critic. Among the notable offspring of Europeans were the Ecuadorian Bishop Gaspar de Villarroel (*c.* 1587–1665); the Chileans Pedro de Oña (1570–*c.* 1643), author of lengthy narrative poems, such as the very florid *El vasauro,* and of *Arauco domado* (Arauco Tamed; Lima, 1596), the first poetic work by a native-born American writer to appear in print; and Francisco Núñez de Pineda Bascuñán (1607–82), who related his happy captivity (*Cauti-*

verio feliz) of seven months (in 1629) among the Araucanians; the Brazilians Friar José de Santa Rita Durão (1722–84), author of the poem *Caramurú* (1781), and José Basílio da Gama (1740–95), author of the poem *Uruguai* (1769), depicting the nature and life of the Indians in America; the Latinist poets Francisco Javier Alegre (1729–88), Diego José Abad (1727–79) —both Mexicans—and Rafael Landívar (1731–93), who in his fine poem *Rusticatio mexicana* (1781–82) describes the landscape and the customs of Mexico and of his native Guatemala; the Brazilian dramatist Antônio José de Lisboa (1705–39), a Jew who was burned at the stake by the Portuguese Inquisition and who has been called "the Portuguese-American Molière." Foremost among the offspring of Europeans was the Mexican Juan Ruiz de Alarcón (*c.* 1580–1639), who went to Madrid when he was about thirty-three and there wrote his plays. He is among the four major figures of the immortal Spanish drama of the seventeenth century, along with Lope de Vega, Tirso de Molina, and Calderón de la Barca. His plays, in the Spanish dramatic tradition of the times, deal with the life of the nobles and the hidalgos. They are of the genre known as the *comedia de capa y espada* (cloak-and-dagger plays), but he gave them the stamp of his reflective mind, adding a note of gravity. His best-known play, *La verdad sospechosa* (Truth Made Suspect) was imitated in France by Corneille in *Le menteur,* and eventually came to influence Molière.

Among the writers who may be considered Americans were Bernardo de Valbuena (*c.* 1562–1627) and Father Antônio Vieira (1608–97), who came to the New World as children and received their education there. Valbuena was one of the most brilliant Spanish-language poets. He was the author of the pastoral novel *Siglo de oro* (Golden Age), which contains a number of charming eclogues; of the heroic and fantastic poem *El Bernardo,* comparable to Edmund Spenser's *Faerie Queene;* and of the short poem "La grandeza mexicana" (The Grandeur of Mexico), a eulogy of the capital of the Viceroyalty of New Spain, Mexico City. Vieira, one of the outstanding orators and masters of prose in Portuguese letters, defended Brazil against the abuses of the governors and of the European merchants, and he advocated the abolition of slavery.

Women, too, had their place in American literature. Among the many women poets of the colonial period, the first was Sister Leonor de Ovando, of Santo Domingo, who was soon followed by the cultivated Peruvians Clarinda and Amarilis, whom we know only by their noms de plume. Among the prose writers, there was the eloquent nun of New Granada, Sister Francisca Josefa de la Concepción, customarily called "Mother Castillo," after her family name. The most illustrious of these literary women was the Mexican poetess Sister Juana Inés de la Cruz (1651–95), the last of the great Spanish-language poets of the Golden Age. Her poetry is delicately expressive of both amorous feelings and religious fervor, or exquisitely imaginative, or ingenious, as in her celebrated defense of women, *"Hombres necios, que acusáis/a la mujer sin razón"* ("You stupid men who accuse/ Women without good reason"). She also wrote plays and *autos sacramentales* (religious dramas) in the manner of Calderón, *villancicos* (brief pieces to be sung) for church use, and magnificent letters, above all, an autobiographical letter in which she recounts the singular story of her studies.

When the Spanish and the Portuguese brought the European drama to America, it had not yet been developed much beyond the forms of the Middle Ages: the religious representations, the moral allegories, the crude farces. As the drama evolved in Europe, its new forms were transported to the colonies of Spain and Portugal. By the end of the sixteenth century, Mexico City and Lima had permanent theaters where works by both European and local authors were performed. In time, all the important cities had their own theaters.

European music and dance, soon after being transplanted to the New World, began to produce new forms: songs and dances such as the *gayumba*, the *zambajalo*, the *chaconne*, which were afterward adopted in Europe. During the sixteenth and seventeenth centuries, polyphonic music was widely cultivated, especially in the churches. After 1700, operas were composed in

Peru and in Mexico. In 1750, the first symphony orchestra was organized in Caracas. Noteworthy composers were found in Mexico, Peru, Cuba, Brazil, and Venezuela. Among the most active in Venezuela toward the end of the eighteenth century were Father Pedro Palacios Sojo, Lino Gallardo, and José Angel Lamas.

The colonial period was also a time of extraordinary productivity in the fine arts. From an early date, architects, sculptors, and painters came to America from Spain and Portugal, and from Italy, France, and the Netherlands, as well. These men practiced and taught the European techniques. In time, groups and schools of artists were formed, the most active being those in Mexico City, Puebla, Guatemala City, Bogotá, Quito, Lima, Cuzco, Potosí, and, in Brazil, São Salvador da Bahia, Recife de Pernambuco, Ouro Preto, and Rio de Janeiro. Quantitatively, the output was enormous: thousands of churches, public buildings, palaces, and private homes; hundreds of fortifications, bridges, and public fountains; thousands of religious paintings, for churches and for homes; hundreds of portraits and hundreds of polychrome statues.

A good many of these works are of high artistic value. Likewise noteworthy are the products of the industrial arts, especially furniture, textiles and embroidery, pottery, silver and gold objects, and work in iron and bronze. In both earthenware and silver tableware, as in jewelry, the heritage of the colonial period survives to the present day. It is even evident in certain artistic forms such as gourd-shaped bowls and painted wooden boxes.

In Mexico, the outstanding painters were the members of the Echave and Juárez families; Juan de Herrera, who was called "the divine," like the Spanish poet of the same surname (seventeenth century); and Miguel Cabrera (1695–1768). In Bogotá, there was Gregorio Vázquez de Arce (1638–1711); in Quito, Miguel de Santiago (d. 1673); in Cuzco, Juan Espinosa de los Monteros (seventeenth century); in Charcas, Melchor Pérez de Holguín (eighteenth century). Among the sculptors: in Guatemala, Alonso de la Paz (1605–86); in Quito, Father

Carlos (seventeenth century), Gaspar Zangurima (eighteenth century), and Manuel Chilli, who was called "Caspicara" (eighteenth century); and in Brazil, Antônio Francisco Lisboa (1738–1814), called "Aleijadinho" (the Little Cripple), who was a fine architect as well as one of the greatest sculptors of the age, famous for his heroic statues of the Prophets in Congonhas do Campo (Minas Gerais).

Architecture in the European style appeared almost immediately in the countries that came under Spanish domination. In the earliest buildings, in Santo Domingo and Puerto Rico, medieval forms (of ogival structure) are combined with Renaissance forms, especially in the portals, with their semicircular arches: this is what the Spaniards call *estilo isabelino,* belonging to the period of Queen Isabella the Catholic. At times, there are traces of the Mudejar, or Spanish-Moorish, style. The Isabelline style was succeeded by the plateresque (from the Spanish word for silver, *plata*), so named because its ornamentation resembles the work done by silversmiths. Later, there was a brief period of a severe classical style in the manner of Herrera, the architect of the Monastery of El Escorial near Madrid. To this class belongs the Cathedral of Mexico City, the most imposing monument of the colonial epoch (it was inaugurated in 1656). With the opening of the seventeenth century, the baroque style took over. In disrepute for several generations, the baroque has now been fully restored to favor by such writers as Heinrich Wölfflin and Sacheverell Sitwell.

After about 1600, the majority of the architects working in the New World had been born there, and they gradually developed original stylistic traits. During the eighteenth century, particularly in Mexico, the baroque style evolved elaborations quite different from the European forms, and ultimately produced what has been called the ultra-baroque, a recent designation to replace the previous, and inadequate, term "churrigueresque" (derived from the name of the Spanish architects Churriguerra). In the elaborations of the American ultra-baroque, the large structural lines retain their definition, and the profusion occurs only in the ornamental portions. There are many structures of great artistic importance in this style. In the opinion of a European critic, four of the eight masterpieces of baroque architecture throughout the world are found in Mexico: the Sacristy of the Cathedral in Mexico City, the College of the Jesuits in Tepoztlán, the Convent of Santa Rosa y Santa Clara in Querétaro, and the Church of San Sebastián y Santa Prisca in Taxco. Eventually, this American style extended its influence to Spain, as several Spanish art critics have pointed out—for example, Enrique Díez-Canedo and Juan de la Encina. Also in Mexico, in Puebla, a local style called *talaveresco* developed and spread through the neighboring region. It was characterized by the use of multicolored tiles to decorate the façades of buildings.

Finally, toward the end of the colonial period, the eighteenth-century classical reaction reached the New World, bringing the neoclassic style. One of the finest specimens of this is the Church of our Lady of Carmen (1802–7) in Celaya (in the state of Guanajuato, Mexico), the work of Francisco Eduardo Tresguerras (1758–1833), the architect who had directed the construction of the Convent of Santa Rosa in Querétaro.

While original forms were being created in the Spanish-speaking countries, architecture in Brazil retained its Portuguese character, save for innovations in details here and there. Excellent baroque buildings were constructed, particularly in Bahia, Olinda, Recife, Rio de Janeiro, and Minas Gerais.

❦{ 4 }❦

Independence
[1800–1825]

THE IDEA that the American colonies would become independent of Spain and Portugal was very old. It was only natural that the Indians, particularly those who belonged to the two great subjugated empires, Mexico and Peru, should think of recovering dominion over their native lands. Indian uprisings, both large and small, began early and broke out repeatedly, reaching a climax in the famous revolt led by Túpac Amaru, a descendant of the Incas, in 1780. The Europeans, and later their descendants, also launched rebellions. The first were those led by Gonzalo Pizarro, brother of the conqueror of Peru, in 1542–44, and by Martín Cortés, son of the conqueror of Mexico, in 1566, in which the rebels went so far as to talk of secession, though there is no evidence that this idea was accepted by the leaders. In any event, none of these uprisings, whether of Indians, of Spaniards, or of *criollos* (Europeans born in the New World), succeeded in seriously jeopardizing the unity of the Spanish empire.

From time to time, someone would put forth the idea that independence was destined to come in the future, but this prophecy was not made in a spirit of rebellion. In 1783, the Count of Aranda, minister to Charles III of Spain, advised the King to create three monarchies, ruled over by Spanish princes of the blood royal: one in North America and two in South America.

Like the Spanish-speaking countries, Brazil experienced various conspiracies and uprisings before the nineteenth century, all of which failed. The most important was the "Infidencia Mineira," which erupted in 1789 in Minas Gerais, under the leadership of Joaquim José da Silva Xavier (1748–92), better known in Brazilian history and legend as "Tiradentes." This revolt was supported by four of the best Brazilian poets: Claudio Manoel da Costa (1728–89), Tomás Antônio Gonzaga (1744–1810), Alvarenga Peixoto (1744–93), and Barbosa Lage (1761–93).

Three events led finally to the movement for secession among the colonies: the United States Declaration of Independence (1776); the French Revolution (1789); and Napoleon's invasion of Spain and Portugal (1807).

Since the middle of the seventeenth century, as we have said, the colonists had been reading the works of French and English thinkers whose writings contained such doctrines as the social contract (which, starting with Grotius and Althusius, had arrived, by way of Spinoza and Locke, among many others, at Rousseau's influential statement), the sovereignty of the people, and the separation of powers in the government of nations. With the revolutionary turn of events in France and North America, these doctrines acquired a dangerous vitality —dangerous for traditional authority. The Spanish Americans not only ignored the injunctions against reading works containing these doctrines, but persisted in reading the documents of both great revolutions and the writings of the thinkers who had participated in them or had supported them, such as Thomas Jefferson. The Declaration of the Rights of Man promulgated by the Constituent Assembly in Paris, translated into Spanish by Antonio Nariño (1765–1823), and printed clandestinely in Bogotá in 1794, circulated throughout a large part of Spanish America.

When Napoleon invaded the Iberian Peninsula, the Portuguese monarchs transferred their court and more than 10,000 followers (counting their retinue and public officials) to Brazil. They left Lisbon at the end of 1807 and arrived in Rio de

Janeiro early in 1808. In March of 1808, the King of Spain abdicated.

The Spanish colonies were now confronted with an unprecedented situation. They had no legitimate government; their king had abdicated, and they refused to recognize the rights of the usurper. At the outset, the tendency was to ignore the authority of Napoleon and to proclaim loyalty to the deposed Spanish monarch through the *ayuntamiento,* or municipal council, the only body whose authority might be said to derive from the people, if only in part. This was especially so when it took the form of the *cabildo abierto,* or town meeting, with the participation of citizens, who, however, exercised no official function. What resulted was a combination of the doctrine of popular sovereignty, very much in favor at the time among enlightened persons, and the old Spanish tradition of the autonomous *cabildo* or *ayuntamiento.*

This movement failed in Mexico (September, 1808). It triumphed temporarily (only to be defeated later) in La Paz (July, 1809), Quito (August, 1809), Caracas (April, 1810), Bogotá (July, 1810), and Santiago de Chile (July and September, 1810). Only in Buenos Aires (May, 1810) did it achieve a lasting success; thenceforth, local power stayed in Argentine hands.

Meanwhile, in Spain, in the region that Napoleon's forces had not managed to dominate, a parliament was convoked (it was modeled on another traditional Spanish concept—the Cortes), and the "overseas provinces" sent their representatives. This parliament, or congress, held its most important meetings in Cádiz, where peninsular Spaniards and Spanish Americans worked together to discuss and draft the first constitution of Spain, promulgated in March, 1812. It was, in the main, liberal. They decreed, furthermore, liberty of the press (November, 1810) and abolished the tribunal of the Inquisition (February, 1813). Among the Spanish Americans, the one who labored most zealously to shape the constitution was the Ecuadorian José Mejía (1777–1813), who was considered the leading orator of the congress.

But Spanish America was restless and could not be satisfied by the Cortes of Cádiz. The desire for independence was felt everywhere, and soon it erupted in violence in many places. In North America, the insurrection began in Mexico in September, 1810; independence was achieved in 1821. As a consequence, Central America was declared free without a struggle; it comprised Guatemala (seat of the captaincy-general from which the rest of the region had been governed), El Salvador, Honduras, Nicaragua, and Costa Rica.

In South America, the movement had two points of departure: Venezuela and Argentina. As early as 1782, the liberation of Spanish America had been envisioned by the Venezuelan Francisco de Miranda (1750–1816), "the Precursor," a man with an extraordinary career. In the name of Spain, he took part in the United States War of Independence in 1781–82, and in 1792, as a general of revolutionary France, he captured the city of Antwerp. (His name is inscribed on the Arc de Triomphe in Paris.) Moreover, he traveled widely in Europe, going as far as Russia, Sweden, and Turkey. He launched the Venezuelan campaign for independence in 1806, and failed; he raised another expedition in 1810, failed again, and died in prison. Either directly or through the Lautaro Lodge (a secret society founded in Buenos Aires to press for independence), he influenced many of the Spanish American liberators, among them Bolívar, San Martín, and O'Higgins. Simón Bolívar (1783–1830), a military genius, finally liberated Venezuela and then New Granada and Ecuador. In the meantime, José de San Martín (1778–1850), another military genius, in 1812 assumed command of the campaign that had begun in Argentina in 1810, and carried the war to Chile (1817), where he was joined by the forces of Bernardo O'Higgins (1776–1842), and then to Peru (1820). The final battles of the South American wars were entrusted to Bolívar, who won the battle of Junín (August 6, 1824), and to his lieutenant Antonio José de Sucre (1795–1830), who triumphed at Ayacucho against a force led by fourteen Spanish generals (December 9, 1824). Aroused by Bolívar's campaigns, the Spanish Antilles, too, tried to achieve independence. Santo Domingo succeeded without a struggle,* but Cuba and Puerto Rico remained subject to Spain until 1898.†

In Brazil, the Portuguese king, João VI, after residing at Rio de Janeiro with his court for thirteen years, returned to Lisbon (April, 1821), leaving his son Pedro as regent of the colony. Pedro was summoned shortly afterward to the Congress of Portugal. However, on the advice of his Brazilian friends, especially José Bonifacio de Andrada e Silva (1765–1838), he chose to remain. He made the historic declaration of his intent—"eu fico" ("I stay")—on January 9, 1822. On September 7, 1822, he proclaimed the independence of Brazil—Grito de Ipiranga (the Cry of Ipiranga)—and on December 1 he had himself crowned emperor. The weak Portuguese attempts at reconquest were easily repulsed. The Empire was organized as a constitutional monarchy, and Pedro I (1798–1834) governed until 1831, when he was deposed. He was succeeded by his son, Pedro II (1825–91), who ruled until 1889, in which year Brazil became a republic.

Political theories had a very important role in the events that led to the independence of Spanish America. The doctrine

* Nevertheless, it was almost immediately taken over by the former French colony of Haiti, which occupies the western portion of the island, and remained under Haitian rule until 1844, when it achieved independence as the Dominican Republic.—TRANS.

† The various countries issued declarations of independence in this order: Venezuela, July 5, 1811; New Granada (present-day Colombia), July 16, 1813 (reconfirmed December 17, 1819, when New Granada was united with Venezuela under the name Republic of Colombia); Paraguay, October 12, 1813; Mexico, November 6, 1813 (at the Congress of Chilpancingo); Argentina, July 9, 1816 (at the Congress of Tucumán); Chile, November 12, 1817; Ecuador, October 9, 1820; Peru, July 28, 1821; Central America, September 15, 1821; Santo Domingo (today the Dominican Republic), November 30, 1821. The Republic of Bolivia—named in honor of Bolívar—was created in August, 1825. Uruguay, in 1811, joined the Argentine revolution of 1810, was invaded by the Portuguese in 1816, but threw off the yoke of the invaders and proclaimed itself an independent republic in 1828. Panama broke off relations with Spain on November 28, 1821, and united with Colombia. Twice, in 1830 and in 1840, it tried to become independent, but both attempts met with failure. Finally, it achieved separation on November 3, 1903, with the help of the United States.

of popular sovereignty, opposed to the tradition that concentrated sovereignty in the monarch, was the theoretical basis upon which the movement for independence rested. It was to be the people who would decide to constitute themselves as a free nation. The inhabitants would thus be transformed from subjects into citizens. Government was to be representative: completely so if the organization was republican, as in France or the United States; partially so if the organization was monarchic, as in England. The latter type was favored by many, including Miranda, and the Argentine Manuel Belgrano, who, along with others, proposed that the monarch should be one of the descendants of the Incas. The monarchic system was tried twice in Mexico, but failed both times: in 1822–23, with Agustín de Iturbide (1787–1824); and in 1864–67, with Maximilian of Habsburg (1832–67).

Liberty, according to the revolutionaries, should be full, and equality complete. Discriminations of class and race were declared null; titles of nobility were abolished. It was decided to abolish slavery, and emancipation was proclaimed by the priest and revolutionary leader Miguel Hidalgo (1753–1811) in Mexico (September, 1810), by Bolívar in Venezuela (July, 1815), and in decrees of the Congress of Chile (1811) and of the triumvirate that governed in Buenos Aires. The order became effective after independence had been achieved.

During the colonial epoch, the races had mixed freely, with the result that there were many distinctions of caste (Negroes, Indians, mulattoes, mestizos, and combinations of these), which even came to be regulated by law. But these regulations were never systematized; they were often, in fact, contradicted by other regulations. Any ordinance concerning the Indians, such as those that attempted to bar their admission to the University of San Marcos in Lima in the eighteenth century, conflicted with the sixteenth-century regulations encouraging marriage between Spaniards and natives (1503 and 1514; confirmed in 1680) and establishing institutions of higher education for the Indians.

In actual practice, these distinctions were subject to infinite variation and modification; fully defined discrimination never existed. "The colonial castes were the result of racial mixing [*mestizaje*]," wrote the Argentine scholar Angel Rosenblat; but, as it persisted, "the process of *mestizaje* itself tended to bring about the dissolution of castes." As a matter of fact, the Spaniard, a man of the Mediterranean—a very ancient meeting place of races and cultures—had no strongly ingrained race prejudice, and the Portuguese probably had even less. The equalitarian doctrines of the eighteenth century reinforced this traditional attitude in Spanish America, and the campaigns of liberation gave it official sanction.

Another consequence of these new trends was the elimination of the tributes and imposts levied on the Indians, such as the *mita* (forced labor) in the Viceroyalty of Peru. An effort was made to end what amounted to the virtual servitude of the natives—a problem that, because it does not depend solely on laws, still remains unsolved. Only in Mexico have steps been made toward a solution.

Freedom was also proclaimed in the economic sphere. One of the greatest hindrances during the colonial regime had been the ban on all commerce except with Spain (this restriction was only partially modified in the eighteenth century); hence the spread of smuggling, practiced on a large scale by the English, the French, and the Dutch. Finally, another important freedom was achieved: freedom of the press.

In Brazil, as much ferment was produced by political principles as in Spanish America. The government became a constitutional monarchy in 1820, even before independence, and the Constitution of the Empire was promulgated in March, 1824. Titles of nobility were retained, but the onus of inferiority attached to manual labor was eliminated, and descent from the working class was no longer a barrier to public office.

While the struggle for independence was going on, efforts were made to replace the colonial system with a modern social organization, not only in the political and economic areas but also in the cultural area. Plans for the reform of public education were included in several of the revolutionary proclamations and new constitutions. Many leaders cherished the ideal of extending cultural benefits to all the people, taking modern scientific thought as a basis. In the midst of the struggle, a number of cultural and educational institutions were founded: in 1821, the Academia Lauretana, which became the University of Arequipa in 1827; in 1822, the University of Antioquia in New Granada; in 1824, by a decree of Bolívar, the University of Trujillo in Peru; the Naval Schools of Cartagena and of Guayaquil; the Public Library of Buenos Aires (September, 1810), a project of Mariano Moreno (1778–1811), leader of the May Revolution in 1810 in Argentina; the Public Library of Montevideo (1816); those of Santiago de Chile and of Lima, founded by San Martín in 1821; and the Museum of Sciences in Bogotá (1823). In various places, it was decreed that the convents should undertake to teach the people reading and writing, as they had in the sixteenth century (only to let the practice lapse in later years).

Not a great deal could be done, naturally, during the struggle. The cultural organ that could best serve the cause of liberty was the press, and during this relatively brief period, more newspapers and periodicals appeared than during the entire colonial epoch. Mariano Moreno founded the *Gaceta de Buenos Aires* in June, 1810; it lasted until September, 1821. Miguel Hidalgo, priest of the parish of Dolores and initiator of the movement for liberation in Mexico, had *El Despertador Americano* published in Guadalajara (December, 1810–January, 1811) under the direction of another priest, Francisco Severo Maldonado (*c.* 1770–1832), a sort of self-proclaimed socialist. Later, at the height of the insurrection, the *Ilustrador Nacional* appeared (April–May, 1812), edited by Dr. José María Cos (1774–1819), who was also a priest and who improvised a printing press, making his own type out of wood. The Mexican insurrection mustered a total of fifteen publications between 1810 and 1821 (the country as a whole had forty). During the period between the *cabildo abierto* of April, 1810, and the declaration of independence in July, 1811, Venezuela had the *Seminario de Caracas* (from November, 1810, until 1811); *El Mercurio Venezolano* (January, 1811); and *El Patriota Venezolano,* organ of the Patriotic Society (June, 1811. Among later Venezuelan periodicals, one of the most outstanding was *El Correo del Orinoco,* edited by Francisco Antonio Zea (1766–1822) and published in Angostura from 1818 to 1821. Camilo Henríquez (1769–1825) published *La Aurora de Chile* (1812–13) in Santiago, the first newspaper in the country; as such, it aroused extraordinary enthusiasm. Many others might be mentioned, such as *El Diario Político de Santa Fe de Bogotá* (1810–11), edited by Caldas, the naturalist, and Joaquín Camacho, which, however, did not appear daily, in spite of its name; the *Argos Americano* of Cartagena de Indias (1810–12), later moved to Tunja (1813–15) and then to Bogotá (1815–16); and *La Bagatela* of Bogotá (1811–12), under the direction of Antonio Nariño. Between 1810 and 1825, nearly fifty newspapers appeared in New Granada (Colombia).

In cities that remained under Spanish domination during the wars for independence, newspapers were published that attacked the patriots. But the freedom of the press decreed by the Spanish Cortes permitted the existence of another kind of publication which, although it might not dare to advocate the cause of independence openly, at least carried a lively discussion of current problems. Among these were, in Lima, *El Cometa* (1811–14), *El Peruano* (1811–12), and *El Argos Constitucional* (1813); in Havana, *El Americano Libre* (1820); in Santo Domingo, *El Telégrafo Constitucional* (1821); in Mexico, the papers run by Carlos María de Bustamante and Joaquín Fernández de Lizardi (1776–1827), who adopted as a pen name the title of his best-known review, *El Pensador Mexicano* (The Mexican Thinker; 1812–14). In addition, many polemical pamphlets were printed; Fernández de Lizardi alone was responsible for some three hundred during his lifetime.

The Spanish American patriots also published newspapers and pamphlets in foreign cities, particularly in London, a haven at the time for many supporters of liberty. Among the periodicals published in London were *El Colombiano* (1810), edited by Francisco de Miranda; *El Censor Americano* (1810), edited by the Guatemalan Antonio José de Irisarri (1786–1868); and the reviews edited by the Venezuelan Andrés Bello (1781–1865) and the Colombian Juan García del Río (1794–1856), the *Biblioteca Americana* (1823) and the *Repertorio Americano* (1826–27). These two important reviews did not confine themselves to defending the cause of independence, but sought to further enlightenment in America by publishing studies on a wide variety of subjects relating to the scientific movement in Europe.

When the Portuguese monarchs established themselves in Brazil, many innovations were introduced. Freedom of commerce with friendly nations was decreed (1808); the Bank of Brazil was created; the gates were opened for foreign immigration; and printing was re-established (1808). In Rio de Janeiro a number of institutions were established: the Naval Academy (1808), the Academy of Surgery (1816), the School of Fine Arts (1816), the National Museum, the Botanical Garden (1811), the Public Library (1811), and the Royal Theater (1809). In Bahia, the School of Medicine was founded in 1816. The first Brazilian newspapers appeared, beginning with the *Gazeta do Rio de Janeiro* in 1808. The most interesting was perhaps the one published in London, the *Correio Brasiliense* (1808–23), in which Hipólito José da Costa Mendonça (1774–1823) advocated the idea of independence.

The leaders of the movement for independence were, for the most part, men of thought as well as men of action; their thought prepared and directed their actions. Several of them were university graduates. Miranda had an immense and insatiable appetite for reading. He was considered to be, in the words of John Adams, "a man of universal knowledge"; Ezra Stiles, the president of Yale College, called him "a learned man and a flaming son of liberty." Bolívar, a great reader and a great traveler, wrote admirable letters, devoted much attention to political principles, and drafted two constitutions: the Republic of Colombia's first one, in 1819 (in collaboration with Francisco

Antonio Zea), and Bolivia's first one, in 1826. Mariano Moreno eloquently explored social and economic problems, particularly in his dissertation "Sobre el servicio personal de los Indios" (On the Personal Service of the Indians), read in Charcas in 1802, and in the *Representación de los hacendados y labradores* (Representation of Landowners and Workers), submitted to the viceroy in Buenos Aires in solicitation of free trade with foreign countries (1809). Hidalgo had undertaken to teach crafts and trades to his parishioners, had been rector of the College of San Nicolás in Valladolid de Michoacán, and had translated plays from French. José Núñez de Cáceres (1772–1846), catalyst of the independence movement in Santo Domingo in 1821, was a jurist and a writer; in 1815, he had been rector of the University of Santo Tomás de Aquino. Among the many other patriots who were jurists, writers, orators, or poets, we should mention, in Mexico, Friar Servando Teresa de Mier (1763–1827), whose autobiography is as lively as a picaresque novel, and Andrés Quintana Roo (1787–1851); in Central America, José Cecilio del Valle (1780–1834) and Friar Matías de Córdoba (c. 1750–1829); in Colombia, Francisco de Paula Santander (1792–1840), "the man of laws," first President of the nation after its separation from Venezuela and Ecuador; in Chile, Camilo Henríquez; in Argentina, Bernardo de Monteagudo (c. 1787–1825), Manuel Belgrano, and José María Paz (1782–1854)—the last two were generals. Even the Venezuelan general José Antonio Páez (1790–1873), who at the outset of his career as a soldier was an uncultured man, devoted himself to learning and in his old age wrote his memoirs.

The period of independence, because of its very brevity and the inevitable anxieties attendant on it, was scarcely a time in which art might flourish: there were no buildings, of course, and few scholarly works; in painting, only portraits of heroes; in music, patriotic songs and national anthems. Literature there was, and in abundance, but, for the most part, it was politically or socially oriented. The first novels written and published in Spanish America date from this period: the four by Fernández de Lizardi, of which the earliest, *El periquillo sarniento* (The Mangy Parrot, published in English as *The Itching Parrot*), is the best known. It is in the tradition of the picaresque novel, but the social lessons it tries to inculcate derive from the Enlightenment of the eighteenth century.

The theater was also enlisted as a means to stimulate patriotism and propagate political and social principles. There are political overtones even in works of scholarship such as the *Biblioteca hispanoamericana septentrional,* by the Mexican churchman José Mariano Beristáin de Souza (1756–1817), which was published during the war (1816–21). It is an exhaustive bibliography, in three volumes, of the writings produced in Mexico, Central America, and the Antilles during three centuries.

Poetry was enlisted in the service of liberty. Part of it has a popular, anonymous origin—for example, the verses in honor of Morelos, another priest turned revolutionary general:

> *Por un cabo doy dos reales,*
> *por un sargento un doblón;*
> *por mi general Morelos*
> *doy todo mi corazón.*

> *For a corporal I'll give two bits,*
> *For a sergeant one doubloon;*
> *For my General Morelos*
> *I'll give all of my heart.*

Other revolutionary poetry was written by cultivated poets in the popular idiom. Bartolomé Hidalgo (1788–1823), an Uruguayan who labored for the independence of Argentina, is the most interesting of these poets. With him begins, in the region of the Río de la Plata, the type of poetry known as *gauchesca,* which must be distinguished from "gaucho poetry" composed by the rural gauchos. *Gauchesca* poetry is about the gauchos, but is written in the cities. Hidalgo wrote a type of verse called *cielito* (little heaven), imitated from folk poetry and intended for singing around the campfire by the soldiers of the revolution; in addition, he wrote dialogues in verse.

The literary poets also celebrated the triumphs of the revolution with numerous hymns and odes. Outstanding among these is "La Victoria de Junín" (The Victory of Junín; 1825), by the Ecuadorian José Joaquín de Olmedo (1784–1847), in praise of Bolívar. It is in the neoclassic style of the eighteenth century, which Olmedo handles masterfully. Olmedo, who was a deputy from Guayaquil in the Cortes of Cádiz, also translated Pope's *Essay on Man* into Spanish. Another poet, the Cuban José María Heredia (1803–39), eulogized Bolívar and Washington. He sang the misfortunes of Cuba, which had not succeeded in gaining its independence. He himself had taken part in the abortive conspiracy of the Order of the Suns and Rays of Bolívar, in 1823. His best odes are "El Teocalli de Cholula" (1820) and "Niágara" (1824). "Niágara" acquired such fame in all Spanish-speaking countries that to this day its author is called "the Bard of Niagara."

No less celebrated than the odes of Olmedo and Heredia are two by the Venezuelan Andrés Bello entitled *Silvas americanas*. The first, "Alocución a la poesía" (Allocution to Poetry), written in 1823, contains a declaration of intellectual independence for Spanish America, comparable to Channing's in his essay *On National Literature* (1823) and Emerson's in his address "The American Scholar" (1837). The second of these odes, titled "La agricultura de la zona tórrida" (The Agriculture of the Torrid Zone; 1826), calls on the "youthful nations" of America to dedicate themselves to the tasks of civilization. In his time, Bello was the most cultured man in the New World. In the field of philosophy—one of the subjects he taught at the university—he produced a work that was both erudite and original: *Filosofía del entendimiento* (The Philosophy of Understanding). In the realm of law—another subject that he taught—he was the principal author of the Civil Code of Chile (1855) and, in addition, wrote one of the first important treatises on international law. He was the author of a comprehensive Spanish grammar (*Gramática de la lengua castellana*)

and of a short study of Spanish prosody (*Métrica*), both regarded as basic works unsurpassed to this day. He undertook
research in literary history and was the first to clarify the
origins of assonance in rhyme; he translated Horace (as did
many of his contemporaries) and Plautus from the Latin, and
also fragments from the *Nibelungen,* the *Orlando* of Boiardo,
and poems by Byron and Victor Hugo. In public life, after having served his native country as an agent of the revolution in
London, where he lived from 1810 to 1829, he settled in Chile,
where he held various official posts, including that of adviser
to the government on judicial matters. In fact, for three decades, he guided the cultural life of Chile, particularly as
teacher and as president of the University of Chile, which he
reorganized in 1843.

José Bonifacio de Andrada e Silva, orator and poet, truly the
father of Brazilian independence, was esteemed as the most
learned man in Brazil, both in the sciences and in letters. His
scientific specialty was mineralogy. Another Brazilian, José da
Silva Lisboa (1756–1836), distinguished himself as an economist
and historian.

{ 5 }

After
Independence
[1825–1860]

INDEPENDENCE EVOLVED without serious difficulties in Brazil. The country began to adopt modern forms in its public and social life; economic activity, free from the trammels of colonialism, expanded; cultural endeavors prospered.

The Constitution of the Empire (1824) established four powers: in addition to the executive, the legislative, and the judicial—the classical powers, known to readers of Montesquieu—there was the "moderative," derived from Benjamin Constant. The moderative power, in this instance, was represented by the monarch. The legislative powers resided in the Assembly, composed of a chamber periodically elected, and a senate whose members held office for life.

This constitution remained in force until the end of the Empire, in 1889; it underwent revision, however, from 1832 to 1888. The organization of the country, unitarian at first, gradually moved toward federalism. The Additional Act of 1834 granted autonomy to the provinces, giving them their own legislative assemblies. The system of government, the Brazilian historian Pedro Calmon wrote, "was implicitly parliamentary, given the attributes possessed by the sovereign for dissolving the Chamber, the broad functions exercised by the latter, and the responsibility of the ministers of the Crown to the Chamber." In 1847, the office of President of the Council of Ministers (Prime Minister) was established; it was responsible to the Assembly.

In 1835 the right of primogeniture was abolished, although titles of nobility were retained, and restrictions were removed on the division of lands.

Emperor Pedro II, a studious man, supporter and protector of the arts and sciences, showed himself at all times respectful of the laws and of freedom of opinion. Bartolomé Mitre, the Argentine statesman and historian, called Brazil "a crowned democracy."

The situation in the Spanish-speaking countries was very different. For them, the struggle to achieve independence was long and bloody. When it ended, the countries were ruined, their populations decimated, the structure of society disrupted. The colonial regime had not organized or educated the people politically; it had ruled by force, and the force was directed from a distant capital in Europe. At the outset of the campaigns for liberation, men of high intelligence and of firm character, capable of daring and of sacrifice, assumed the leadership and gave shape and direction to the struggle. The masses honored their values because they too aspired to liberty. But once independence was achieved, the forces of anarchy were unleashed and a long period of political unrest ensued, oscillating between despotism and civil strife. The political unity of some of the newly created nations was dissolved. Central America, for example, upon declaring its independence in 1821, had chosen to unite with Mexico. But in June, 1823, it dissolved the union; and in 1838–39, it split into five small republics: Guatemala, El Salvador, Honduras, Nicaragua, and Costa Rica. (One of the obstacles to reunification was the opposition of the United States, in 1882 and 1885.) In 1836, Mexico lost Texas, which seceded and constituted itself a separate republic. When it was annexed by the United States in 1845, war with Mexico ensued (1846–48), as a consequence of which the former Viceroyalty of New Spain lost half its territory. Gran Colombia,* organized under the aegis of Bolívar, split into three new nations: Colombia (formerly called New Granada), Venezuela, and Ecuador.

At times, it has been observed that the remedy for this chaotic situation would have been either a monarchy, as in Brazil, or dictatorial rule by the revolutionary leaders (*caudillos*), duly established by law. In truth, every form of government was tried—monarchy, dictatorship, democracy, unitarianism, federalism—and they all failed. The tyrants, such as Juan Manuel de Rosas (1793–1877) in Buenos Aires† and Antonio López de Santa Ana (1791–1876) in Mexico, fell from power, and so did the more democratic rulers. However, after 1850, the countries began to grow somewhat calmer. Unrest did not disappear entirely—it is still with us—and occasionally there were violent outbreaks, but only rarely has there been a recurrence of the extreme conditions that prevailed immediately following independence.

Not all was anarchy or tyranny even then, however. In addition to Brazil, where the monarchy existed without too much disturbance during the reign of Pedro II, Chile quieted down after 1830, with a series of oligarchical governments, strong but

* The nomenclature of present-day Colombia has a long and complicated history. Originally, the country formed part of the New Kingdom of Granada, which became a viceroyalty in 1717. As reorganized in 1740, the Viceroyalty of New Granada included the present republics of Colombia, Panama, Venezuela, and Ecuador. By 1810, however, after the creation of the Captaincy-General of Venezuela and the Presidency of Quito, the viceroyalty consisted only of present-day Colombia and Panama. In 1819, New Granada achieved independence from Spain under the leadership of Bolívar, and on December 17 of that year, by decree of the Congress of Angostura, New Granada and Venezuela were united as the Republic of Colombia—generally known as Gran Colombia. This union was dissolved in 1830, with the secession of Venezuela and Ecuador, which became independent nations. On February 29, 1832, the Republic of New Granada was established. Then, with the constitution of May, 1863, the name United States of Colombia was adopted. Finally, the constitution of 1885 provided that the country should henceforth be known as the Republic of Colombia.—TRANS.

† Rosas became governor of the Province of Buenos Aires in 1829; from this vantage point he was able to make himself virtual dictator of Argentina until his overthrow in 1852.—TRANS.

not despotic. And in other countries, there were leaders clearly inclined toward democracy and sometimes truly liberal, like Bernardino Rivadavia (1780–1845) in Argentina, Valentín Gómez Farías (1781–1858) and Benito Juárez (1806–72) in Mexico, Vicente Rocafuerte (1783–1847) in Ecuador, Francisco de Paula Santander and Tomás Cipriano Mosquera (1798–1878) in Colombia.

In the midst of this ferment, the men of thought who attained to positions of influence in the governments or in the congresses accomplished an extraordinary task of social transformation. The leaders of the independence movements had projected these reforms; now they had to be made a reality. In the intervals between anarchy and despotism, or even in the midst of them, legislation was passed in an effort to establish orderly rule. The trend was predominantly democratic, with occasional concessions to authoritarianism, as in the Chilean constitutions of 1818, 1822, 1823, and 1833. The law was at times too far in advance of the facts; it represented the ideal rather than reality. In the long run, however, it imposed forms of political coexistence.

The juridical knowledge acquired in the universities and by reading seldom had any practical application during the colonial regime, save in exceptional cases such as that of Antonio León Pinelo in the seventeenth century—compiler, systematizer, and historian of the legal code of the Indies; and the Mexican Francisco Javier Gamboa (1717–94), author of the Carolingian Code on the treatment of slaves. Now, with independence, this knowledge was manifested in a prodigious legislative effort.

The first concern of the organizers of the new nations was to adopt constitutions. During the wars of independence the first constitutions were drafted and promulgated; afterward came many others.* The general political instability also affected

* In 1814, the first constitution of Mexico was proclaimed (at the Congress of Chilpancingo). The first constitutions of other nations came into effect as follows: Chile, 1818, replaced in 1822, 1823, and 1833; Argentina, which was then known as the United Provinces of the Río de la

these fundamental charters, and in several countries the custom persists of changing them each time a new current of opinion (real or imaginary) is imposed, either by way of new statutes (as in Bolivia and the Dominican Republic) or through constitutional amendments (as in Mexico and Guatemala).

The models for these constitutions were the Spanish Constitution of 1812 (particularly in the case of the Chilean Constitution of 1822, the Mexican Constitution of 1824, and the Dominican Constitution of 1844), and the constitutions of France and the United States; at times, influences from all three were combined. In successive emendations and revisions, changes of local origin began to appear. A few countries adopted the federal system: Brazil after 1889; Mexico from 1824 to 1836 and in 1857; Argentina after 1853; Venezuela after 1864; Colombia from 1863 to 1886. The rest adopted a unitarian or centralized system. All of them have the presidential system, as in the United States, with the exception of Chile, which for a long time had the parliamentary system of

---

Plata, with a centralized government, 1819 (at the Congress of Tucumán, later moved to Buenos Aires); Gran Colombia, 1819 (at the Congress of Angostura, replaced in 1821 by the constitution of the Congress of Cúcuta); and Peru, 1823. In the Dominican Republic and Central America, which had no wars of independence, the first constitutions were proclaimed, respectively, in 1821 and 1824. Later came the constitutions of Bolivia, drafted by Bolívar, 1826; Uruguay, 1830 (it was in effect until 1916); and Paraguay, 1844 (before that, there had been only the Government Regulations of 1813). A new constitution was proclaimed in Argentina in 1826, making it a unified republic; in 1827, the provinces became virtually autonomous, except for foreign affairs, which were entrusted to the local government of Buenos Aires—and remained so until they were reunited under the new constitution of 1853. New constitutions came into effect as follows: Mexico, 1824, followed by those of 1836, 1843, and 1857; Peru, 1828, followed by those of 1834, 1839, 1856, and 1860; Bolivia, 1831, followed by six more, up to 1861; Chile, 1828 and 1833 (the last, drafted chiefly by Mariano Egaña, 1793–1846, was in force until 1925); the Dominican Republic, 1844, 1854, and 1858; Venezuela, 1830, revised in 1857 and 1858; Ecuador, 1830, revised six times up to 1861; and Colombia, 1832, revised in 1843 and 1853. The last three were adopted after these countries separated politically, as was the case also in Central America, where Guatemala and Nicaragua adopted their first constitutions in 1838, El Salvador and Honduras in 1839, and Costa Rica in 1844 (followd by two others, in 1847 and 1859). El Salvador and Honduras had new constitutions in 1848, and Guatemala in 1851.

ministerial responsibility to an elected congress, as in England with its Parliament. Universal suffrage was an aspiration of most authors of these constitutions, but in practice, suffrage was limited to that part of the population that could read and write. Such was the case in Chile, Bolivia, Ecuador, and Venezuela. One of the interesting innovations in Hispanic American constitutional law is the *recurso de amparo,* found in the Mexican legislation. It is a suit, brought before a federal court, against any authority or law that infringes on the rights of the individual. As a guaranty of personal safety, it has been no less efficacious than the right of habeas corpus.

The aim of legislative activity during the wars of independence and in the years immediately following was to realize the ideal of liberty, both of nations and of individuals. In Mexico, Venezuela, Chile, and Buenos Aires, as we have said, it was decreed that slavery would be abolished, and abolition was implemented successively throughout the countries of Spanish America.* In each case, these countries anticipated the action taken by the United States in the Emancipation Proclamation (1862). Under the Spanish regime, however, slavery was retained in Puerto Rico and Cuba until 1872 and 1880, respectively. In Brazil, slavery was maintained during the Empire. But it should be observed that slavery left no strong racial prejudices in Brazil. The experience in Brazil indicates that prejudice between races disappears with the elimination of all discrimination in practice—a solution reflecting both common sense and the brotherhood of man.

Throughout Hispanic America, moreover, measures were taken or confirmed to abolish the imposts borne by the natives (in Peru, the final abolition of Indian tribute had to wait until

---

* In Gran Colombia, by the constitution of 1819 (confirmed subsequently by the three republics into which this country was divided: Colombia, 1851; Ecuador, 1853; Venezuela, 1854). In Central America, at that time federated, by a decree of the Constituent Assembly, 1823. In Chile, by the constitution of October, 1823. In Bolivia, by the constitution of 1826. In Mexico, by the decree of President Vicente Guerrero in 1829. In Uruguay, by a decree of 1843, complying with a provision in the constitution of 1830. In Argentina, by the constitution of 1853. In Peru, by a decree of 1854.

1854). The Indians and the Negroes were thus no longer set apart as a servile class, though they continued to be exploited, like the poor in all parts of the world.

Equality before the law was sanctioned by legislation throughout the whole of Hispanic America; so was social equality, in principle, with the suppression of privileges, of titles of nobility (in Brazil they persisted solely as a form of distinction under the Empire), of the rights of primogeniture (which in Chile—an anomalous case—were established in 1833, but abolished in 1857), and of every kind of hereditary distinction. The movement toward social democracy, then, has been steady and continuous, while the advance toward political democracy has been uneven.

Along with the establishment of a firm basis for liberty and equality, it was also necessary to modernize the judicial structure of society with respect to relations among individuals. Spain and Portugal had bequeathed to the peoples of America a vast and confused body of laws of every period, from the Middle Ages to the beginning of the nineteenth century. These laws had to be simplified. France had set the example with the codification of civil law (1804), commercial law (1807), and penal law (1810); and of civil proceedings in 1806, and criminal proceedings in 1808. Following this trend, Bolivia enacted a civil code in 1830, Peru in 1851, and Chile—the most original of all—in 1855, largely the work of Andrés Bello. Commercial codes were formulated in Bolivia in 1834, in Costa Rica in 1853, and in Argentina in the 1850's. The Argentine code was the work of Dalmacio Vélez Sarsfield and Eduardo Acevedo; Bolivia drafted its penal code in 1834, and Guatemala, around 1836. The process of codification was to continue throughout the century.

Brazil began the task of codification in 1850, with commercial legislation. The year 1857 saw the appearance of the *Consolidação das Leis Civis* (The Consolidation of the Civil Laws), compiled, classified, and elucidated by Augusto Teixeira de Freitas. The civil code, however, was not enacted until 1916.

In addition to the questions of political and juridical structures, the governments were confronted with three fundamental problems: public economy, the relations of Church and state, and the education of the people. It was necessary to restore prosperity to the ruined countries. On the economic front, liberal principles were adopted. The first step, taken at the outset of the wars for independence, was to establish complete freedom of commerce. Afterward, there was much to abolish: monopolies, both official and private; the *alcabala,* a sales tax which in some cases (in Mexico, for example) required a kind of internal customs service to make collections; and the mortmain,* which prohibited the alienation of certain property. In general, an attempt was made to modify the system of taxes (among others, the tithes imposed by the Catholic Church, as well as the Indian tributes, were abolished); public works and public services were projected; and efforts were made to attract foreign capital. Progress was very slow until after 1860 because of the political unrest. And loans from abroad were of little help; foreign capitalists were often dishonest in fulfilling the terms of their contracts.

In matters of religion, many statesmen endeavored to establish complete liberty of worship. At first, such efforts were not everywhere successful; eventually, however, freedom of religious worship was incorporated in all the constitutions of Spanish America, even in the countries that have an official religion, such as Costa Rica and Paraguay, and in those where a recognized religion receives government support, such as Argentina, Bolivia, and the Dominican Republic. The Spanish American clergy, which had supported, and even in certain instances promoted, the movement for independence, did not always concur with the separation of Church and state. Neither did it approve of tolerance toward religions other than Roman Catholicism. (There were some admirable exceptions, however, such as the Peruvian Father Francisco de Paula Vigil, 1792–

---

* Literally, "dead hand," referring to the hand or possession of ecclesiastical corporations, since ecclesiastics in early law were considered civilly "dead." At one time, only the sovereign had power to alienate lands in mortmain.—TRANS.

1875.) But that was not the only difficulty. The laws concerning mortmains affected above all the Church and the religious orders, which had large holdings in real estate, and there was a dispute over whether or not these holdings belonged to the state. There were also disputes about the establishment of a civil register for births, marriages, and deaths, and particularly about the law establishing civil matrimony. And disputes would arise in the twentieth century, or shortly before, about the laws establishing divorce: in the Dominican Republic (1897), in Honduras (1898), and thereafter in Venezuela, Nicaragua, Cuba, Uruguay, Panama, Mexico, Peru, and Bolivia. Difficulties ensued over the secularization of cemeteries, and over lay teaching. However, these principles finally prevailed, with very few exceptions. The properties of religious orders were taken over by the state in Mexico (after 1859), and in Guatemala, Honduras, and Venezuela. They were closed in Paraguay during the government (1814–40) of Dr. José Gaspar Rodríguez de Francia (1766–1840).

A final area requiring reform was public education, both its methods and its content, with modern science taking a prominent place. The transformation was slow, but constant. In the first phase, the chief innovation in method was the introduction of the Lancastrian system of mutual instruction, which helped to offset the scarcity of teachers. Joseph Lancaster, a British Quaker (1778–1838), was in Caracas in 1824 at Bolívar's invitation. Even before that, his method was introduced by the Scotsman James Thompson, who resided in Argentina, at the invitation of Rivadavia, from 1818 to 1821, and who also spent some time in Chile (where the Lancastrian method had been introduced in 1821 by Friar Sebastián de Mora), Peru, and Colombia, until his return to Europe, in 1825.

Schools to train teachers were organized in Gran Colombia in 1822, in Peru and Uruguay in 1827, and in Bolivia, but the first true normal school was established in Chile in 1842, under the direction of the Argentine educator Domingo Faustino Sarmiento (1811–88); similar establishments were being projected in Colombia at the time. If public education did not grow apace, it was because of the lack of resources. Nevertheless, in Colombia, from 1827 to 1837, Santander succeeded in increasing the number of schools from about five hundred to more than a thousand.

At times, the universities that had been founded during the colonial epoch stood in opposition to the innovating spirit ushered in by independence, and it was necessary to reform them. As a general rule, those under the direction of the clergy—the majority—were secularized, and nearly all the faculties of theology were abolished. Theological teaching was confined to the Tridentine seminaries. In Mexico City, the university was closed in 1833; its component schools survived separately until 1910. The University of Chile was closed in 1842, but reopened the following year after being reorganized on the French model, under the direction of Andrés Bello. It then began to publish its scholarly *Anales* (Annals). New universities were founded in Buenos Aires (1821), in Montevideo (1833), and in Medellín and Cauca, Colombia, and in Costa Rica (1843). Schools of law and of medicine were founded in various cities, and in 1831, Mexico opened its National Museum of Archaeology, History, and Ethnology, which in time was to attain to an extraordinary development.

In Brazil, several educational institutions were established during the residence of the Portuguese monarchs in the colony. The period of the Empire also saw the founding of law schools in São Paulo (1827) and Olinda (1827), of the School of Medicine in Rio de Janeiro (1830), the Lyceum of Arts and Crafts (1856), and many provincial schools (after 1836).

The desire for far-reaching innovations found political expression in two great movements: the Reform (*Reforma*) in Mexico and the Organization (*Organización*) in Argentina. In Mexico, the conflict of ideas—and of arms—between conservatives and liberals lasted from 1833 to 1867. The conservatives were trying to retain as much as possible of the colonial system; the liberals wanted the elimination of privileges, the separation of Church and state, freedom of worship, freedom of speech and of the press, and the alienation of the lands in mortmain. (As mentioned, the Mexican government at length took possession of all ecclesiastical property.) The liberals succeeded in drafting and ratifying the admirable constitution of 1857; the conservatives, who triumphed in 1864 with the help of the troops of Napoleon III, had Maximilian of Habsburg installed as emperor. The conflict ended with the fall of the Empire and the triumph of the liberal party (1867). The leaders of the Reform were Valentín Gómez Farías, Benito Juárez, Father José María Luis Mora (1794–1850), Ignacio Luis Vallarta (1830–93), known for his opinions from the bench on constitutional questions, Melchor Ocampo (1813–61), and the Lerdo de Tejada brothers, Miguel (1812–61) and Sebastián (1827–89).

In Argentina, the initial attempt at modern organization was carried out by Bernardino Rivadavia, first as secretary of the Triumvirate (September, 1811–October, 1812), then as minister in the province of Buenos Aires (1821–24), and finally as President of the Republic (February, 1826–July, 1827). He founded the University of Buenos Aires, the Academy of Medicine, the School of Agriculture, and in 1822, the Sociedad de Beneficencia, a benevolent association under the direction of a woman of unusual energy and intelligence, María Sánchez de Mendeville (1786–1868). (This society is still in operation.) He also established the Museum of Natural History (1823), a great many schools for both boys and girls, the discount bank, the national currency system, the mercantile exchange, and four cities. He drafted regulations governing the practice of medicine (1822) and the administration of hospitals (1822), and made reforms in Church matters, abolishing ecclesiastical immunity and tithes, and imposing regulations on the number and age of the members of monasteries and convents. In 1821, he established the Recoleta Cemetery, the first in Buenos Aires; previously, the dead had been interred in courtyards or porches, or in churches or buildings of the religious orders. He encouraged the immigration of farmers and craftsmen and improved the breeding of sheep by importing merinos. He set up guarantees for labor contracts and for apprenticeships, and established the type of contract known as emphyteusis, whereby lands were granted in usufruct to those who would work them and who were in a position to pay for them (although payment was not actually required). He even proposed to aid the liberals in Spain in 1823 against the absolutist excesses of Ferdinand VII, who was supported by the foreign troops of the Holy Alliance.

In 1827, when the political unity of the nation was disrupted, the work of Rivadavia was attacked and partly rescinded. The system of emphyteusis disappeared, and land was distributed arbitrarily; immense holdings (latifundia) were then created for the benefit of a few. The provinces suffered for years under *caudillaje,* the rule of local despots. Under the *caudillo* Juan Manuel de Rosas, who was the most powerful of these dictators as governor of the province of Buenos Aires, the University of Buenos Aires and the Public Library practically ceased to exist. After 1838, thinking men, particularly the younger ones, went into exile and did not return until 1852, after the overthrow of Rosas.

Then, at long last, the Argentine Republic was established under the constitution of 1853, which is still in force, though it was drastically revised by Juan Perón in 1949. Three of the former exiles played highly important roles in the republic, which gave the nation a long period of peace and prosperity: Juan Bautista Alberdi (1810–84), author of the *Bases* (1852), which served, substantially, as the foundation of the constitution; Bartolomé Mitre (1821–1906), President from 1862 to 1868; and Domingo Faustino Sarmiento, President from 1868 to 1874.

Literary reviews and literary societies were an important part of the cultural activity of the time. Although they were chiefly concerned with belles-lettres, their sphere of interest extended to include philosophy and even the sciences. Such was the case with the Academy of San Juan de Letrán in Mexico City (1836 to 1856) and the Literary Salon in Buenos Aires (1837). Organized by the Uruguayan bookseller and pedagogue Marcos Sastre (1809–87), the Salon was forced to close in short order when Rosas began to persecute its members. Other progressive societies were the various "Amigos del País" (Friends of the Country), first organized during the eighteenth century. These latter were typical of the Enlightenment; their main interest was in economic development. There were also associations whose interests were strictly scientific, such as the Society of Geography and Statistics, founded in Mexico City in 1833, which still exists.

Many fine reviews flourished, especially in Chile. Among these were: the *Semanario de Santiago* (1842–43); the *Revista de Valparaíso* (1842); the *Museo de Ambas Américas,* edited by the Colombian Juan García del Río in Valparaíso (1842); *El Crepúsculo,* edited by the political thinker José Victoriano Lastarria (1817–88) in Santiago (1843–44); the *Revista de Santiago* (1848–51 and 1855); the *Revista de Ciencias y Letras* of Santiago (1857–58); the *Revista del Pacífico* of Valparaíso (1858–61), and *La Semana* of Santiago (1859–60).*

The best was the *Revista Bimestre Cubana* (1831–34), organ of the Economic Society of the Friends of the Country, in Havana. Its contributors were liberal men, many viewed with suspicion by the Spanish authorities, such as Domingo del Monte (1804–53), José Antonio Saco (1797–1879), and José de la Luz y Caballero (1800–1862). Reviews devoted to particular sciences began to appear. The *Memorial de Ciencias Naturales,* for example, was edited in Lima by two mineralogists, Nicolás de Piérola (d. 1857) and Mariano Eduardo Rivero

---

* There were many others: *La Moda de Buenos Aires* (1837–38), written by the members of the Literary Salon; *El Iniciador* of Montevideo (1838–39), edited by Uruguayan and Argentine exiles who opposed Rosas; *El Plata Científico y Literario* of Buenos Aires (1854–55); *El Mosaico* of Caracas (1854–57); the *Revista de La Habana* (1853–57). The large publishing houses of Mexico also issued several: Cumplido published the *Revista Mexicana,* 1835; *El Mosaico Mexicano,* 1836–42; *El Museo Mexicano,* 1843–46; *El Album Mexicano,* 1849; *La Ilustración Mexicana,* 1851–52; and also the famous liberal daily *El Siglo XIX.* Galván published *El Año Nuevo,* 1837–40; and *El Recreo de las Familias,* 1838. García Torres issued *El Ateneo Mexicano,* organ of the association of that name, 1844; the *Biblioteca Mexicana Popular y Económica,* 1851–52; and the liberal daily *El Monitor.*

(1798–1857). There were also the *Repertorio Médico Habanero*
(1840–43), founded by Nicolás José Gutiérrez (1800–1890). In
Mexico, there were, curiously, periodicals devoted to theatrical
activities.*

Among Brazil's outstanding cultural organizations were the
celebrated Historical and Geographical Institute, established
in 1838 under the patronage of Pedro II, who took part in its
activities, and the Velosian Society,† established in 1850 for
research in the natural sciences. The Institute began to publish its journal in 1839 and its records in 1845. Among literary
reviews, two are especially notable: *Marmota* of Rio de Janeiro,
and *Niteroi,* published in Paris in 1836, which was involved
in the beginnings of Brazilian Romanticism.

The supreme cultural achievement of this period is to be
found in the work of political stabilization and social reform
carried out by legislators, statesmen, and jurists. The times
were less propitious for the sciences, philosophy, and linguistic
studies. Nevertheless, there were distinguished scholars in these
fields of learning as well. In addition to Andrés Bello, these
scholars included the Mexican astronomer and engineer Joaquín Velázquez de León (1803–82); the Peruvian mathematician Miguel Garaicoechea (1816–61), author of a work on the
binomial calculus; the Dominican botanist Manuel de Monte-
verde (1793–1871); the Uruguayan naturalist Dámaso Lar-
rañaga (1771–1846), who described the flora of the region of
the Río de la Plata and the southern coasts of Brazil; the
Argentine naturalist Francisco Javier Muñiz (1795–1871), who
excavated and studied fossil remains of South American
species of the tiger, the horse, and other animals, and who

* In countries outside Spanish America there were publications edited by
Spanish Americans residing abroad, such as *El Habanero* (1824–26), under
Father Félix Varela (1788–1853), in Philadelphia and later in New York;
El Mensajero Semanal (1828–30), under Saco and Varela, in New York;
and *Revista Española de Ambos Mundos* (Spanish Review of Both Worlds),
in Madrid from 1853 to 1855, under the Uruguayan novelist and poet
Alejandro Magariños Cervantes (1825–93).

† Named after the Brazilian scientist José Mariano da Conceição Velosa
(1742–1811).—TRANS.

wrote the valuable work *El ñandú o avestruz americano* (The Nandú or American Ostrich; 1848) and frequently assisted Darwin through correspondence; the grammarians José Gómez de la Cortina (1799–1860), a Mexican, and Antonio José de Irisarri (1786–1868), a Guatemalan, who was also a journalist and politician; the Dominican geographer and lexicographer Esteban Pichardo (1799–*c*. 1880), author of the first American dictionary of regionalisms (1836); the Peruvian mineralogists Nicolás de Piérola and Mariano Eduardo Rivero, who discovered silicate of magnesia and oxalate (or humboldtine), introduced sodium nitrate to Europe, and did pioneer work in archaeology with his *Antigüedades peruanas* (Peruvian Antiquities; 1851); the Mexican chemist and physician Leopoldo Río de la Loza (1807–73), who systematized the pharmacopoeia of the country and published studies on potable and mineral waters. The eminent Mexican philologist, ethnographer, and historian Manuel Orozco y Berra (1816–81) made the first classification of the indigenous languages of Mexico barely forty years after Franz Bopp had classified the Indo-European languages. This valuable work, outlined in 1853 (according to the *Diccionario universal de historia y geografía*) and completed in brief in 1857, was given its final form in 1864, under the title *Geografía de las lenguas y carta etnográfica de México* (Linguistic Geography and Ethnographic Map of Mexico). The wealth of linguistic data now available has emended this work considerably, but at the time it represented a daring scientific feat.

In Cuba, still under Spanish dominion, the most distinguished philosophers were Father Félix Varela and José de la Luz y Caballero, also an exceptional teacher. The outstanding zoologist was Felipe Poey (1799–1871), who classified a great number of species of the Antilles and wrote the *Memorias sobre la historia natural de Cuba* (Memoirs on the Natural History of Cuba; 1856–58) and *Iciologia cubana* (Cuban Ichthyology) —fishes were his specialty.

If the times were not propitious for the sciences, philosophy, and linguistics, they were no more propitious for the arts. The political and economic upheavals prevented the development of architecture. Very few houses were built, and no public buildings or churches, or almost none. Brazil is the exception. During the reign of Pedro II, a number of important buildings were erected: the Church of the Glória, the Theater of São Pedro, the Palace of Boa Vista, and the Academy of Fine Arts. The last was the work of the French architect Auguste Henri Victor Grandjean de Montigny (1776–1850), who was very influential in Brazil. Another French architect, Louis Léger Vauthier (b. 1815), constructed three fine theaters: Santa Isabel in Recife (Pernambuco), and Belem del Pará and São Luis in Maranhão.

Sculpture and painting were not in demand for churches and so diminished in importance. Painters turned to other subjects; in addition to portraits, which were plentiful in the colonial period, they painted landscapes, regional scenes, and historical compositions. Juan Cordero (1824–84) in Mexico and Prilidiano Pueyrredón (1823–70) in Argentina cultivated these genres. The folk life of Lima is depicted in the watercolors and caricatures of Pancho Fierro (1803–79).

Literature, on the other hand, flourished, and publishers made money, especially in Mexico, where, along with works written locally, many reprints of European books appeared. Among the outstanding publications was an illustrated Bible in several volumes, and the magnificent *Diccionario de historia y geografía* (Dictionary of History and Geography; 1853–56), to which many learned writers contributed articles that are still consulted. Some of the contributors were Orozco y Berra, Gómez de la Cortina, Lucas Alamán, Miguel Lerdo de Tejada, Guillermo Prieto, José Fernando Ramírez, Joaquín García Icazbalceta, and José Bernardo Couto. In Santiago de Chile, the erudite Argentine scholar and critic Juan María Gutiérrez (1809–78) compiled *América poética* (1846), the first comprehensive anthology of Spanish poetry published in the New World in the nineteenth century. In this period, as during the wars for independence, literature was closely linked to political and social changes. It is hardly necessary to mention the newspapers, by now very numerous, and oratory, in even greater supply. Most men in public life were, at least on occasion, both orators and journalists. Part of this literature is a literature of combat—even the poetry—as for example, the resounding verse of José Mármol (1818–71) and the clever lines of Hilario Ascasubi (1807–75) against the dictator Rosas; the poetry of José Eusebio Caro (1817–53) and Julio Arboleda (1817–61) in Colombia; and that of the conservatives and liberals in Mexico, prominent among whom are the "men of the Reform" Ignacio Ramírez (1818–79), Guillermo Prieto (1818–97), Ignacio Manuel Altamirano (1834–93), and Vicente Riva Palacio (1832–96). Ramírez and Altamirano were also notable prose writers. The urgency of the conflict also makes itself felt in plays, short stories, and novels such as *El matadero* (The Slaughterhouse) by the Argentine Esteban Echeverría (1805–51), and *Amalia* by Mármol; in the essays such as the sensational *Sociabilidad chilena* (Social Organization in Chile; 1844), by Francisco Bilbao (1823–65); and in historical works such as those of Lucas Alamán (1792–1853), Lorenzo de Zavala (1788–1836), and José María Luis Mora in Mexico. *Facundo* (1845), Sarmiento's work, is both polemical and constructive, both a program and a prophecy,

The literary current of the period was Romantic. Romanticism reached Spanish America in 1832—directly from France and somewhat before it reached Spain—through the work of Esteban Echeverría. After the publication of his poem *La cautiva* (The Captive; 1837), the tide of Romanticism swept up all the young writers of Argentina and Uruguay. In 1823, Bello had proclaimed the intellectual independence of Spanish America; the young writers now felt that the liberation had been only partial. Bello, Olmedo, and Heredia wrote on American themes, but their style was derived from European academic classicism. Advocates of Romanticism now proposed that each nation create its own style, drawing on its native traditions. This was the aim of young writers in the region of the Río de la Plata and elsewhere in Spanish America. If they did not succeed, it was because a style is not created simply by willing it. They abandoned the classical models and standards, but in the forms they tried to invent, one can discern the influence of the European Romantics. At times, the creole flavor of America flowed from their pens when they were least aware of it. In their subjects, they did indeed undertake a methodical exploration of their own countries: the landscape, from inaccessible cordilleras to interminable plains; the indigenous and the colonial traditions, and the impact of the Conquest; the heroic deeds of the wars for independence and the ideals of liberty and progress nourished by the struggle; the folkways of the countryside and of the city.

Though Echeverría launched Romanticism in Spanish America, he is not its best poet. Far superior are the Colombians José Eusebio Caro, with the soul of a generous puritan, Julio Arboleda, author of the spirited though unfinished narrative poem *Gonzalo de Oyón,* dealing with the Conquest, and Gregorio Gutiérrez González (1826–72), author of the delightful *Memoria sobre el cultivo del maíz en Antioquia* (Memoir on the Cultivation of Maize in Antioquia), in which he describes with simplicity and typical creole vivacity the routine of rural labor; the Venezuelan José Antonio Maitín (1804–74), author of the well-known "Canto fúnebre" (Dirge) on the death of his wife; and the celebrated Cuban Gertrudis Gómez de Avellaneda (1814–73), who, while living in Spain, wrote, in addition to splendid lyrical poems, such powerful dramas as *Munio Alfonso* (1844), *Saúl* (1849), and *Baltasar* (1858).

The drama, which had flourished since the colonial period, held its own now with the plays of the Mexican Manuel Eduardo de Gorostiza (1789–1851), who, while in Spain, had written classical comedies in the tradition of Molière and, after returning to his homeland, made adaptations of European stageworks; with the Peruvians Felipe Pardo (1806–68) and Manuel Ascensio Segura (1805–71), who depicted creole life with the wit characteristic of the *limeño* (inhabitant of Lima); and with the Romantics Fernando Calderón (1809–45) of Mexico, whose comedies were better than his serious dramas, and José Jacinto Milanés (1814–63) of Cuba. There were excellent actors and actresses, such as the Argentine Trinidad Guevara, who retired from the stage in 1826, and her pupil Juan Aurelio Casacuberta (1799–1849), who became the teacher of the celebrated Spanish tragedienne Matilde Díez. The novel, which had begun with Fernández de Lizardi during the wars of independence, proliferated, especially after 1845. There was a spate of *cuadros de costumbres* (sketches of local customs) in the form of articles and short essays, particularly in Colombia, Venezuela, Peru, and Chile.

Historians endowed with wide philosophical vision were active, seeking the causes of the complex events they were witnessing and involved in. Some of those in Mexico have already been mentioned. They include Lucas Alamán, *Disertaciones sobre la historia de México* (Dissertations on the History of Mexico; 1844–52), and *Historia de México* (1849–52); Lorenzo de Zavala, *Ensayo histórico de las revoluciones de México* (Historical Essay on the Revolutions of Mexico; 1831); José María Luis Mora, *México y sus revoluciones* (Mexico and Its Revolutions; 1836); and Manuel Orozco y Berra, *Historia de la dominación española en México* (History of the Spanish Domination in Mexico), and *Historia antigua de la conquista de México* (The Ancient History and the Conquest of Mexico). In Venezuela, there were Rafael María Baralt (1810–60), who was also a philosopher and a grammarian (*Historia de Venezuela;* in collaboration with Ramón Díaz; 1841–43); Juan Vicente González (1811–66), author of a biography of José Félix Ribas, and Felipe Larrazábal (1817–73), who wrote *Vida del Libertador Simón Bolívar* (Life of the Liberator Simón Bolívar). In Argentina: Bartolomé Mitre, *Historia de Belgrano y de la independencia argentina* (History of Belgrano and of Argentine Independence; 1857; completed and corrected in 1876–77), and *Historia de San Martín y de la emancipación sudamericana* (History of San Martín and of the Emancipation of South America; 1887). In Chile: Diego Barros Arana (1830–1907), author of *Un decenio de historia de Chile* (A Decade of Chilean History), and the monumental *Historia general de Chile* (General History of Chile; 1884–1902), and Benjamín

Vicuña Mackenna (1831–86), whose works include *El ostra-cismo de los Carreras* (The Ostracism of the Carreras; 1857), *Historia de Santiago* (1869), and *Historia de Valparaíso*. Al-though they began to publish at this time, two other historians wrote their most important works in the following period. They are the Argentine Vicente Fidel López (1815–1903), au-thor of *Historia de la República Argentina* (1883–93), and the Cuban José Antonio Saco, author of *Historia de la escla-vitud* (History of Slavery; 1875–92).

The impressive output of these historians is distinguished by loftiness of thought and decorous patriotism, whatever the political leanings of the authors—whether conservative, as in the case of Alamán, or liberal, as in López' case. Later genera-tions have rarely succeeded in achieving anything comparable. The main effort has been concentrated on research and on the analysis of documents; only here and there has an exceptional historian, like Justo Sierra, risen to the philosophical heights of those earlier writers.

The Argentine Domingo Faustino Sarmiento stands out among all his contemporaries in Spanish America as a writer of genius, because of his fertility of ideas, range of imagination, and wealth of expression. His three chief works are: *Facundo* (1845), *Recuerdos de provincia* (Provincial Recollections; 1850), and *Viajes* (Travels; 1849). The first is a superb description of the social and political life of Argentina, with a penetrating in-quiry into its causes and a daring prediction regarding its im-mediate future. The second consists of memories of the author's childhood and youth, and portrays the people who lived around him and the world in which they moved. The third contains keen and ever varied observations on Europe and America; the longest portion is devoted to the United States, whose freedom and progress he considered to be a magnificent example for Spanish America. Sarmiento was, moreover, a tire-less advocate of literacy, the founder of numerous schools and libraries, zoological gardens, astronomical observatories, and even cities. No one in America has carried out, through the government, a more effective or fruitful task than he. Fortune was on his side, as it had not been with Rivadavia, who was forced to abandon the greater part of his projects soon after they were conceived.

In Brazil, as in Spanish America, literature was concerned with social problems. The abolition of slavery was preached by poets such as Antônio Gonçalves Dias (1823–64), Tobias Barreto de Meneses (1839–89), Luís Nicolau Fagundes Varela (1841–75), and Antônio Castro Alves (1847–71). The theme of the Indian aroused a great deal of interest, both scientific and humanitarian. This was reflected in the literature, notably in the poems of Gonçalves Dias ("Y-Juca-Pirania,"* "Canção do Tomoio," "Os Timbiras") and in the novels of José Martiniano de Alencar (1829–77): *O Guaraní* (1856), *Iracema* (1865). Gonçalves Dias and Alencar are the two main figures of Brazilian Romanticism, which, ushered in by the *Suspiros Poéticos e Saudades* (Poetic Sighs and Longings; Paris, 1836) of Domingos José Gonçalves de Magalhães (1811–82), reached its full splendor in these two writers. In the theater, the pleasant comedies of manners by Luis Carlos Martins Penna (1815–48) enjoyed considerable popularity. Dramas by Alencar and Gonçalves Dias were produced with varying success. The most celebrated actor was João Caetano.

* According to the poet, the meaning in Tupí (a native Indian language of Brazil) is: "He who is put to death and is worthy thereof."—TRANS.

{ 6 }

Organization
and Stability
[1860–1890]

B ETWEEN 1850 AND 1870, the particular form of organization
characteristic of each nation of Spanish America took
definite shape. In Argentina, the process that began with the
constitution of 1853 closed in 1862 with the end of dissension
between Buenos Aires and the other provinces. In Mexico, the
Reform came to a close with the overthrow of the Empire, in
1867. Henceforth, institutions were stabilized, with only a few
changes. Although civil disorder did not disappear, it at least
diminished. Although some governments were still excessively
authoritarian, there was respect for legal forms, and where this
was lacking, there was at least a pretense of respect. Legislative
activity continued; in addition to constitutional revisions and
emendations (not always strictly necessary), legal codes were
drafted.*

* In addition to the codes mentioned in the previous chapter, legal codes
were enacted during this period in Venezuela (1862), Uruguay (1868),
Argentina (1869), Paraguay (1869), Mexico (1870, for the Federal District;
thereafter copied by the states, with a few exceptions, such as Veracruz),
Colombia (1875), Guatemala (1877), El Salvador (1880), Costa Rica (1886),
and Ecuador (1887). Commercial codes were drafted in Venezuela (1862),
Chile (1865), Uruguay (1866), Nicaragua (1869), Colombia (1869, for over-
land commerce; 1873, for maritime commerce), Guatemala (1877), El Salvador (1882), Ecuador (1882), and Mexico (1889). Penal codes were drawn up

In international law, Latin America made an especially distinguished contribution through the doctrines of the Argentine jurist Carlos Calvo (1824–1906), author of the internationally known treatise *Derecho internacional teórico y práctico* (The Theory and Practice of International Law; 1868) and of the *Diccionario de derecho internacional público y privado* (Dictionary of Public and Private International Law; 1885). Calvo advanced the principle that no government should use armed force to support financial claims against another nation. This principle, now universally accepted, won world-wide attention in 1902, when it was invoked by the Argentine minister of foreign affairs, the jurist Luis María Drago (1859–1921), in connection with the conflict between Venezuela and England. Argentina, moreover, had advocated the principle of compulsory arbitration at the Pan-American Conference of 1889. The idea later received the support of Brazil, and even though it has not become mandatory, it has made considerable headway in international opinion.

Political and institutional stability brought the beginning of economic recovery. Two indications of this were the increase in the number of banks and the growth of railroads. Argentina and Uruguay, which in 1860 were the least populated countries in America (Argentina had less than one inhabitant per 250 acres), received waves of European immigration. Agriculture and cattle raising were developed; the first exports of grain and meat were shipped from Argentina during the presidency (1874–80) of the jurist and writer Nicolás Avellaneda (1837–85). There was no immigration of any significance in the other countries of Spanish America, because immigrant labor could not compete with the natives, whose standard of living, as a consequence of centuries of exploita-

---

in Peru (1862), Venezuela (1863), Mexico (1871, for the Federal District), Chile (1874), Costa Rica (1880), El Salvador (1881), the Dominican Republic (1884), Argentina (1886), Uruguay (1889), Guatemala (1889), Colombia (1890), and Paraguay (1890). The most important are the civil code of Argentina, the work of Dalmacio Vélez Sarsfield (1801–75); the civil code of Uruguay, the work of Tristán Narvaja (d. 1877); and the Mexican penal code, the work of Antonio Martínez de Castro (d. 1879).

tion, was at an irreducible minimum. Nevertheless, the power of economic development in the modern world made its influence felt everywhere, and around 1880, prosperity, to a greater or a smaller degree, began to appear or to revive.

Brazil, which had embarked on an independent existence in a much better condition than its neighbors, continued its prosperous development right to the end of the imperial epoch. Nor did the abolition of slavery in 1888 cause any serious disturbances in the national economy; previous laws and events had by then reduced slavery to negligible proportions. In 1850, a ban had been placed on the slave trade, and many investors were therefore obliged to seek out more profitable fields for their capital. In 1871, "freedom of the womb" was decreed, whereby the children of slaves were born free. In 1885, slaves more than sixty years old were emancipated; in 1883, abolition had been proclaimed in Ceará. An "underground railroad" was active, such as the United States had had earlier, and voluntary manumission, practiced by generous owners, was frequent (between 1872 and 1876, there were 30,000 instances of it). Emperor Pedro II had asked for abolition as early as 1867, and finally it was voted amid great popular enthusiasm. For many years, the ground had been prepared by poets, orators, journalists, and statesmen—established or aspiring—such as the Viscount of Rio Branco (1845–1912), José do Patrocínio (1854–1905), Ruy Barbosa (1849–1923), and Joaquím Nabuco (1849–1910).

The southern part of Brazil benefited strikingly from European immigration. "In 1912," Pedro Calmon wrote, "the largest Brazilian fortunes were to be found in Bahia and Pernambuco. From 1850 to 1870, north and south were on a par. After 1870, the economic hegemony of the south was indisputable, and as a consequence, political predominance ensued." In 1889, the republic was peacefully established, and its democratic constitution was adopted in 1891.

The fundamental cultural need was to extend education by increasing the number of schools. The first countries that showed noteworthy progress in this respect were Colombia and

Chile. Argentina surpassed them during the administration of Sarmiento (1868–74) and since then has retained its lead, at least in primary instruction.

Education had gradually freed itself from the colonial traditions. Now the trend was decidedly toward the sciences, while the humanities were neglected. The predominance of science was reinforced by the influence of positivism, beginning with the philosophy of Comte and followed by that of John Stuart Mill and Herbert Spencer.

This was especially apparent in Chile. In Argentina, positivism was propagated by the French philosopher Amédée Jacques (1813–65), whom President Mitre named director of the first National College of Buenos Aires (1863); in Mexico, by the physician and philosopher Gabino Barreda (1818–81), designated director of the National Preparatory School by Juárez (1867); in Brazil, by the poet and thinker Tobias Barreto de Meneses (1839–89), by Luis Pereira Barreto (1840–1923), author of voluminous works on the evolution of human thought, and by Benjamin Constant Botelho de Magalhães (1838–91), one of the founders of the republic; in Venezuela, by the physician Rafael Villavicencio and by the German naturalist and ethnologist Adolf Ernst, who founded the Museum of Natural Sciences in Caracas. In Uruguay, positivism spread through discussions at the Ateneo (Athenaeum), around 1880. In the Dominican Republic, it was introduced by the Puerto Rican thinker Eugenio María Hostos (1839–1903), founder and director of the Normal School (1880–88). Even in Cuba it spread, outside the official curriculum imposed by Spain, through the lectures (1880–82) on logic, psychology, and ethics given by Enrique José Varona (1849–1903). In Mexico, positivism became virtually an official philosophy shortly before 1890 and retained this status until 1910. In Brazil, the same thing happened, to the extent that the legend on the flag of the republic, "Order and Progress," was taken from Comte. Specialized reviews were devoted to spreading the doctrines of Comte in Brazil, where even today there are centers dedicated to Comte's "religion of humanity" (dating from 1881). A simi-

lar review was published in Chile, edited by Juan Enrique
Lagarrigue, and another in Mexico, edited by Agustín Aragón.
Hostos and Varona, meanwhile, gradually drew away from
positivism: Hostos toward his distinctive ethical rationalism;
Varona toward his theoretical skepticism, which never pre-
cluded useful human action.

Cultural associations were also active and influential. Examples are the Liceo Mexicano, under the direction of the
noted teacher of the young, Ignacio Manuel Altamirano; in
Caracas, the Academy of Social Sciences and Belles-Lettres
(1869), the Venezuelan Academy of Literature (1872), and the
Society of the Friends of Learning (1882); in Santiago de Chile,
the Club (1859–64 and 1869–70) and the Academy of Belles-
Lettres (1873–80); in Santo Domingo, the Society of the Friends
of the Country (1871–1903); in Montevideo, the Athenaeum
of Uruguay, which published its annals from 1881 to 1886; in
Lima, the Literary Club with its annals (1873–76), the Athenaeum of Lima, whose organ was published from 1886 to 1890,
and the Literary Circle, active in the same years, with its
Revista Social (Social Review). Associations for scientific studies
were organized, such as the Geographical Society of Lima
(1887); the Society of Naturalists of New Granada in Bogotá;
the Geographical Society (1885) in Rio de Janeiro; and in
Mexico, the societies named for distinguished Mexican scientists of the past: "José Antonio Alzate" (1884), "Andrés del
Río," "Leopoldo Río de la Loza," and "Pedro Escobedo"
(1872).

The Spanish Academy of Madrid encouraged the creation
of similar bodies in America, which it designated "corresponding academies"; thus were organized the Colombian Academy
(1871), the Mexican Academy (1875), the Ecuadorian (1875),
the Venezuelan (1883), the Peruvian, the Chilean, the Argen-
tinian, and later a number of others. At first, they were active
and published reviews or annals containing valuable studies—
especially the Colombian and Mexican academies—and they
collaborated on the *Diccionario de la lengua castellana* (Dictionary of the Spanish Language), issued by the Academy in

Madrid. But later they lost momentum, and now they are moribund, or, as in the case of the Argentine Academy, have ceased to exist.

As the nineteenth century passed its midpoint, newspapers increased and multiplied. Daily papers, which until 1860 were the exception, began to be widespread and to appear regularly. This period saw the founding of the two great daily newspapers of Buenos Aires, which were to grow so remarkably and to become notable for the attention they devoted to cultural manifestations: *La Prensa* (October, 1869) and *La Nación* (January, 1870), the latter edited by Bartolomé Mitre. This period also saw the rise of *El Comercio* of Lima, founded in 1839 by Manuel Ascensio Segura, and of the Chilean paper *El Mercurio,* founded in Valparaíso (1827) and later moved to Santiago, with editions in both cities. In Brazil, the oldest daily is the *Diario de Pernambuco;* it was followed by the *Jornal do Comercio* of Rio de Janeiro, founded in 1827. The reviews, mostly literary, likewise increased both in volume and in importance.*

* Of the reviews, these are the most outstanding: in Mexico, *El Renacimiento* (1869), edited by Ignacio Manuel Altamirano; in Venezuela, the *Revista Literaria* (1864–66), edited by Juan Vicente González; in Colombia, *El Mosaico* (1850–60, 1864–65, 1871–72), the *Revista de Bogotá* (1871–72), *La Patria* (1877–82), edited by Adriano Páez (1844–90), and the notable *Repertorio Colombiano* (1878–84, 18[?]–1899), edited by the historian Carlos Martínez Silva (1847–1903), the *Papel Periódico Ilustrado* (1881–87), and the *Revista Literaria* (1890–94), edited by the critic and bibliographer Isidoro Laverde Amaya; in Ecuador, *El Cosmopolita* (1866–69) and *El Regenerador* (1876–78), both edited by Juan Montalvo (1832–89); in Peru, the *Revista de Lima* (1860–68, 1873–[?]), *El Correo del Perú* (1871–75), and the *Revista Peruana* (1879–80); in Chile, the *Revista de Sud América* in Valparaíso (1861–63), the new *Revista de Santiago* (1872–73), the new *Revista de Valparaíso* (1873–74), the *Revista Chilena* (1875–80), edited by the historians Miguel Luis Amunátegui (1828–88) and Diego Barros Arana, and the *Revista de Artes y Letras* in Santiago (1884–90); in Argentina, the *Revista de Buenos Aires* (1863–71), edited by the historian Vicente Gregorio Quesada (1830–1913) and the jurist Miguel Navarro Viola, the *Revista del Río de la Plata* (1871–78), edited by Juan María Gutiérrez, Vicente Fidel López, and the Uruguayan historian Andrés Lamas (1820–91), and the new *Revista de Buenos Aires* (1881–85), edited by Vicente Quesada and his son Ernesto, a historian and sociologist (1858–1934); in Santo Domingo, the *Revista Científica, Literaria y de Conocimientos Utiles* (1883–84); in Cuba,

Worthy of note as the first effort of its kind is the *Anuario bibliográfico de la República Argentina* (Bibliographical Yearbook of the Argentine Republic; 1880–88), founded by the poet Alberto Navarro Viola (1858–85). Outstanding among the purely scientific reviews is the *Repertorio Físico-natural de la Isla de Cuba* (1865–68), edited by Felipe Poey.

The universities also published reviews, annals, and reports. Following the lead of the University of Chile, which began to publish in 1843, were the universities of Lima (1862), Bogotá (1868), Quito (1883), Buenos Aires (1888), and Montevideo (1891). The National Museum of Archaeology, History, and Ethnology of Mexico began to publish its annals in 1877.

The scientists of this period were no less active than the philosophers, their influence even equaling that of such major figures as Varona and Hostos. The most eminent scientist is the Argentine paleontologist Florentino Ameghino (1854–1911), a scholar of formidable and heroic efforts. He acquired renown as a result of his weakest book, *La antigüedad del hombre en el Plata* (The Antiquity of Man in the La Plata Region; 1880), in which he maintained—with insufficient data—that the indigenous American races originated in the New World. In that part of his work that is indisputably sound—the study of mammalian fossils in the region of the Río de la Plata—he proved to be a pioneer. With few exceptions, the mammals he de-

---

the *Revista Habanera* (1861–62), edited by the poet Juan Clemente Zenea (1832–71), the *Revista Crítica de Ciencias, Literatura y Artes* (1868), edited by the philologist Néstor Ponce de León (1837–99), the *Revista de Cuba* (1877–84), edited by José Antonio Cortina (1852–84), the *Revista Cubana* (1885–95), edited by Enrique José Varona, *La Habana Elegante* (1883–96), and the *Hojas Literarias* (1893–94), the very personal publication of Manuel Sanguily (1848–1925). Noteworthy, too, are the periodicals published in foreign lands by Spanish Americans: in Paris, the *Revista Latinoamericana* (1874–75), edited by Adriano Páez, and *El Espectador,* sounding board for Juan Montalvo (1886–88); in New York, *El Mundo Nuevo* (1871), edited by the Cuban historian and critic Enrique Piñeyro (1839–1911), the *Revista Ilustrada de Nueva York* (*c.* 1889–*c.* 1892), edited by the Venezuelan observer of manners and customs Nicanor Bolet Peraza (1838–1906), and *La Edad de Oro* (1889), an incomparable album of stories, instructive articles, and children's verses, all written by the Cuban patriot and man of letters José Martí (1853–95).

scribed had never been classified before. He was not merely a descriptive naturalist, but a theorist as well. In such works as *Filogenia* (1884), he contributed to the discussion and formulation of biological laws.

Another Argentine naturalist, William Henry Hudson (1841–1922), is famous throughout the world—for his literary more than his scientific achievements. He wrote in English, with a clear and enchanting style. He was born about twenty miles from Buenos Aires, but he spoke English from childhood —his parents were from the United States—and when he was thirty-three, he settled permanently in England. He did not write in the language of his native land, but he used South American themes for his books: in novels, such as *The Purple Land* (1885) and *Green Mansions* (1904), in short stories, such as those in the volume entitled *The Ombú* (1902), in autobiographical narratives, such as *Idle Days in Patagonia* (1893) and *Far Away and Long Ago* (1918), in zoological treatises and reports, such as *Argentine Ornithology* (in collaboration with P. L. Sclater; 1888–89), *The Naturalist in La Plata* (1892), *Adventures Among Birds* (1913), and *Birds of La Plata* (1920). Hudson, like Buffon, is a naturalist who will always be read because in reading him one discovers unexpected forms and aspects of life on this earth.

Other men of science were: in Argentina, the geographer Francisco Paula Moreno (1852–1919), founder of the Museum of La Plata (1884), known throughout the cultivated world for its superb collections in natural history, ethnology, and archaeology; the naturalist Eduardo Ladislao Holmberg (1852–1937), author of *Flora y fauna de la República Argentina* (Flora and Fauna of the Argentine Republic) and of studies of fish, insects, and arachnids, in addition to several works of science-fiction in the manner of Jules Verne and H. G. Wells; in Mexico, the geographer Antonio García Cubas (1832–1912) and the astronomer Francisco Díaz Covarrubias (1833–89), who determined the geographical location of the federal capital, directed the geodesic triangulation of the valley of Anáhuac (which had been attempted, with insufficient resources, in the eighteenth century by Joaquín Velázquez de Cárdenas y León, 1732–86), made valuable observations on eclipses and on the orbits of the planets around the sun, founded the Astronomical Observatory, and published, among other works, *Tablas geodésicas de la República Mexicana* (Geodesic Tables of the Mexican Republic) and *Nuevos métodos astronómicos* (New Methods in Astronomy); in Colombia, the naturalist Florentino Vega (1833–90), author of *Botánica indígena* (Indigenous Botany), *La Expedición Botánica* (The Botanical Expedition) —an account of the expedition directed by José Celestino Mutis (1732–1808) in the eighteenth century—and *La botánica en Nueva Granada* (The Botany of New Granada); in Puerto Rico, the botanist Agustín Stahl (1842–1917); in Cuba, the zoologist Rafael Arango (1837–93); in Peru, the physician Daniel Carríon (1859–85), who did research on the infectious diseases known locally as *verruga* and who died in the course of his work. To these must be added the ethnologists, philologists, and archaeologists who studied the indigenous peoples, their languages, and their cultures: in Colombia, Ezequiel Uricoechea (1834–80) and Liborio Zerda (1834–1919); in Peru, Pablo Patrón (1855–1910); in Venezuela, Gaspar Marcano (1850–1916), equally distinguished for medical research on blood, and Arístides Rojas (1826–94), who in addition was a historian with an inquiring mind and a writer with a pleasing style. In Mexico, along with Manuel Orozco y Berra, there were José Fernando Ramírez, the extraordinary historian and researcher who established the basis for the hieroglyphic interpretation of the Aztec codices; Alfredo Chavero (1841–1906); Francisco de Borja del Paso y Troncoso (1842–1916); and Nicolás León, who produced valuable linguistic studies and extensive bibliographical works. In Puerto Rico, there were Cayetano Coll y Toste (1850–1930), also a historian; in Argentina, Samuel Lafone Quevedo (1835–1920), Adán Quiroga (1863–1904), and Juan Bautista Ambrosetti (1865–1917).

Spanish philology reached its highest point in the nineteenth century with the work of the Colombian Rufino José Cuervo (1844–1911). No one in Europe or America, not even Andrés

Bello, had as thorough a grasp as he of the history of the Spanish language, of each word and each idiom. He began as a grammarian, correcting errors, in his *Apuntaciones críticas sobre el lenguaje bogotano* (Critical Annotations on the Language of Bogotá; 1867). In its five subsequent editions, right to the posthumous one of 1914, this work was progressively transformed into a masterwork on philology. In his *Diccionario de construcción y régimen de la lengua castellana* (Dictionary of the Construction and Regimen of the Spanish Language), he compiled the largest syntactic repertory of the language. (He was able to publish only volumes I and II, A-B-C-D; the rest remained in manuscripts.) In monographic studies, he exhausted such questions as the history of complementary pronouns, clarified problems of Spanish pronunciation and writing prior to the eighteenth century, and noted significant facts about the spread of the Spanish language in America. He was the first to reject, for example, the assumption that the Andalusians had predominated in the Spanish Conquest and colonization of America.

Classical philology was cultivated by distinguished humanists, such as the Colombian Miguel Antonio Caro (1843–1909), author, in collaboration with Cuervo, of the best Latin grammar written in Spanish, and masterly translator of the *Aeneid* and the *Georgics* of Vergil. During the colonial period, all men of letters, all university graduates, had a mastery of Latin and, more often than not, used it for writing both prose and verse. After independence, classical studies declined, but there was no dearth of humanists who translated the ancient authors, especially in Mexico.

Among Mexican humanists, we should mention Alejandro Arango y Escandón (1821–83), who, besides Greek and Latin, also studied Hebrew and wrote on biblical subjects; José Sebastián Segura (1822–89); José María Roa Bárcena (1827–1908); José María Vigil (1829–1909), translator of Martial and Persius; Joaquín Arcadio Pagaza (1839–1918); Ignacio Montes de Oca (1840–1921), translator of complete editions of Pindar, Theocritus, Bion, Moschus, Coluthus of Lycopolis, and Apollonius of Rhodes; Francisco de Paula Guzmán (1844–84); Joaquín Diego Casasús (1858–1916), translator of Catullus, Tibullus, Propertius, "Lygdamus," and Sulpicia; Ambrosio Ramírez (1859–1913); and Federico Escobedo. Of the many others from various countries who might be cited, it will suffice to mention the Argentine poet Carlos Guido Spano (1829–1918), who adapted epigrams from the Greek Anthology. Almost all the men of letters translated Horace (in particular, Pagaza and Ramírez), and many translated Vergil.

In Brazil, the outstanding humanists include João Gualberto Fereira dos Santos (b. 1787), Manoel Ignacio Suares Lisboa, João Nunes de Andrade (*c.* 1800–1861), and Manoel Odorico Mendes (1799–1865), who wrote Portuguese versions of the *Aeneid,* the *Iliad,* and the *Odyssey.*

The important historians were men from the previous period who were still active: Mitre, López, Saco, Orozco y Berra, Barros Arana, Vicuña Mackenna. In addition to the exhaustive volumes they produced, collective works were undertaken, such as the *Historia de Chile* in five volumes (1866–82), edited by Vicuña Mackenna, and *México a través de los siglos* (Mexico Through the Centuries), also in five volumes, under the direction of Vicente Riva Palacio, with the collaboration of (among others) Alfredo Chavero (1841–1906) and José María Vigil. To this period also belong the authors of another great collective work: *México: Su evolución social* (Mexico: Its Social Evolution), which was published some years later (1900–1901). Outstanding among its contributors was Justo Sierra (1848–1912), with his profound and masterly study *La evolución política del pueblo mexicano* (The Political Evolution of the Mexican People), reprinted afterward as a separate volume (third edition, 1948).

A special place is occupied by another Mexican historian, Joaquín García Icazbalceta (1825–94), who devoted himself to a study of the beginnings of Spanish culture in Mexico, and wrote biographies of missionaries, teachers, and literary men, and monographs on public education, the theater, agriculture, cattle raising, and many other subjects. His most ambitious works are the biography (1881) of the first archbishop of Mexico, Juan de Zumárraga (1468–1548), and the *Bibliografía mexicana del siglo XVI* (Mexican Bibliography of the Sixteenth Century; 1886), "a work, in its line, that ranks with the most perfect and excellent produced by any nation whatsoever," in the opinion of the well-known Spanish critic Marcelino Menéndez y Pelayo.

Another historian whose specialty was colonial history is the Chilean José Toribio Medina (1852–1930). He published a series of exhaustive works dealing with printing throughout Spanish America (in seventeen volumes, 1891–1912), another on the books about America published in Europe from 1493 to 1810 (in seven volumes, 1898–1907), a third on the Inquisition (in six volumes, 1887–1914). He also compiled the *Diccionario biográfico colonial de Chile* (Colonial Biographical Dictionary of Chile; 1906) and studies of historical figures, such as the explorer Sebastián Cabot.

On the whole, the best literature of this period was in prose, and the representative writers were of the stature of Bello, Sarmiento, Francisco Bilbao, Ignacio Ramírez—men of thought and action who might be described as both fighters and builders. Such were the Brazilians Ruy Barbosa and Joaquim Nabuco, the Ecuadorian Juan Montalvo, the Peruvian Manuel González Prada (1848–1918), the Mexican Justo Sierra, the Puerto Rican Eugenio María Hostos, the Cubans Varona and Sanguily. All of them enriched Spanish prose with unique touches; in particular Montalvo, who reanimated the opulent vocabulary and the turns of phrase of the Golden Age with the impetus of his American imagination; Justo Sierra, eloquent, great-souled, and generous; González Prada, concise and energetic; Varona, limpid and persuasive; Hostos, ardent and luminous. Ruy Barbosa, writing in Portuguese, displayed a style that was at once rich and precise.

All these writers took part in the movements for freedom and for culture, as teachers, journalists, or orators, or by direct political action: Ruy Barbosa and Joaquim Nabuco worked for the abolition of slavery (Ruy Barbosa, in addition, strove for the establishment of a republic in Brazil); Varona and Sanguily for the independence of Cuba; Hostos for the independence of Cuba and Puerto Rico; Montalvo and González Prada against the "vested interests" who used all their power to support injustices. And they all worked for the cultural improvement not only of their native countries but also of other lands, as in the case of Hostos. They are men of moral as well as literary grandeur.

Just as in Romantic poetry Spanish America had been ahead of Spain, so it now took the lead in the realistic novel, with the works of the Chilean Alberto Blest Gana (1830–1920), *La aritmética en el amor* (The Arithmetic of Love; 1860), *Martín Rivas* (1862), and *El ideal de un calavera* (The Ideal of a Rake; 1863), which antedate by some years the first novels of the Spanish master Benito Pérez Galdós. It was also in this period that the Romantic novel produced its most exquisite work: the delicate and polished *María* (1867), by the Colombian Jorge Isaacs (1837–95).

In Brazil, the realistic novel appeared even earlier, with *Memórias de um sargento de milícias* (Memoirs of a Militia Sergeant; 1854) by Manuel Antônio de Almeida (1830–61), and culminated in the works of Joaquim Maria Machado de Assis (1839–1909), a novelist with the maturity and refinement of an old civilization. Machado de Assis was more than a mere realist; he was a great creator of literary personages, a painter of character, an acute analyst of feelings. His *Memórias Póstumas de Brás Cubas* (Posthumous Memoirs of Brás Cubas; 1881), *Quincas Borba* (1891; translation, *Philosopher or Dog?*, 1954), and *Dom Casmurro,* (1900; translation, 1953) are novels of the first order in any literature, seldom equaled and never surpassed in Hispanic America.* After Machado de Assis, and influenced by French naturalism, came Raúl Pompeia (1863–95), with *O Ateneu* (recollections of school life); Aloísio Azevedo (1857–1913), with *O Mulato* (The Mulatto; 1881) and *O Cortiço* (1890; translation, *A Brazilian Tenement*, 1926);

---

* See also his collection *The Psychiatrist and Other Stories,* tr. W. L. Grossman and H. Caldwell (Berkeley, Calif., 1963).—Trans.

and Júlio César Ribeiro (1845–90), with *A Carne* (The Flesh; 1888).

Novels dealing with indigenous themes included works of high quality during this period: *Cumandá* (1871), by the Ecuadorian Juan León Mera (1832–94); *Enriquillo* (1879–82), by the Dominican Manuel de Jesús Galván (1834–1910), which takes place during the Conquest; and *Aves sin nido* (Birds Without a Nest; 1889), by the Peruvian Clorinda Matto de Turner (1854–1904), which depicts the sufferings of the exploited Indian race in contemporary times. Not a novel, but a delightful narrative of real events, rich in picturesque description and wise observations, is *Una excursión a los indios ranqueles* (An Excursion Among the Ranquel Indians; 1870), by the Argentine army officer Lucio Victorio Mansilla (1837–1913), a nephew of Rosas but a friend of Sarmiento. The *Tradiciones peruanas* (Peruvian Traditions) written by Ricardo Palma (1833–1919) over a period of more than forty years, beginning in 1860, are very original. In these brief narratives, he relates—always with ingenuity—events of the colonial epoch.

With Romanticism now established as a tradition, poets continued to explore native themes, bucolic and urban. Along with novels dealing with indigenous themes were such works in verse as *Fantasías indígenas* (1877), by the Dominican José Joaquín Pérez (1845–1900), and *Tabaré* (1886), by the Uruguayan Juan Zorrilla de San Martín (1857–1931), a poem admirable for its constant inventiveness in imagery and its musical quality, which, without disturbing the easy flow of the narrative, enhance the wealth of emotion and feeling. Among poems of a personal nature, there were some of exceptional merit, such as those of the Colombian Rafael Pombo (1833–1912) and the "Vuelta a la patria" (Return to the Fatherland) of the Venezuelan Juan Antonio Pérez Bonalde (1846–92). Some poets, seeking to revive Romantic expression (now worn out by repetition), returned to classical forms. Such were the humanists Miguel Antonio Caro and Joaquín Arcadio Pagaza (who knew how to evoke the latent feelings of repose and of

vigor in the mountains and valleys of his native Mexico), and
Manuel José Othón (1858–1906), who projected his tragic view
of life on the desolate landscape of northern Mexico, as for
example, in his poem titled "En el desierto: Idilio salvaje"
(In the Desert: A Savage Idyl).

Themes of public and civic interest were not missing from
the poetry of this period. In the Dominican Republic, Salomé
Ureña de Henríquez (1850–97) exhorted her fellow citizens to
revere peace and to dedicate themselves to work and study.
The famous Spanish critic Menéndez y Pelayo called her "an
eminent poetess whose feminine arms firmly uphold the lyre
of Quintana, drawing from it robust sounds in praise of civilization and of her native land." As an educator, she collaborated with Hostos in founding the first normal school for
training women teachers (1881). The Argentine Olegario Víctor Andrade (1839–82) hymned the glory of San Martín in his
poem "El nido de cóndores" (The Condors' Nest) and, with
a magnificent prophetic vision, sang, in "Atlántida," "the
future of the Latin race in America."

The greatest poetic originality of the period is to be found
in the works of the *gauchesco* poets of Argentina: José Hernández (1834–86) and Estanislao del Campo (1834–80). They
were both city men, but they wrote in the language of the
countryside, using the rural idioms of the gaucho, the herds-
man of the Argentine pampas. Rafael Obligado (1851–1920)
treated similar themes but in literary language. His *Santos
Vega* (1877–1885) is noteworthy for the richness of its imagery.
Estanislao del Campo, in his *Fausto* (1866), retold the medieval
legend of Faust in the words of a gaucho who has attended a
performance of Gounod's opera at the Teatro Colón in Buenos
Aires and is recounting the experience to a friend. The time-
less folklore theme fits in easily with the mentality and the
speech of the pampas dwellers, for whom the Devil is a familiar
being, capable of every kind of trickery and disguise. José
Hernández, in *Martín Fierro* (1872) and *La Vuelta de Martín
Fierro* (The Return of Martín Fierro; 1879), used literature
for political propaganda. He depicted the gaucho as a victim

(an unexpected paradox!) of the new social order created by
agencies seeking to promote progress. But the two poems go
far beyond mere polemics; they become large frescoes of the
rural life of the pampas, imbued with strange vigor and rude
grandeur.

In Brazil, the last group of Romantic poets was humorously
known to their critics as *condoreiros,* because they chose the
condor of the Andes as a symbol. They were poets with robust
lungs, interested in social questions. The two representative
figures in this movement are Tobias Barreto de Meneses and
Antônio de Castro Alves (1847–71). This group was succeeded
by the refined Parnassians (influenced by the French school of
that name): Machado de Assis (the novelist), Luís Guimarães
(1847–98), and Teófilo Dias (1857–89).

Latin America has given Europe a number of eminent
writers, some of whom came to adopt a language not their
own, as was the case with William Henry Hudson. Some, however, settled in Spain, for example, the dramatist Ventura de
la Vega (1807–65), who was born in Argentina. Others settled
in Portugal, such as the poet Antônio Gonçalves Crespo (1847–
83), born in Brazil. Some settled in France and wrote in
French: the Cuban-born José María de Heredia (1843–1905)—
cousin of the "Singer of Niagara," whose name he shares—who
joined the French Parnassians and became famous for his son-
nets; the Symbolist poet Jules Laforgue (1860–87) and the precursor of the Surrealists, Comte de Lautréamont (pen name of
Isidore Ducasse, 1846–70), both born in Uruguay; the Cuban
writer Mercedes Santa Cruz, Countess of Merlin (1789–1852),
who preceded them and who had one of the most celebrated
literary salons of the time in Paris; and, later, the Uruguayan
poet and novelist Jules Supervielle (1884–1960). There have
been—and are—many others, of less importance, writing in
French, English, Italian, or German.

After the economic recovery that marked this period, architecture revived. The Spanish style gave way to the French,
which, in Brazil, had already taken precedence over the Portuguese style. The cities in the southern part of South America

began to develop rapidly: Rio de Janeiro, São Paulo, Montevideo, Buenos Aires, Santiago de Chile, Valparaíso; there was pronounced growth also in two cities of the north, Caracas and Mexico City, and in Havana, still in the hands of Spain.

In painting, classical traditions persisted, either in opposition to or in fusion with Romantic tendencies. Representative painters were the Mexican José María Velasco (1840–1912), whose characteristic canvases were vast landscapes of the valley of Mexico, and the Uruguayan Juan Manuel Blanes (1830–1901), whose favorite subject was the countryside around the Río de la Plata. In popular pictorial art, there was unusually interesting work, such as the drawings of the Mexican José Guadalupe Posada (1851–1913) which illustrated broadsides containing ballads or stories, and his caricatures for satirical periodicals.

Other painters, too, deserve to be remembered, such as the Mexicans Félix Parra (1845–1919), creator of the celebrated work that depicts Father Bartolomé de Las Casas as protector of the Indians, and Santiago Rebull (1829–1902); the Venezuelan Arturo Michelena (1863–98); the Chileans Pedro Lira (1845–1912) and Alfredo Valenzuela Puelma (1856–1908); the Brazilians Pedro Américo de Figueiredo (1843–1905) and Vítor Meireles (1832–1903); and the Argentine Eduardo Sívori (1847–1918). The influence of French Impressionism was first evident in the Argentine Martín Malharro (1865–1911) and the Dominican Luis Desangles (1862–1937).

There was very little sculpture. Public monuments, as a rule, were commissioned from French, Italian, or Spanish artists, as for example, the Bolívar by Pietro Tenerani in Bogotá, and the Columbus by Henri-Charles Cordier in Mexico City. In the twentieth century, Rodin made the statue of Sarmiento, and Bourdelle that of General Alvear, for Buenos Aires. A significant exception is Miguel Noreña, sculptor of the statue of Cuauhtémoc and of the monument to the seventeenth-century engineer Enrico Martínez in Mexico City.

Devotion to music was widespread, as in the colonial period. An orchestra was founded in Caracas around 1760, and there is mention of one in Guatemala City in 1800. Although the symphony orchestras did not become permanent organizations, during the nineteenth century symphonic concerts were held in the principal cities. In Buenos Aires in the time of Rivadavia, from 1821 to 1827, symphonies by Haydn and Mozart were performed; there were concert orchestras in Mexico City and in Bogotá; music by Palestrina and Victoria, Bach and Handel, was performed in the churches.

In this period, Spanish America produced musical performers of international renown: among pianists, the Venezuelan Teresa Carreño (1853–1917), the Cubans Fernando Aristi (1828–88) and his daughter Cecilia, Ignacio Cervantes (1847–1905), and José Manuel Jiménez (1855–1917); among violinists, the Cubans José White (1836–1918), Rafael Díaz Albertini, and Claudio Brindis de Salas (1852–1912); among singers, the Mexican Angela Peralta (1845–83).

There were many composers—of religious music, symphonies and quartets, pieces for piano and for violin, and songs. Among those who wrote operas were the Mexicans Cenobio Paniagua (1822–82), with his *Catalina de Guisa;* Aniceto Ortega (1823–75), with his *Guatimozín* (on an indigenous subject, 1871); and Melesio Morales (1839–1909), with his *Indegonda,* produced in Florence around 1868, and three operas produced in Mexico: *Romeo y Julieta* (1863), *Gino Corsini* (1877), and *Cleopatra* (1891). The Colombian José María Ponce de León wrote the Biblical opera *Ester* (1874). The Cuban Gaspar Villate (1851–91) wrote *Zilia* (Paris, 1877), *Baldessare* (Madrid, 1885), and *La Czarine* (The Hague, 1888). The only composer whose operas have survived is the Brazilian Carlos Gomes (1836–96), who had nine operas produced in Europe and in America. Critics maintain that his masterpiece is *Lo schiavo* (The Slave; 1889), but his best-known opera—especially its picturesque overture—is *Il Guarany* (La Scala, Milan, 1870), which has an indigenous subject based on the novel by José Martiniano de Alencar. It has an admirable score in the manner of Verdi during his transitional period, when he wrote *Aïda.*

Rural folk music and urban popular music continued to flourish, as in the past. Its outstanding contribution is the *danza habanera,* which emerged in Cuba as a transformation of the French *contredanse,* and which spread to all the Antilles and beyond, particularly along the Atlantic coast of South America, where it eventually engendered the Argentine tango. In Europe, the *habanera* became known through the versions published by the Spanish-Basque composer Sebastián Iradier, who lived for many years in Cuba. Iradier is noted as the composer of "La paloma" as well as being Bizet's source for the famous "Habanera" in his opera *Carmen.* Among other European composers later attracted by the *habanera* are Chabrier, Saint-Saëns, and Ravel. In America, beginning with Cuba, stylized forms of the *danza habanera* (also called *danza cubana*) were written for piano by Manuel Saumell (1817–70) and by Ignacio Cervantes (1874–1905), whose compositions in this form are masterpieces of their kind. In Puerto Rico, the composer who chiefly saw the *danza* as a form for piano was Juan Morel Campos (1857–96), who brought to this music an attractive melodic inventiveness. Another Cuban composer, Eduardo Sánchez de Fuentes (1876–1944), at the age of sixteen wrote a song in *habanera* rhythm, called "Tú" (Thou), which became famous throughout the world. The *danza* was cultivated in Colombia by Enrique Price (1819–63), and in Mexico by Ernesto Elorduy (1853–1912), Ricardo Castro (1866–1907), and Felipe Villanueva (1863–93). These composers were also partial to the waltz, a celebrated Mexican example of which is "Sobre las olas" (Over the Waves), by Juventino Rosas (d. 1895). Besides the *habanera,* other creole types of music proved attractive to Latin American composers. Around the middle of the nineteenth century, and particularly in Mexico, Cuba, Colombia, and Brazil, composers began to imitate local songs and dances, and to utilize regional melodies and rhythms. This was to produce an abundant harvest in the twentieth century.

{7}

Prosperity and
Renewal
[1890–1920]

IN LATIN AMERICA, as throughout the Western world, the
1890's were marked by a general prosperity. Which groups
received the benefits of this prosperity varied from country to
country. In Argentina and Uruguay, many strata felt its benefits; in Mexico and Brazil, only the upper classes. Political
organization gave the impression of stability; institutions en-
dured, and were respected, outwardly at least. In the realm
of law, society had adapted to the existing system, based on
the French model, and few legislative changes were made. At
the same time, in those human relationships that are not regulated by law, Spanish and Portuguese traditions persisted. In
Brazil, the establishment of republican institutions met with
no obstacles. In many respects the Empire had been democratic; the change of regime made very little difference in
public life.

The only possessions that Spain had retained in the New
World were lost in 1898, as a consequence of the Cuban insurrection (1895–98) and the Spanish-American War. Cuba became independent and began to function as a republic in 1902
(its constitution was adopted in 1901). Puerto Rico came under
the control of the United States but retained its Hispanic

character, and the English language, in spite of official efforts to promote it, is little used there even today.

At the beginning of the twentieth century, Latin America, like the rest of the world, presented an appearance of stability that promised to last indefinitely. There were political disturbances here and there, but they were regarded as remnants of a turbulent past, destined to disappear. Shortly, however, the picture began to change, even before Europe plunged into the conflict of 1914. With economic prosperity, new social groups rose in Spanish America. A "middle class" was formed, primarily defined by economic standing. (In Spanish America, and in Brazil, there were no "classes" in the traditional, political sense that prevailed in Europe.) These new groups were eager to exert their influence in public life. As always, it was in Mexico and Argentina that significant movements developed.

The movement known as "the Revolution" started in Mexico shortly before 1910; it was to have deep repercussions and vast consequences throughout America. Beginning in 1908, the Mexican people showed signs of a determination to put an end to the long dictatorship of Porfirio Díaz, which had lasted since 1876 (including the four years, 1880–85, of the presidency of Manuel González). This regime had been peaceful, but it had suppressed public liberties. It had been liberal at its outset, but had ended by creating a new kind of political conservatism. Now the "middle class" demanded the restoration of the democratic liberties proclaimed by Benito Juárez and Sebastián Lerdo de Tejada. In its initial phase, the Revolution triumphed within a few months (November, 1910–May, 1911), but the government that resulted was of short duration; it was overthrown by the conservative reaction in February, 1913. For five years, the civil war went on, bringing numerous reverses to both sides; it came to an end, in 1917, except for occasional outbreaks, some of them very serious.

Meanwhile, to the demands of the "middle class" had been added the championing of the proletariat, for socialist principles had been incorporated in the program of the Revolution.

The demands of the rural worker had found a voice through the rebellion in 1910 led by Emiliano Zapata (1879–1919) in the state of Morelos, one of the regions devoted to the sugar industry. In 1916, in the midst of the civil war, a constitution was drafted, although its promulgation was delayed until February, 1917—exactly seventy years after the adoption of the venerable and venerated constitution of the Reform. The new constitution contained articles that provoked—and still provoke—controversy: Article 3, which established the socialist character of public (official) instruction; Article 27, which regulated the ownership of land and of water and decreed that the ownership of mines and oil fields rested exclusively with the nation; and Article 123, which spelled out the rights of the worker. Socialism, however, was not rooted in the Mexican economic order except in the system of the *ejido*, or rural communal property, which had existed during the colonial epoch as a Spanish system imposed on an Aztec tradition and which had been rescinded, at the time of the Reform, by the laws pertaining to mortmain. The *ejido* was restored, but lands were also distributed to the peasants on an individual basis, and private ownership of small holdings was encouraged.

In Argentina, after the exemplary administrations of Mitre, Sarmiento, and Avellaneda, from 1862 to 1880, an oligarchy was established that maintained itself in power for thirty-six years, until President Roque Sáenz Peña (1851–1914) obtained from the Congress a reform of the electoral law that ensured freedom of the ballot. In this way, the Radical Party came to power in 1916; but it was not "radical." Despite its name, it represented, above all, the "middle class," which consisted principally of the descendants of immigrants. The University Reform began in 1918; it was to be a far-reaching movement.

Socialist doctrines were not new to Latin America in the twentieth century; even before the middle of the nineteenth century, the theories of Saint-Simon, Fourier, and Proudhon were known. In Argentina, the program of the Asociación de Mayo, founded in 1838 by Echeverría and his friends, was called *Dogma socialista;* in Colombia, socialist clubs were organized during the liberal government (1849–53) of José Hilario López (1798–1869); in Mexico, there were writers and poets with socialist orientations, such as Pantaleón Tovar (1828–76) and Juan Díaz Covarrubias (1837–58); the Frenchman Taudonnet had published a *Revista Socialista* in Rio de Janeiro (1845). But these socialists rarely ventured so far as to accept the doctrines of European socialism *in toto;* the economic implications were too great. Echeverría, for example, never went beyond the liberal viewpoint. And all the legislation of this period confirmed the respect for private property, which had been threatened by the abuses of absolutism.

In the twentieth century, the situation changed. The brand of socialism that is studied and is influential is no longer the "utopian" kind of the French thinkers, but the "scientific" kind of Marx and Engels. This new variety of socialism spread rapidly, and by 1910, it had representatives in the congresses of Chile and Argentina. The Argentine Socialist Party was founded by Juan Bautista Justo (1865–1928), a professor of medicine at the University of Buenos Aires and author of several important books, among them *Teoría y práctica de la historia* (The Theory and Practice of History; 1909). Its first congressional representative (deputy) was Alfredo Lorenzo Palacios (1879–1965), who began in 1905 to sponsor and put through laws favoring the workers; later he became professor of law and president of the University of La Plata. The first Socialist Party senator, in 1913, was another professor, Enrique del Valle Ibarlucea (1878–1921), a jurist who drafted the labor code in collaboration with Joaquín V. González (1863–1923), a liberal thinker and politician who was minister of justice and public instruction (1904–06) and founded the University of La Plata. The Party's newspaper, *La Vanguardia,* began publication in 1894.

In philosophy, positivism was still dominant at the beginning of the twentieth century, and it even made new converts. The most notable were the Argentine psychologist and sociologist José Ingenieros (1877–1925) and the Peruvian sociologist Mariano H. Cornejo (1883–1946). But soon new theories arose in opposition to the limitations of positivism; the writings of Boutroux, Bergson, Croce, William James, began to find acceptance. The new trends started by these writers were given direction by Raimundo de Farías Brito (1862–1917) in Brazil; Alejandro Deústua (1849–1945) in Peru; Alejandro Korn (1860–1936) in Argentina; Carlos Vaz Ferreira (1873–1958) in Uruguay; and, in the next generation, Antonio Caso (1883–1946) and José Vasconcelos (1881–1959) in Mexico; Víctor Andrés Belaúnde (1883–1966) and Francisco García Calderón (1883–1953) in Peru. To their number should be added Enrique José Varona and Justo Sierra, who watched the process of renewal with interest. All these thinkers produced notable, and at times original, works. Especially marked by originality were the ideas of Korn, with his *La libertad creadora* (Creative Freedom; 1922); Vaz Ferreira, with his *Lógica viva* (Living Logic; 1910); and Caso, with his *La existencia como economía, como desinterés y como caridad* (Existence as Economy, as Disinterest, and as Charity; 1919). Also included in this movement, at least in his role of moral thinker, was the great Uruguayan writer José Enrique Rodó (1871–1917), who in his *Motivos de Proteo* (1909; translation, *The Motives of Proteus,* 1928) expounded the doctrine of spiritual renewal as a duty: the "ethics of becoming."

In public education, as the influence of positivism waned, philosophical freedom asserted itself; but in secondary teaching, the dominance of the sciences persisted. Pedagogy as a subject in its own right began to attract attention; interest was displayed in new methods and ideas. Pedagogical experimentation and research acquired special importance in Chile, Argentina, Mexico, Cuba, and specialized reviews were published. In 1858, Sarmiento had founded the *Revista de Educación,* organ of the provincial authorities of Buenos Aires, and later, in 1880, he was responsible for establishing *El Monitor de la Educación Común.* Both publications still exist.

New universities were founded, the most important in the Argentine city of La Plata (1902). In 1910, the University of Mexico City was reconstituted, thanks to the efforts of Justo

Sierra; in 1914, the University of Santo Domingo, which in 1866 had been restored as a "Professional Institute," was reconstituted. In Cuba, after the departure of the Spanish, Varona reorganized the system of public instruction, from the university to the elementary schools. The latter quadrupled in number; the island then had "more teachers than soldiers."

The movement of University Reform, initiated in Argentina in 1918, exerted its influence in neighboring countries, particularly in Peru, where another movement arose under the same name (1919). It demanded and obtained the participation of the students in the government of the university, and it tried to bring the university closer to the people. Even before 1918, Argentina had had the Popular Universities established by the Socialist Party.

Scientific research was systematized in institutions such as the National Museum of Mexico, the Museum of La Plata, the Astronomical Observatory of Córdoba in Argentina (which Sarmiento had established during his administration) and its counterpart in Tacubaya in Mexico, and in new establishments such as the Institutes of Geology, of Biology, and of Bacteriology in Mexico, the Institute of Physics and the Astronomical Observatory of La Plata (affiliated with the University, as was the Museum, although the latter was older), and the Ethnographic Museum, the Pharmacological Museum (where the materia medica of the Indians was studied), the Institute of Physiology, the Institutes of Normal Anatomy and of Pathological Anatomy, the Model Institute of Clinical Medicine, and the Institute for Historical Research—all affiliated with the University of Buenos Aires.

As official institutes for research increased in number, there was a corresponding decline in private associations devoted to cultural interests. The private groups had played a vital role at the beginning and in the middle of the nineteenth century, and some still exercised considerable influence, particularly three bearing the name Ateneo (Athenaeum): the Ateneo de Montevideo, which is still active; the Ateneo de la Habana, where many excellent lectures were given; and the Mexico

City association (1907–14), which served as the vehicle for the youthful intellectual revolution that preceded the political revolution of 1910, and under whose auspices the first Popular University in Mexico was founded (1912–20). The Ateneo in Mexico City, at first called the Sociedad de Conferencias (1907–8), counted among its principal members Antonio Caso, Alfonso Reyes, José Vasconcelos, Martín Luis Guzmán (b. 1887), and Enrique González Martínez (1871–1952). Two of them, Jesús Tito Acevedo (c. 1888–1918) and Federico E. Mariscal (b. 1881), initiated the movement for the study of the colonial architecture of Mexico. The Ateneo in Havana, on the other hand, was supplanted, at least in the public's awareness, by the Sociedad de Conferencias (1910–15), founded by the essayist and short-story writer Jesús Castellanos (1879–1912) and the Dominican writer Max Henríquez Ureña (b. 1885).

In the annals of medical science, one of the most eminent figures was the Cuban research scholar Carlos Juan Finlay (1833–1915). In 1883, he had demonstrated experimentally (in the case of Father Urra) that the yellow-fever virus is transmitted by means of a common mosquito (*Aëdes aegypti*). His thesis was confirmed in 1900 by the work of a commission of doctors from the United States and Cuba; in charge were Walter Reed, Jesse W. Lazear, James Carroll, and Arístides Agramonte. Finlay's methods were applied in the sanitation programs undertaken in Havana and later in Panama and, under the supervision of the great hygienist Oswaldo Cruz (1872–1917), in the seaports of Brazil. Finlay made many other studies of various diseases. In 1905, he was nominated for the Nobel Prize by Sir Ronald Ross, famous for his research on malaria. Finlay and his assistant Claudio Delgado, as well as Domingos Freire (1849–99) in Brazil (1880), and Manuel Carmona y Valle (1827–1902) in Mexico, attempted to isolate the malaria virus. In 1927, Rockefeller Foundation researchers in Africa (Adrian Stokes, J. H. Bauer, and N. Paul Hudson) made the first studies toward reliable diagnosis of the disease and, therefore, its ultimate control.

Also of great importance are the works of the Argentine

biologist Angel Gallardo (1867–1934), with his *Interpretación dinámica de la división celular* (The Dynamic Interpretation of Cellular Division; 1903), and of two Argentine physicians, Luis Agote (1869–1954) and Pedro Chutro (1880–1937). Agote was the first to add citrate of sodium to the blood to prevent coagulation in transfusions (1914); Chutro, in World War I, devised, applied, and propagated the "rationalization" of operating techniques, for the purpose of gaining time in operating on the wounded.*

As always, there were numerous ethnologists, archaeologists, and philologists engaged in studying the indigenous peoples and the cultures and languages of America: in Venezuela, the geographer Alfredo Jahn (1867–1940) and the historian Lisandro Alvarado; in Colombia, Ernesto Restrepo Tirado (1862–1948); in Argentina, Salvador Debenedetti (1884–1930) and Luis María Torres (1878–1937).

A major contribution from Brazil was made by the great precursor of modern aviation, Alberto Santos Dumont (1873–1932), who, after experimenting successfully with flights in dirigible balloons (in 1901, he flew from Saint-Cloud to Paris and back), made airplane flights on October 23 and November 12, 1906.

By the end of the nineteenth century, daily newspapers and magazines were proliferating at an astounding rate—all the more so because so many of them were short-lived. Noteworthy among publications that attained some importance in the lit-

---

* Among other men of science of this period are: in Cuba, the zoologist Carlos de la Torre y Huerta (1858–1950), the biologist and physician Juan Guiteras (1852–1925), the botanists Manuel Gómez de la Maza (1867–1916) and José Tomás Roig y Mesa (b. 1878), co-authors of *Flora de Cuba* (1914); in Mexico, the geologists José G. Aguilera and Ezequiel Ordóñez (1867–1950), who supervised the triangulation of the national territory, the physicist and astronomer Valentín Gama (1868–1942), the biologist Alfonso Luis Herrera (1868–1944); in Venezuela, the biologists and physicians Luis Razetti (b. 1862) and Guillermo Delgado Palacios (1865–1934); in Colombia, the botanist Joaquín Antonio Uribe (1858–1935), author of the *Flora sonsonesa;* in Argentina, the botanist Miguel Lillo (1862–1931), the physicians Abel Ayerza (1861–1918) and Marcelino Herrera Vegas (born in Venezuela in 1870), author of studies on hydatid cysts.

erary movement that bore the rather inexpressive name *modernismo* were, in Mexico, the *Revista Azul* (1894–96), one of whose editors was the poet Manuel Gutiérrez Nájera (1859–95), and the *Revista Moderna* (1898–1911), edited by the poets Jesús E. Valenzuela (1856–1911) and Amado Nervo (1870–1919); in Cuba, *La Habana Elegante* (already mentioned), *El Fígaro* (1885–1925), and *La Habana Literaria* (1891–92); in Caracas, *El Cojo Ilustrado* (1892–1915) and *Cosmópolis* (1894–95); in Montevideo, the *Revista Nacional de Literatura y Ciencias Sociales* (1895–97); in Buenos Aires, the *Revista de América* (1896), edited by the great Nicaraguan writer Rubén Darío (1867–1916) and the Bolivian poet Ricardo Jaimes Freyre (1868–1933), and *El Mercurio de América* (1898–1900). The cause of the new literature was also aided, in part, by *La Biblioteca* (1896–98) of Buenos Aires, organ of the National Library of that city, under the direction of the eminent Franco-Argentine historian Paul Groussac (1848–1929). Among the reviews that appeared after the beginning of the twentieth century were, in Buenos Aires, *Nosotros* (1907–34; second series, 1936–43); in Lima, *Colónida* (1915–19[?]), edited by the Peruvian writer Abraham Valdelomar (1888–1919); in Santiago de Chile, *Los Diez* (1916–19[?]); in Havana, *Cuba Contemporánea* (1913–27).

Other reviews appeared in countries outside Latin America: for example, *Las Tres Américas* (1894–97), edited by Nicanor Bolet Peraza, in New York. Also in New York, a review of current events called *Las Novedades* flourished for forty years, starting in 1876; in its final years of publication (1915–16), it had an interesting literary section. There were also the publications of the Cuban independence movement, the best of which was *Patria* (1892–98), founded in New York by José Martí and afterward edited by Varona. In the twentieth century, there were *El Nuevo Mercurio* (1907–19[?]), edited by the Guatemalan Enrique Gómez Carrillo (1873–1927); *Mundial* (1912–14), edited by Rubén Darío; and the *Revista de América* (1912–14), edited by the Peruvians Francisco and Ventura García Calderón—all published in Paris. Publications devoted to the sciences, to law, and to history became more numerous. Many of these were organs of institutes or societies for research and study.

The literature of this period was extraordinarily brilliant. In the development of *modernismo,* a true literary renascence, the Spanish American countries were more than fifteen years ahead of Spain. Signs of a change in taste may be discerned in poets such as González Prada and Manuel José Othón; in the Argentine Almafuerte (pseudonym of Pedro Bonifacio Palacios, 1854–1917); in the Dominican Gastón Fernando Deligne (1861–1913), with his keenly perceptive psychological and philosophical poems; in the Mexican Salvador Díaz Mirón (1853–1928), who in his first writings was impetuously Romantic in the manner of Victor Hugo and in his second phase was serene in expression but rigorous in form; and in Francisco Asís de Icaza (1863–1925), also a Mexican, who, as a critic, was especially distinguished for his studies of the *Novelas ejemplares* of Cervantes, published in 1901.

The *modernista* movement in its apogee may be said to have had five leading representatives: José Martí and Julián del Casal (1863–93) of Cuba; Manuel Gutiérrez Nájera of Mexico; José Asunción Silva (1865–96) of Colombia; and Rubén Darío of Nicaragua. Among their followers were the Colombian Guillermo Valencia (1873–1943), the Mexicans Luis Gonzalo Urbina (1868–1934), Amado Nervo, and José Juan Tablada (1871–1945)—all from countries north of the Equator. Later, in 1893, the movement extended south, when Rubén Darío went to live in Buenos Aires. At that time appeared Leopoldo Lugones (1874–1938) of Argentina, Julio Herrera y Reissig (1875–1910) of Uruguay, Ricardo Jaimes Freyre of Bolivia, José Santos Chocano (1875–1934) of Peru, and Carlos Pezoa Véliz (1879–1908) of Chile. These men represent, as a whole, the highest poetic level Spanish America has ever reached.

Concurrently in Brazil, a similar movement developed, but with scarcely any connection with its counterpart in the Spanish language. The best Brazilian poets—as a group—are part of this movement: Olavo Bilac (1865–1918),* Alberto de Oliveira (1857–1937), Raymundo Correia (1860–1911), Bernardino Lopes (1859–1916), and João de Cruz e Sousa (1862–1918).

In addition to the poets, many writers of prose emerged throughout Latin America. They did not compare, as a group, with the figures of the previous period, which included Justo Sierra, González Prada, Montalvo, Hostos, Varona, Ricardo Palma, and Jorge Isaacs in Spanish America, and Ruy Barbosa, Joaquim Nabuco, and Machado de Assis in Brazil. But there were some outstanding figures, notably the Uruguayans José Enrique Rodó and Horacio Quiroga (1879–1937), the Colombian Baldomero Sanín Cano (1861–1957), and the Venezuelan Manuel Díaz Rodríguez (1868–1927). Among the poets, some were also distinguished prose writers: Martí, Gutiérrez Nájera, Rubén Darío, Nervo, Urbina, Valencia, and Lugones.

This movement completely transformed the forms of prose and poetry: vocabulary, turns of speech, types of verse, paragraph structure, themes, embellishment. Versification developed with an unprecedented variety. All existing verse forms were employed, and new forms were invented; poets even wrote "free verse" in the manner of Walt Whitman and also used the "fluctuating" verse characteristic of Spanish poetry in the twelfth and thirteenth centuries. At first, these new forms were tried timidly; later, with full liberty, as in the "Canto a la Argentina" (Song to Argentina; 1910), by Darío. Prose lost its rigid forms of semijocose narration and solemn oratory with lengthy paragraphs; it acquired brevity and agility.

Of the great figures of the movement, the first, chronologically, is José Martí, liberator of Cuba, who gave impetus to his country's final struggle for independence with his extended speechmaking campaigns, his work as a journalist, and his activity as an organizer and unifier of the national will. He died in the struggle, shortly after it began. His life was a life of sacrifice, dedicated to Cuba and to *nuestra América* ("our

* His real name was Brás Martins dos Guimarães.—TRANS.

America"), an expression that he coined to designate Hispanic America. As a writer, he is one of the most masterly in the Spanish language. His style displays constant and felicitous invention, with a wealth of ideas, a wide emotional range, a deep faith in humanity, liberty, justice, and goodness.

Rubén Darío is generally regarded as the greatest poet Latin America has produced.* During his lifetime, he enjoyed immense fame, not only on this continent, but also in Spain, where he exerted a strong personal influence (from 1899) and brought about a literary revolution. Since his death, opinions about him have been divided, but few deny him a place in the front rank. His youthful work, particularly *Prosas profanas* (1896), is marked by brilliance, color, and joy. He wanted to embrace all the beauty of the world, all the refinements of civilization, from China and India to Florence and Paris. He was reproached for being excessively fond of the exotic, and he himself believed that he was spiritually cut off from America and from his own times; actually, he represented the desire— very much a part of "our America"—to taste all the fruits of culture. Later, his stay in Spain made him feel that he was "the poet of the race" (the inaccurate expression then in vogue), and he began to deal with themes that had not previously interested him, such as public affairs, and with great visions of the future of the Spanish-speaking peoples: "Salutación del optimista" (Salutation of the Optimist; 1902), "A Roosevelt" (1903), "Oda a Mitre" (Ode to Mitre; 1906), "Viaje a Nicaragua" (Journey to Nicaragua; 1907), "Canto a la Argentina" (1910). With the years, his early joyfulness gave way to the bitterness of life that is passing, of youth that is disappearing, and his verses began to strike deep and sorrowful notes: "Nocturnos" (Nocturnes), "Fatalidad" (Fatality), "Poema del otoño" (Autumnal Poem)—some of the deepest and most sorrowful in all Spanish poetry.

If Rubén Darío was considered the greatest poet of his time,

* English translations of representative work may be found in *Selected Poems of Rubén Darío*, trans. Lysander Kemp. *See* Bibliography under "Central America."—TRANS.

José Enrique Rodó was judged the greatest prose writer. Like Darío, he has been the victim of critical reaction by later generations; and like him, he retains, in spite of his detractors, a very high place. As a stylist, Rodó gave the Spanish language new tones; as a critic, he brought new life to the formal appreciation of literature. Among his important critical works are *Rubén Darío,* 1898, and *Juan María Gutiérrez y su época* (Juan María Gutiérrez and His Times); as a thinker, he originated the doctrine of the "ethics of becoming" and made important studies of events and trends in the social and cultural life of Spanish America, particularly in his best-known work, *Ariel* (1900), and in his monographs on Montalvo and Bolívar.

Among the other prose writers and poets of this period (it would be impossible to study them all without converting this volume into a treatise on literary history), we must briefly note the serene and polished poetry of Gutiérrez Nájera, and his prose, amazing in its variety of forms, ranging from the ornamental and picturesque to the minute and fine, in this last anticipating the prose of the Spanish Azorín a generation later; the poetry, at times opulent with color, at times sorrowful and plaintive, of Casal; the emotional originality, expressed in unique form, of the third "Nocturno" of Silva, the one that begins: *"Una noche . . .";* the verbal and descriptive mastery of Lugones; the inventive images in Julio Herrera y Reissig; the multicolored images of America in Chocano; the strange and personal emotions of Amado Nervo, in contrast to the ordinary emotions so limpidly expressed by Urbina; the delicate shadings in the prose of Díaz Rodríguez; the mature and liberal wisdom of Sanín Cano.

The prose writers showed a preference for essays (Rodó, Darío, Sanín Cano, Díaz Rodríguez); for *crónicas,* or commentaries on current affairs, either local or global (Martí, Gutiérrez Nájera, Darío, Urbina, Enrique Gómez Carrillo); and for the short story (Martí, Gutiérrez Nájera, Casal, Silva, Darío, Nervo, Lugones, Díaz Rodríguez, and Horacio Quiroga, whose original and vigorous stories deal with men and animals in the jungle).

The novel was cultivated less; its outstanding practitioners were Reyles, Quiroga, Díaz Rodríguez, the Venezuelan Rufino Blanco Fombona (1874–1944), the Dominican Tulio Manuel Cestero (1877–1955), the Argentines Enrique Larreta (1873–1961), with his historical novel *La gloria de Don Ramiro* (The Glory of Don Ramiro; 1908), and Roberto José Payró (1867–1928), with his narratives and descriptions of Spanish American life.

In Brazil, Olavo Bilac was a typical poet of the tropics, with lively emotions and brilliant imagery; Alberto de Oliveira achieved perfection in form and depth in concept; the work of Raymundo Correia is fine and delicate. All three were admirable poets of the landscape. In fiction, after the realists and naturalists, came José Pereira da Graça Aranha (1868–1931), whose celebrated novel *Canaã* (1902; translation, *Canaan*, 1920) is one of the earliest examples of the "problem novel," with discussions on the future of the country. The most important prose writer was Euclides da Cunha (1866–1909). His great work *Os Sertões* (1902; translation, *Rebellion in the Backlands*, 1944) relates the tragic history of the religious fanatic Antônio Conselheiro and his followers; it is at the same time a profound study of the rural milieu and its inhabitants, which are depicted with vigorous strokes.

The theater has always been a favorite form of entertainment for the public in Latin America, and during the nineteenth century and the early part of the twentieth, Spanish and Portuguese theatrical companies appeared in the principal cities, along with local troupes. Furthermore, after 1870, there were frequent visits by renowned actors and actresses from Italy (Adelaide Ristori, Giacinta Pezzana, Tomasso Salvini, Ernesto Rossi, Ferruccio Garavaglia, Ermete Novelli, Ermete Zacconi, Eleonora Duse, Italia Vitaliani, Virginia Reiter, Teresa Mariani, Irma and Emma Grammatica, Giovanni Grasso, Mimi Aguglia, Ruggero Ruggeri); from France (Sarah Bernhardt, the two Coquelins, Gabrielle Réjane, Julie Baret, Lucien Guitry, Suzanne Desprée, Aurelien Lugné-Poë); and, occasionally, German- or English-speaking actors (the most

notable of these was the German actor Alexander Moissi).
Among notable native-born actors in Spanish America were
the Cubans Paulino Delgado and Luisa Martínez Casado, and
the Panamanian Germán Mackay. Local production of dramas
and comedies, which was considerable in the years after independence, subsequently declined, except for the *sainetes* (short
dramatic sketches or farces) and the *zarzuelas breves* (operettas),
such as were produced in Mexico and Cuba. Theatrical activity
was revived in an unexpected fashion in Argentina and Uruguay through the circus. The Uruguayan impresario José
Podestá (1858–1937) conceived the idea of offering to the public, as part of the circus under his management, dramatic
pantomimes dealing with gaucho life. The first of these, *Juan
Moreira* (1884), was performed with spoken dialogue in 1886.
Many more dramas of this type were written, their popularity
increased, and several companies organized by the Podestá
family toured Argentina and Uruguay. Finally, in 1901, they
made the transition from the circus and the neighborhood
theaters to the downtown theaters of Buenos Aires, and in
1902, they abandoned the gaucho pieces to produce plays of
all kinds by Argentine and Uruguayan authors. The output
was abundant and the success enormous. Among these playwrights—and there were many—the leading one was the Uruguayan Florencio Sánchez (1875–1910). His dramas are somber
and powerful, especially the magnificent *Barranca abajo* (Down
the Gully; 1905), comparable to the great realistic works of the
European theater. Noteworthy among his comedies are *La
gringa* (The Immigrant Girl), and *M'hijo el dotor* (My Son,
the Lawyer; 1903).*

In music and the plastic arts, this was a period of transition.
The composers divided their attention between France and
Germany as models in the production of formal works such as
the symphony, the string quartet, and the lied; in opera, the
influences were French and Italian, with emphasis on post-
Wagnerian tendencies. The study and utilization of elements

* The three plays mentioned here are available in translation. *See* Bibliography.—TRANS.

of popular music were now heading in new directions, particularly with the compositions of Julián Aguirre (1869–1924) in Argentina and of Manuel M. Ponce (1882–1948) in Mexico. Aguirre became internationally known for his stylized versions of two typical dance songs of northern Argentina, "Huella" and "Gato" (orchestrated by Ernest Ansermet); he composed a number of other piano pieces and some attractive songs. Ponce, famous for his song "Estrellita" (in the style of the German lied), made fine transcriptions and arrangements of Mexican folksongs between 1912 and 1920. Later, he turned to more complex forms of instrumental composition.

Turn-of-the-century architecture displayed very little originality, copying European styles. French models were preferred for large buildings, public or private, in the cities. Houses in the country and in the suburbs were modeled after English, Swiss, or Basque (Spanish and French) styles.

In painting, Impressionism appeared with artists such as the Argentines Martín Malharro (1865–1911)—when he is successful, perhaps the best of them all—and Fernando Fader (1882–1935), influenced by the German school; the Uruguayan Pedro Blanes Viale (1879–1926); the Dominican Luis Desangles; the Mexicans Joaquín Clausell (1866–1935), Alfredo Ramos Martínez (1875–1947), and Gerardo Murillo, or, "Dr. Atl" (1875–1964), who afterward went off in other directions.* Impressionism also produced the original Uruguayan painter Pedro Figari (1861–1938), one of the most important artists of the Americas. Figari discovered distinctive traits in the South American landscape and evoked scenes of bygone days; his sense of color is exquisite.

* By 1910 he had become a leading spirit in the art movement of the Mexican Revolution.—Trans.

{ 8 }

The
Immediate
Past
[1920–1945]

I N THE PERIOD BEGINNING around 1920, two contradictory tendencies were evident in Latin America. One was the championing of the cause of the proletariat, which in Mexico and
Peru was usually called "the redemption of the Indian"; the
other was the reappearance of dictatorships in countries that
had rid themselves of tyrants, such as Argentina and Brazil.

The Mexican Revolution of 1910 was original. It was the
third great democratic movement, after the Independence and
the Reform, which included in its program the rehabilitation
of the oppressed. The first two, Independence and Reform,
were liberal movements inspired by eighteenth-century principles that were upheld and disseminated during the nineteenth century. The Revolution of 1910 combined liberal
principles with a socialist outlook. Its theoretical culmination
was the constitution of 1917. After that came its practical accomplishments through government action: land distribution
in communal *ejidos* and small private holdings; nationaliza-
tion of oil deposits (1938); dissemination of culture by increasing the number of libraries and of schools of all kinds, begin-

ning with the efforts of José Vasconcelos as minister of public
education, in 1920–23; satisfaction of the demands of industrial workers, who were represented chiefly by the Mexican
Confederation of Workers (CTM), under the leadership of
Vicente Lombardo Toledano (b. 1894; also noted as a political
orator and a writer with a broad philosophical background,
author of a treatise on ethics, in 1922, and of studies on the
theoretical foundations of law).

In Peru, as in Mexico, the demands of the proletariat figured
in the program—a vast scheme of general social reforms—of
the most forward-looking political party: the Alianza Popular
Revolucionaria Americana (APRA), whose aims, as its name
indicates, reached beyond the limitation of geographic boundaries. Its leader, Víctor Raúl Haya de la Torre (b. 1895), was,
like Lombardo Toledano, an orator and a writer with a solid
philosophical background. The APRA movement (*aprismo*)
engaged widely in ideological propaganda and founded Popular Universities (as the CTM did later in Mexico) before it
had an opportunity (in 1944) to intervene directly in legislative
matters.

The Russian Revolution, which came after the adoption of
the constitution of 1917, was influential throughout Latin
America, manifesting its strength in the formation of Com-
munist parties, the most important being those in Brazil, Chile,
Cuba, Argentina, Uruguay, Venezuela, and Peru. Socialist
parties existed much earlier. The Socialist Party of Argentina
has a brilliant and dignified history, with leaders such as Justo,
Palacios, and Valle Ibarlucea, Nicolás Repetto (1871–1965),
Mario Bravo (1882–1943), Enrique Dickmann (1874–1955), and
Américo Ghioldi (b. 1899). The totalitarian dictatorships of
Italy (1923–45) and Germany (1933–45) also exerted an influence in Spanish America; and the Spanish Civil War of 1936–
39 and World War II stirred public opinion and provoked
ideological conflicts.

Woman suffrage was established in Panama, Uruguay (1934),
Cuba (1940), Ecuador, and the Dominican Republic (1942).
Uruguay, Cuba, and the Dominican Republic were among the

first to have women representatives in Congress. Partial woman suffrage was established in Brazil (for employed women), Chile (in municipal elections, with eligibility for public office; a woman was at one time mayor of the capital), Peru and Venezuela (in municipal voting), and Mexico (but only in a few states). The constitutions of El Salvador and of Nicaragua, both adopted in 1939, provided for woman suffrage. Argentina had woman suffrage in the province of San Juan, but it was abolished.*

The population of Latin America had increased rapidly since the beginning of the century; this increase was largely concentrated in the cities. By 1945, Buenos Aires, with 3.1 million inhabitants, Rio de Janeiro, with 1.9 million, and Mexico City and São Paulo, with 1.5 million each, ranked among the largest cities in the world. The population of Havana and of Santiago de Chile had passed the million mark, and that of Montevideo was approaching it.†

* In Argentina, a law enacted on September 25, 1947, established equal political rights for women. This was confirmed by an electoral law in 1957. In addition, woman suffrage has been confirmed, or established for the first time, in Bolivia (supreme decree, 1952), Brazil (federal constitution of 1946), Colombia (legislative decree, 1957), Costa Rica (constitution of 1949), Chile (electoral law, 1958), Cuba (basic law, 1959), Dominican Republic (constitution of 1960), Ecuador (constitution of 1946), El Salvador (constitution of 1950), Guatemala (constitution of 1956), Honduras (constitution of 1956), Mexico (political constitution of 1917; federal election law, 1951, amended 1953), Nicaragua (constitutional amendment, 1955), Paraguay (electoral law, 1959), Peru (constitution of 1933 as amended September 7, 1955), Panama (constitution of 1946), Uruguay (constitution of 1951), and Venezuela (electoral law, 1958).—TRANS.

† The estimated population of Buenos Aires in 1962 was 3.8 million (metropolitan area, 7 million); of Rio de Janeiro, 3.3 million (metropolitan area, 4.7 million); of São Paulo, 3.3 million (metropolitan area, 4.4 million); of Mexico City, 3.3 million (Federal District, 4.8 million); of Montevideo, 1.7 million; of Lima, 1.7 million; of Santiago, 2 million; of Havana, 1.2 million; of Bogotá, 1.5 million; of Caracas, 1.5 million. For the next largest cities, the estimated 1965 population figures were: Recife, 797,000; Rosario, 761,300; Porto Alegre, 700,000; Medellín, 690,000; Salvador (Bahia), 655,700; Guatemala City, 637,841; Córdoba, 635,000; Monterrey, 597,000; Guayaquil, 510,000; Santo Domingo, 462,000; Barranquilla, 456,000; San Juan, 432,300; La Plata, 410,000; Belem, 402,000; La Paz, 347,400; Asunción, 305,000; Managua, 274,900; Valparaíso, 267,600; San Salvador, 255,700; San José, 167,000; Tegucigalpa, 140,000.—TRANS.

The press mushroomed, spreading to all the cities and towns. Many daily newspapers had a long and stable existence; the oldest of these were in Brazil, Argentina, Chile, and Peru. The principal newspapers of Rio de Janeiro, São Paulo, Buenos Aires, and Santiago de Chile are comparable to the best in Europe and the United States. Magazines, on the other hand, seldom lasted very long, but at times they had great importance within various literary movements.

Among the more important periodicals are the *Revista do Brasil* (started in 1916) in Rio de Janeiro, *Fronteiras* (started in 1932) in Recife, and *Plan-Alto* (started in 1941) in São Paulo; *Valoraciones* (1923–28) in La Plata; *Martín Fierro* (1925–28), spokesman for avant-garde literature, and *Sur* (started in 1930), edited by Victoria Ocampo, in Buenos Aires; *Alfar* in Montevideo; the *Revista Chilena* (1917–28) in Santiago, and *Atenea* of the University of Concepción (started in 1923); *Kollasuyo* in La Paz; the new *Mercurio Peruano* (started in 1918) and *Amauta* (1927–c. 1930) in Lima; *Revista de las Indias* (started in 1936) and *Revista de América* (started in 1945), both founded by Germán Arciniegas in Bogotá; *Cultura Venozolana* (1918–c. 1927) and *Revista Nacional de Cultura* (started in 1938) in Caracas; the new *Revista Bimestre Cubana* (started around 1906) as the organ of the very old Sociedad Económica de Amigos del País, the new *Revista Cubana* (started in 1935), and the *Revista de Avance* (1927–30) in Havana; the *Ateneo Portorriqueño* in San Juan; *México Moderno* (1920–22), *Contemporáneos* (1928–31), *Letras de México* (started in 1937), *Cuadernos Americanos* (started in 1942), and *El Hijo Pródigo* (1941–46) in Mexico City; the *Repertorio Americano* (started in 1920), edited by Joaquín García Monge, in San José de Costa Rica; the *Revista de Guatemala* (started in 1945). We can regard also as reviews the Sunday supplements of the two great morning newspapers of Buenos Aires, *La Nación* and *La Prensa*. Not to be overlooked, finally, are the innumerable publications of official institutions and private associations.

Publishing houses were important in Latin America, especially in Mexico, from 1840 to 1880, but afterward declined. Editions of Spanish and Portuguese books printed in Paris, books issued in Madrid, Barcelona, and Valencia, and Portuguese editions issued in Lisbon, Oporto, and Coimbra captured the market from local American publishers. But in the twentieth century, the lost ground was regained, and today the principal publishing centers for Latin America are in Brazil, Argentina, Mexico, and Chile.

In this period, literary societies did not have the extensive influence they had exerted in previous periods. But groups with combined interests were formed, in which—characteristically—women predominated: among them, the Lyceum of Havana and the Association of Friends of Art in Buenos Aires, which from 1924 to 1942 was a center for exhibits of painting, sculpture, architecture, photography, and books, for lectures and readings, and from time to time for theatrical and cinematographic novelties. Particularly effective were the associations devoted to the performance of music, such as Música Viva in Rio de Janeiro, the Pro Arte Society (founded in 1918) and the Society for Contemporary Music (founded in 1930) in Havana, and the Wagnerian Association (founded in 1913) in Buenos Aires.

In education, no innovations of great importance appeared during this period, but there was interest in new methods and ideas, ranging from John Dewey's to Maria Montessori's. There was a great deal of experimentation, including schemes for adapting the Indians to Western civilization while preserving all that could be salvaged from the indigenous cultures (and speaking to the Indians, if necessary, in their native languages, as did the missionaries of the sixteenth century). An attempt was made to cultivate spontaneous expression in Indian children, chiefly in artistic forms, through the teaching of painting in the Indian school of Xochimilco; by means of the method of drawing devised in 1921 by Adolfo Best Maugard (b. 1891), using the "seven lineal elements" of Aztec art and of the folk arts of Mexico; and in the teachings of Jesualdo in Uruguay, and of Olga Cossettini in Argentina.

Government efforts in matters of education were concentrated on increasing the number of schools, which was a peremptory need. Except for Argentina and Uruguay, much still remains to be done to bring the rate of literacy up to the level of the best-educated countries. Meanwhile, the universities were growing; the University of Buenos Aires, for example, had a student body almost as large as the largest in the United States, and its school of medicine was equal in scientific standards and technical equipment to the most advanced in any country. Research centers were developed. After the National Museum of Mexico, the Institute of Physiology in Buenos Aires, and the Historical and Geographical Institute of Brazil, many others were established, such as the Museum of Anthropology in Lima, the National Institute of Anthropology in Mexico City, and the Laboratory of Biological Sciences in Montevideo.

The Institute of Philology of the University of Buenos Aires, founded in 1923, was directed, beginning in 1927, by the Spanish-Argentine philologist Amado Alonso (1896–1952). Among its publications were the series "Estudios Estilísticos" (Stylistic Studies)—a discipline of which Alonso was the founder in the Spanish language—and the "Biblioteca de Dialectología Hispanoamericana" (Library of Hispanic-American Dialectology), in addition to the "Revista de Filología Hispánica" (first published in 1939). Today it is renowned throughout the world as the foremost center for Hispanic philological research; in addition to the studies by Alonso, it has published important monographs by María Rosa Lida (b. 1910), Raimundo Lida (b. 1908), Angel Rosenblat (b. 1902), and Eleuterio F. Tiscornia (1879–1945). At the University of Cuyo (in Mendoza, Argentina), in Santiago de Chile, in Montevideo, and in Bogotá, similar institutes were organized, based on this model.

The College of Mexico brought together research scholars rigorously selected from every part of the nation and Spanish scholars in exile. It is interesting to note in passing that the dispersion of Spanish professors and writers that resulted from the Spanish Civil War of 1936–39 has given them an opportunity—perhaps a compensation—to render valuable service to culture in Spanish America, notably in Mexico, Colombia, Argentina, Cuba, and the Dominican Republic. In Buenos Aires, the Free College of Higher Studies, maintained through private support, has, since 1930, offered hundreds of courses on a wide variety of subjects. Its faculty includes many of the country's most eminent men, as well as a number of distinguished visiting professors.

In philosophy, after the lengthy struggle first to impose positivism and then to dislodge it, a climate of free inquiry and universal curiosity ensued. From 1910 to 1925, Bergson's theories were the dominant influence. After that, philosophy became more diffuse in its orientation, embracing previously little known German philosophers (Dilthey, Husserl, Scheler, Heidegger), French thinkers (Meyerson, Maritain, Marcel), the Russian Berdyaev, and the Englishmen Whitehead and Russell. Through Heidegger, Kierkegaard was discovered—whom, let it be said, the Spanish philosopher Unamuno had earlier discovered through Ibsen. Other Spanish thinkers who were influential include Ortega y Gasset and, later, Santayana, who was educated in the United States and who wrote in English; influential, too, were the philosophers of a later generation who left Spain during the Civil War.

The great classical works of philosophy were also studied: Plato, Aristotle, Plotinus, St. Thomas Aquinas, Descartes (studies by Euryalo Cannabrava and Ivan Lins in Brazil; tributes, on the occasion of the tercentenary of the *Discourse on Method,* by the Universities of Buenos Aires—with a publication in three volumes—of La Plata, and of the Litoral, in Argentina), Spinoza (a study by León Dujovne in four volumes, Buenos Aires, 1941–45), Pascal, Leibniz, Kant, Hegel. Histories and anthologies of philosophical thought were published, notably those of Caso and Vasconcelos in Mexico and Leonel França (b. 1893) in Brazil. The history of thought in Latin America also received serious attention, in works by Samuel Ramos (1898–1959) and Leopoldo Zea (b. 1912) in

Mexico; Medardo Vitier (b. 1886) in Cuba; Clóvis Bevilaqua (1861–1944) in Brazil; in addition to earlier works, especially those by Korn and Ingenieros in Argentina, Emeterio Valverde Téllez (1864–1948) in Mexico, and Sílvio Romero (1851–1914) in Brazil. Emphasis was given to special branches, such as logic, the philosophy of culture, the philosophy of history, the philosophy of law; specialized studies in logic were undertaken by Lidia Peradotto and by the mathematician Claro Cornelio Dassen (1873–1941) in Argentina, and by Francisco Miró Quesada (b. 1918) in Peru. The outstanding Argentine philosopher was Francisco Romero (1891–1962), author of *Teoría del hombre* (Theory of Man; 1952), who was concerned with "transcendancy and value" and "the philosophy of the person."

Scientific study developed as a rigorous discipline. An eminent product of this discipline is the Argentine physiologist Bernardo Alberto Houssay (b. 1887), winner of the Nobel Prize for Medicine in 1947, whose studies embrace many branches of physiology: circulation, respiration, digestion, metabolism, blood, immunization, the nervous system. He has concentrated on the glands of internal secretion (suprarenal, thyroid, parathyroid, pancreas) and particularly on the hypophysis, to which he has devoted more than a hundred monographs. Of special importance are his studies on the role of the hypophysis in the metabolism of carbohydrates and as the generator of *diabetes insipidus*. Houssay has trained a large number of distinguished colleagues and followers in the Institute of Physiology of Buenos Aires. Another eminent scientist is the Mexican physicist Manuel Sandoval Vallarta (b. 1899), whose special field is research on the expansion of the universe. In collaboration with the Belgian Georges Edouard Lemaître, he formulated a theory concerning the trajectory of rays as they near the earth; the trajectory assumes the form of a conic spiral under the influence of the magnetic poles. Sandoval Vallarta worked in Belgium, in Germany, and in the United States (at the Massachusetts Institute of Technology) before returning to his native country to teach and to direct research. Outstanding work has also been done by the Peruvian biologist Carlos Monge (b. 1884), with his studies on the influence of high altitudes on the human organism.

In the ethnology, archaeology, and linguistics of the indigenous peoples of America, mention should be made of the work of the Argentine Félix Faustino Outes (1878–1939), the Peruvians José Uriel García (b. 1890) and Julio C. Tello (1880–1947), and the Mexicans Manuel Gamio (b. 1883) and Alfonso Caso (b. 1896). It was Caso who discovered the ruins of Monte Albán, which brought about a reinterpretation of many aspects of the ancient cultures of Mexico.

Scientific research developed to such an extent, especially in Brazil, Argentina, Mexico, and Peru, that an account of all its phases would be far too lengthy. It will suffice to mention the names, chosen at random, of the Brazilian naturalist Edgardo Roquette-Pinto (1884–1954), author of important works on Brazilian anthropology, especially *Randônia* (1917) and *Ensaios de Antropologia Brasiliana* (1933); the Argentine physicists Enrique Gaviola (b. 1900) and J. Cortés Pla; the Peruvian biologist and physician Juan B. Lastres (b. 1902), author of *Historia de la medicina peruana* (History of Peruvian Medicine; 1951); the Uruguayan biologist Clemente Estable (b. 1894), author of *Psicología de la vocación* (Vocational Psychology; 1941); the Argentine bacteriologist Alfredo Sordelli (b. 1891); the Argentine botanist Cristóbal Hicken (1876–1932), who bequeathed to his country the Darwinian Museum; Lorenzo Parodi (b. 1895), the Argentine botanist; the botanist Carlos E. Chardón (b. 1897) of Puerto Rico; the Dominican botanist Rafael María Moscoso (b. 1874), author of a definitive work on the flora of the Dominican Republic, *Catalogus florae dominigensis* (New York, 1943); the Mexican botanist Isaac Ochoterena (b. 1885), editor since 1930 of the *Anales del Instituto de Biología* of the National University of Mexico; the botanists César Vargas of Peru and M. Pio Correia of Brazil; the Ecuadorian archaeologist Jacinto Jijón y Caamaño (1880–1950); the Brazilian ethnologists Ulíses Pernambucano and Artur Ramos (1903–49), author of *O Negro Brasileiro* (1934; translation, *The Negro in Brazil*, 1939); the Argentine astronomer Félix Aguilar (1884–1944); the Cuban sociologist Fernando Ortíz (b. 1881), a specialist in Afro-Cuban culture; and the Peruvian geologist Carlos I. Lisson.

In literature, the *modernista* movement began to disintegrate after 1910, as dissensions arose. The opposition to the aristocratic attitude of Rubén Darío's youthful period—which he himself afterward abandoned—was formally embodied in the celebrated sonnet "Tuércele el cuello al cisne" (Twist the Neck of the Swan), by the Mexican Enrique González Martínez (1871–1952), a meditative and serene poet, polished and strict in form. Opposition was also implicit in the descriptions of the life of the common people, in poets such as the Colombian Luis Carlos López (1880–1950), the Argentine Baldomero Fernández Moreno (1886–1950), and the Mexican Ramón López Velarde (1888–1921). Another dissenting trend was represented by the "vehement" poets, a sort of new Romantics. Among them were the Colombian Miguel Angel Osorio (1883–1942), who wrote under the names Ricardo Arenales and Porfirio Barba-Jacob; the Argentine Arturo Capdevila (b. 1889); the Uruguayan Carlos Sabat Ercasty (b. 1887); and, above all, the women poets: the Uruguayans María Eugenia Vaz Ferreira (1875–1924), Delmira Agustini (1887–1914), and Juana de Ibarbourou (b. 1895); the Argentine Alfonsina Storni (1892–1938); and the Chilean Gabriela Mistral (1889–1957), whose work, imbued with nobility both in verse and in prose, was awarded the Nobel Prize for Literature in 1945.

Around 1920, a new movement in poetry began, which has been given various names: *ultraísmo, creacionismo, vanguardia*. Its distinctiveness resides in its use of images, in which, as a rule, disparate elements are unexpectedly associated. Among the principal poets who anticipated the movement or participated in it are the Peruvians José María Eguren (1882–1942) and César Vallejo (1895–1938); the Mexicans Alfonso Reyes (1889–1959), who was also a distinguished essayist and literary historian (concerned especially with Spain and Greece), Jaime Torres Bodet (b. 1901), who is also a fine novelist, José Gorostiza (b. 1901), and Carlos Pellicer (b. 1897); the Argentine

Jorge Luis Borges (b. 1899), another keen and very original essayist; the Chileans Vicente Huidobro (1893–1948) and Pablo Neruda (b. 1904), who today exerts a vast influence on the younger poets with his powerful lyric output.

This movement to transform Spanish American poetry was linked to the movement in Spain represented by Federico García Lorca, Jorge Guillén, and Rafael Alberti (b. 1903), who settled in Argentina as a result of the Spanish Civil War. But there is no priority of Spain over America, as in the colonial era, or of America over Spain, as in the *modernista* movement of 1880–90. There was a separate but similar movement in Brazil, led by Manuel Bandeira (b. 1886) and Mário de Andrade (1893–1945). The new poets of this period are prolific and brilliant—notably Carlos Drummond de Andrade (b. 1902).

While poetry was being remade, prose literature acquired great variety in its forms. As in other countries, the drama did not maintain the momentum it had had at the beginning of the century. The best efforts, and in general the best works, were now to be found in the experimental theaters.

Part of the new literature aspired to be "pure literature," especially in poetry: literature stripped of all ends that were not strictly artistic, and stripped especially of "anecdote," that is, of reference to events that might be interesting in themselves rather than for the manner in which they are interpreted by the poet. Another part of this literature, however, dealt with human problems, both individual and collective. Such was the poetry of Neruda and Vallejo, of the *indigenistas* (the defenders of the Indian), whose work commenced with the "¡Quién sabe!" ("Who knows?") of José Santos Chocano in 1913 and reached its apogee with poets like Jorge Carrera Andrade (b. 1903) in Ecuador and Jacinto Fombona Pachano (b. 1901) in Venezuela. Paralleling this were some of the writers of so-called *poesía negra,* poetry that sings the joys and the griefs of the African race in America, chiefly in the Antilles: Nicolás Guillén (b. 1904), Emilio Ballagas (1908–54), and Luis Palés Matos (1898–1959). In prose, there are the writings of the Brazilian Gilberto Freyre (b. 1900), author of substantial essays and of admirable books, such as *Casa-Grande e Senzala* (1934; translation, *The Masters and the Slaves*), which have a solid sociological foundation; the essays of the Cuban José María Chacón y Calvo (b. 1893), and the Argentines Victoria Ocampo, Ezequiel Martínez Estrada (b. 1895), whose original and keen *Radiografía de la pampa* (1933) and *La cabeza de Goliat* (1940) analyzed, respectively, Argentina and its capital, and Eduardo Mallea (b. 1903), who is, moreover, an intense novelist (see Chapter 9). These essays, like comparable literature in the United States, revolve around the problem of understanding America.

The novel served as the medium for a great many writers in this period. Some represented man confronting savage Nature and probed its influence upon him, as in *La vorágine* (1924; translation, *The Vortex*, 1935) by the Colombian José Eustasio Rivera (1888–1928); in *Doña Bárbara* (1929; translation, 1931) by the Venezuelan Rómulo Gallegos (b. 1884); and in the stories of the Peruvian Ventura García Calderón (1887–1959). Others represent him in the midst of Nature domesticated, as in *Don Segundo Sombra* (1926; translation, subtitled *Shadow on the Pampas*, 1935), by the Argentine Ricardo Güiraldes (1886–1927). Still others describe the world of the worker, in the country or in the city; this theme is particularly frequent among the Brazilian novelists: Graciliano Ramos (1892–1954), author of *Vidas Sêcas* (Parched Lives) and *Memórias do Cárcere* (Prison Memoirs); José Lins do Rêgo (1901–57), who portrayed life on the sugar plantations; Raquel de Queirós (b. 1912), who has written chiefly about the Northeast; Jorge Amado (b. 1912), from Bahia, author of *Terras do Sem Fin* (translation, The Violent Land, 1945); and Erico Veríssimo (b. 1905; *see Bibliography*).

Many novelists have depicted the tragic situation of the Indian, eternal victim of exploitation. This was the theme—in Bolivia, Peru, Ecuador, and Mexico—of novelists such as Alcides Arguedas (1879–1948), Ciro Alegría (1909–67), Jorge

Icaza (b. 1906), and Gregorio López y Fuentes (1895–1966). The
Mexican Revolution of 1910–20 inspired many novelists. Especially prominent were Mariano Azuela (1873–1952), who wrote
Los de abajo (1916; translation, *The Underdogs,* 1929); and
Martín Luis Guzmán (b. 1887), author of *La sombra del caudillo* (The Shadow of the Leader; 1930) and *El águila y la
serpiente* (1928; translation, *The Eagle and the Serpent,* 1930),
his best work, which appears to be a novel but is in reality a
fictionalized autobiography.

In its musical compositions, Latin America during this
period grappled with two fundamental problems: that of em-
ploying all the modern resources of structure, both melodic
and harmonic; and that of utilizing native material. The first
problem was rather easily solved through a close study of all
the current innovations. The second admits of various solu-
tions, ranging from the old way, which limited itself to tran-
scribing, with or without embellishments, folk tunes or popular
themes, including archaic pre-Columbian elements when possible, to the more recent procedure, which consists of inventing
forms of expression based on the vernacular, "converting the
local factor into stylistic elements with which the composer
works in order to create independent forms, more or less
removed from the original popular forms."

Two composers of this period became widely known outside
Latin America: the Brazilian Heitor Villa-Lobos (1887–1959)
and the Mexican Carlos Chávez (b. 1899). The former was
characterized by the Spanish musicologist Adolfo Salazar as
"a prodigious and robust personality, marked by mental agility
and creative spontaneity." Among the most important compositions of Villa-Lobos (whose total catalogue comprises more
than seven hundred items) are the two series of works, for various instrumental and vocal combinations, that he titled *Choros*
(from the name given to a band of popular street musicians in
Brazil) and *Bachianas Brasileiras* (in tribute to Johann Se-
bastian Bach, whose principles of architectural composition
Villa-Lobos tried to fuse with the spirit of Brazilian popular

music). Between 1920 and 1945, Carlos Chávez wrote a number of the thoroughly modern, yet thoroughly Mexican compositions on which his reputation largely rests, notably the Aztec ballet *El fuego nuevo* (1921), the indigenous ballet *Los cuatro soles* (1926), the "dance symphony" *H.P.* (Horsepower; 1926–27), the *Sinfonía de Antígona* (Symphony No. 1, 1933), the *Sinfonía india* (Symphony No. 2, 1935–36), the *Concerto for Piano and Orchestra* (1938–40), *Xochipilli-Macuilxóchitl* for a Mexican orchestra including replicas of ancient Aztec instruments (1940), and the ballet *La hija de Cólquide* (The Daughter of Colchis; 1943–44). During these twenty years, he also wrote a number of works designed to reach the masses through a simplified presentation of familiar Mexican tunes, as in the *Obertura repúblicana* (1935), or through an appeal to the socialistic spirit of the Mexican Revolution, as in *Llamadas,* for large orchestra and mixed chorus (1934), which is subtitled "Proletarian Symphony."

Other noteworthy composers of the period are, in Argentina, Juan José Castro (b. 1895), author of the programmatic symphonies *Sinfonía argentina, Sinfonía de los campos,* and *Sinfonía bíblica,* and Juan Carlos Paz (b. 1897), leader of the avant-garde movement and a consistent follower of the twelve-tone method of composition; in Chile, Humberto Allende (1885–1959), who combined post-Impressionist and nationalist tendencies, and Domingo Santa Cruz (b. 1899), predominantly neoclassical; in Mexico, Manuel M. Ponce (1886–1948), José Rolón (1883–1945), Candelario Huízar (b. 1889), and especially the original and brilliant Silvestre Revueltas (1899–1940); in Colombia, Guillermo Uribe Holguín (b. 1880) and Antonio Valencia (1902–52); in Peru, Daniel Alomía Robles (1871–1942), Teodoro Valcárcel (1900–1942), and Andrés Sas (b. Paris, 1900); in Venezuela, Vicente E. Sojo (b. 1887) and Juan Bautista Plaza (1898–1965); in Cuba, Amadeo Roldán (1900–1939) and Alejandro García Caturla (1900–1940), who initiated the modern movement in Cuban music, with strong emphasis on Afro-Cuban elements, as in Roldán's *La rebambaramba* and

Caturla's *Bembé*. In Brazil, where a strong nationalist movement closely allied to the country's folk and popular music
manifested itself (Villa-Lobos was its foremost representative),
leading composers of this period include Oscar Lorenzo Fernández (1897–1948), Francisco Mignone (b. 1897), and Camargo Guarnieri (b. 1907). Some of these composers, Castro
and Chávez in particular, are also excellent conductors and
have been active in that capacity.

There are perhaps fewer internationally famous interpreters
of music than during the nineteenth century. Outstanding
among the pianists are Angélica Morales (b. 1911) of Mexico,
Rosita Renard (1894–1949) and Claudio Arrau (b. 1903) of
Chile, Guiomar Novaes (b. 1895) of Brazil, and Jesús María
Sanromá (b. 1903) of Puerto Rico; among singers, the Brazil-
ians Elsie Houston (d. 1942) and Bidu Sayão (b. 1908), and the
Argentine Isabel Marengo (b. 1897).

Popular music continually produced new types of song and
dance in Latin America. In this century, Europe and the
United States adopted the maxixe and the samba of Brazil;
the tango of Argentina and Uruguay; the son, the rumba, and
the conga of Cuba; the pasillo of Colombia; and many more.
Popular songs also gained wide currency, for example, "¡Ay,
ay, ay!" by the Chilean Osmán Pérez Freire (1878–1930), and
"Siboney," by the Cuban Ernesto Lecuona (1896–1953).

Sculpture was cultivated, and public monuments were as a
rule commissioned from artists in the country where the monument was to be located. Outstanding among the sculptors was
the Argentine Rogelio Irurtia (1879–1950), whose technique
was masterly and vigorous. He is responsible for the monument to Rivadavia, the statue of Dorrego, and the "Canto al
trabajo" (Song to Labor), all in Buenos Aires.

Architecture, after the various experiments in every kind of
style that occupied architects for the greater part of the nineteenth century and the beginning of the twentieth, now divided into two tendencies: the colonial, which seeks inspiration
from the era of Spanish and Portuguese domination; and the

innovational, which seeks functional form. Earlier—and later also—there were independent initiatives, such as the houses built in Havana by the architects Morales and Mata, of white stone with black grillwork and wide galleries, adapted to the tropical climate. The colonialist tendency has yielded its best results in Mexico, where it was easy to take up the thread of this tradition. Later, this tendency receded before the advance of functionalism, strongly entrenched in Mexico, as it is in Argentina, Uruguay, and Brazil. The Brazilians have constructed buildings that are among the most daring and the most successful of contemporary architecture, such as the Ministry of Education and Health and the Press Association Building in Rio de Janeiro. Special attention is given to the problems of lighting and ventilation; these problems, writes the American critic Edward Alden Jewell, "are resolved logically and with genuine imagination."

Of all the forms of cultural expression in Latin America in this century, painting had the widest repercussions. The extent of its maturity began to become apparent when, in 1921, the Mexican government commissioned Diego Rivera (1887–1957) and other young artists to decorate the walls of several public buildings with mural paintings. Rivera had lived for fourteen years in Europe, chiefly in Paris, assiduously studying all forms of modern art and of the art of the past. Upon returning to Mexico, in 1921, he devoted himself to local traditions, the indigenous as well as the colonial and the popular. Nor did he overlook the forgotten painters of the nineteenth century, becoming in particular a consistent champion of the merits of José María Velasco (1840–1912). With his technical mastery and his personal vision, he achieved a powerful and brilliant series of works. Moreover, he made his painting an expression of Mexican life and of its social problems.

Beside Rivera there soon arose the figure of José Clemente Orozco (1883–1949), educated exclusively in Mexico, who revealed a profound and mordant vision of Mexican reality, along with a dazzling mastery of execution. Later came David

Alfaro Siqueiros (b. 1898), a vigorous and audacious painter. Many public buildings in Mexico were adorned with mural paintings, and the fame of this movement spread to the United States and Russia, both of which have invited Mexican artists to paint murals. According to a publication of the Museum of Modern Art in New York, it was the Mexican school that exercised the strongest influence on art in the United States from 1920 to 1940. Mexico has produced many other painters, some of whom continued to work with murals while others cultivated easel painting and drawing. Among them are Miguel Covarrubias (1904–57), well known in the United States for his imaginative designs and his theatrical sets; Manuel Rodríguez Lozano (b. 1896), Angel Abraham (1905–24), Julio Castellanos (b. 1905), Jesús Guerrero Galván (b. 1910), and María Izquierdo (1906–56), to mention only a few.

While this major revolution was going on in Mexico, the artists in other countries of Latin America were exploring post-Impressionist trends. Later, however, the work being done in Mexico stimulated an attempt to express aspects of American life. This was the case in Brazil, with Cândido Portinari (1903–62), a powerful painter of heroic forms; in Ecuador, with Camilo Egas (b. 1895); in Peru, with José Sabogal (1888–1956), leader of the *indigenista* movement, Julia Codesido (b. 1892), and Camilo Blas (b. 1903), who seek their subjects in the life of the natives both in cities and in rural areas.

In the region of the Río de la Plata, there was extraordinary artistic activity, and hundreds of painters appeared, especially after modern currents began to prevail, following the first exhibitions by Emilio Pettoruti (b. 1894), in 1924. Pettoruti is regarded as the precursor of the modern movement in Argentine painting. The contemporary Argentine school is characterized by technical mastery, as may be seen, for example, in the works of Miguel Carlos Victorica (1884–1955), Lino Spilimbergo (1896–1964), Ramón Gómez Cornet (b. 1898), Horacio Butler (b. 1897), Antonio Berni (b. 1905), Raúl Soldi (b. 1905), and Norah Borges (b. 1903), noted for her delightful "ingenuous" paintings. In neighboring Uruguay, abstract painting was represented by Joaquín Torres García (1874–1949).

This abundant and continuous activity has placed Latin America in the forefront of contemporary painting. Without question, four or five of its painters may be counted among the great artists of our time.

The
Approximate
Present
[1945–1965]

BY GILBERT CHASE

THE POLITICAL ARENA of this period was marked by the disappearance of many dictators: Vargas in Brazil (1954), Perón in Argentina (1955), Somoza in Nicaragua (1956), Rojas Pinilla in Colombia (1957), Pérez Jiménez in Venezuela (1958), Batista in Cuba (1959), and Trujillo in the Dominican Republic (1961). But "disappearance" is a word that covers many things, from suicide (Vargas) and assassination (Somoza) to political exile cushioned by the spoils of dictatorship (Perón and others). That a fallen dictator in exile can still be a powerful and disturbing influence was demonstrated in the Argentine national elections of 1962, when the followers of Perón (the *peronistas*), allowed to present their candidates for the first time since 1955, succeeded in electing a surprisingly large number of deputies and governors, including the governor of the key province of Buenos Aires. These unforeseen results precipitated a crisis; the military were determined to prevent the elected *peronistas* from assuming office, and President Arturo Frondizi was forced to resign. His successor became a front for the military, and Argentina's troubled progress toward democratic government was dealt another setback.

In 1962, the presidential election in Peru likewise revealed the chronic crisis of democracy in Latin America. The three leading contenders were Manuel Odría, a general who seized power in 1948 and had himself elected for a six-year term in 1950; Fernando Belaúnde Terry, a member of the oligarchy and an architect by profession, who had achieved political celebrity by narrowly losing the presidential election of 1956; and Víctor Raúl Haya de la Torre, the famous and aging leader of the APRA (Alianza Popular Revolucionaria Americana), who obtained the largest number of votes. The military, nursing a bitter long-standing feud with the APRA, called upon President Manuel Prado to annul the elections. When he refused, a military junta deposed him and took over the reins of government. In the new presidential election finally held in June, 1963, Belaúnde was elected by a clear majority.

The overthrow of the Cuban dictator Batista in January, 1959, by the revolutionary leader Fidel Castro resulted in the establishment of a Communist regime in Cuba, closely tied to Russia and China. The Marxist revolution in Cuba has made itself felt in every phase of that country's cultural activity, from primary education, and a crash program for reducing illiteracy, to the ideological controls imposed upon higher education, the arts, and all the media of communication. But it is too soon to attempt, in a general survey such as this, an evaluation of the results of Communism as applied to Cuban culture by the Castro regime.

Whatever the problems of Latin America may be—and they are grave, numerous, and urgent—they are continually being probed and analyzed, pondered and discussed, by the *pensadores* (thinkers), who often tend to be, like their predecessors Bello and Sarmiento, both men of thought and men of action. These "action-thinkers" (to borrow a term from the vocabulary of contemporary painting) tend generally to fall into two classes: intellectuals who become involved in politics, like Rómulo Gallegos in Venezuela; and politicians who take to writing books, like Haya de la Torre in Peru. Gallegos, famed as a novelist, became President of Venezuela for ten months in 1948, until he was ousted by reactionary elements. Juan José Arévalo, before becoming President of Guatemala (1945–51), lectured at Argentine universities and in 1939 published a philosophical work on the values of pedagogy (*La filosofía de los valores en la pedagogía*); his later writings are more political, as in his study of democracy and imperialism in Guatemala (1954), the anti-American *Fábula del tiburón y las sardinas* (1956; translation, *The Shark and the Sardines*, 1961), and *Anti-Komunismo en América Latina* (1959; translation, 1963). Eduardo Santos, President of Colombia from 1938 to 1942, in addition to being director of the newspaper *El Tiempo* of Bogotá, has written much on American problems and was one of the contributors to the volume *Responsible Freedom in the Americas* (1955), together with such representative Latin American intellectuals as Jaime Benítez of Puerto Rico, Jorge Mañach of Cuba, Gabriela Mistral of Chile, Mariano Picón-Salas of Venezuela, Arturo Torres Rioseco of Chile, and Rafael Heliodoro Valle of Honduras. Rómulo Betancourt, President of Venezuela from 1945 to 1948 and from 1958 to 1964, has written voluminously on political and economic subjects, including an explanation of his "popular and democratic doctrine" (*Posición y doctrina,* 1958).

Withal, it is probably as *pensadores* rather than as officials that these intellectuals have rendered their most valuable service; by bringing their knowledge and intelligence to bear upon national and hemispheric problems, such as illiteracy, economic inequality, political instability, and the plight of the indigenous populations in certain countries—notably Bolivia, Ecuador, Peru, Guatemala, and Mexico. The Argentine historian Enrique de Gandía (b. 1906) addressed himself to the problem of the indigenous masses in a work published in 1943 (*Problemas indígenas americanos*), while Manuel Gamio (1883–1960) studied the problem in Mexico (*Consideraciones sobre el problema indígena mexicano;* 1948). Gamio was director of the Instituto Indigenista Interamericano, created in

1940 with headquarters in Mexico City, to serve as a coordinating center for the study of the indigenous cultures and peoples of the Americas.

Perhaps no Latin American *pensador* has been more persistent in analyzing the sociocultural problems of his country than Jorge Basadre (b. 1903), in such works as *Perú: Problema y posibilidad* (Peru: Problem and Possibility; 1931); *Meditaciones sobre el destino del Perú* (Meditations on the Destiny of Peru; 1947); and *La multitud, la ciudad y el campo en la historia del Perú* (The Multitude, the City, and the Country in the History of Peru), consisting mainly of an address the author delivered at the University of San Marcos in 1929 (republished in 1947). Basadre has also written the standard multivolume history of Peru.

In Argentina, the eminent historian Ricardo Levene (1885–1959), in addition to writing the monumental *Historia del derecho argentino* (History of Argentine Law), in eleven volumes (1945–58), and editing the comprehensive *Historia de América*, in fourteen volumes (1940–42), published many monographs on national and international political, economic, and legal affairs. Although Ricardo Rojas (1882–1957) is known above all for his multivolume *Historia de la literatura argentina*, in which he treated literature as a manifestation of the "national soul," he also wrote two important biographies, one of San Martín (translation *San Martín: Knight of the Andes*) and the other of Sarmiento (*El profeta de la pampa*, 1945). He defined the essence of Argentine nationalism in *La argentinidad* and developed an Indo-American theory of aesthetics in *Eurindia*. José Luis Romero (b. 1909) is the author of *Las ideas políticas en Argentina* (1946; translation, *A History of Argentine Political Thought*, 1963).

In Mexico, Leopoldo Zea has been especially concerned with the hisory of ideas in America and with defining a specifically American point of view in philosophical thought (*América como conciencia*, 1953; *América en la historia*, 1957). His study of positivism and Romanticism in Latin America, *Dos etapas del pensamiento en Hispanoamérica* (1949), was translated into English as *The Latin-American Mind* (1963).

The Cuban writer José Antonio Portuondo (b. 1911) has dealt particularly with the question of the "generations" in cultural history (*La historia y las generaciones,* 1958), and with the social content of literature in Cuba (*El contenido social de la literatura cubana,* 1944). The late Jorge Mañach (1898–1961) was a distinguished writer on both history (*Historia y estilo,* 1944) and philosophy (*Filosofía de la vida,* 1951); his biography of José Martí was published in an English translation as *Marti, the Apostle* (1950).

In Brazil, Francisco José de Oliveira Viana (1883–1951) was a historian whose interests ranged over many fields, including social psychology, ethnology, industrial organization, labor relations, political science, and law. His work of most general interest is probably *Evolução do Povo Brasileiro* (1922; fourth edition, 1956), a social history of the Brazilian people. Eminent among present-day Brazilian historians is Pedro Calmon (b. 1902), who has attempted to describe what he calls the "spirit of society" in his two-volume work *História Social do Brasil* (1935–37). Calmon's *História do Brasil na Poesia Popular* (1954) is in fact a history of the Brazilian people as reflected in their folk songs. Fernando de Azevedo (b. 1894) is the author of a large and impressive work, *A Cultura Brasileira* (1944), which has been translated into English as *Brazilian Culture: An Introduction to the Study of Culture in Brazil* (1950). The first part, dealing with the social and political evolution and the psychology of the Brazilian people, serves as background for a discussion of art, literature, science, education, and religion. Gilberto Freyre brought his sociological knowledge to bear on an analysis of modern Brazilian culture in *New World in the Tropics* (1959), written especially for English-speaking readers. The poet Manuel Bandeira published in 1940 a work titled *Noções de História das Literaturas* (Elements of Literary History). The section dealing with Brazil was acclaimed for its clarity of presentation and its fine critical judgment—this section has been translated into English (*A Brief History of Bra-*

zilian Literature, 1958) and serves as an admirable introduction to the subject. The most comprehensive history of Brazilian literature remains that of Sílvio Romero, *História da Literatura Brasileira,* of which the fifth edition, in five volumes, appeared in 1953–54.

Since the death of Francisco Romero, the leading Argentine philosopher is Risieri Frondizi (b. 1910), who has given particular attention to psychological theory. His work, *Substancia y función en el problema del yo* (1952), has been translated into English as *The Nature of the Self* (1953). Carlos Cossio (b. 1903) has specialized in the philosophy and ethics of law. Among the numerous works that he has published on this subject, the most important is *Teoría de la verdad jurídica* (Theory of Juridical Truth, 1954). Catholic thought is represented in Argentina by Nicolás Derisi (b. 1907), whose Neo-Thomist works include *Los fundamentos metafísicos del orden moral* (The Metaphysical Foundations of the Moral Order; 1941) and *La persona: Su esencia, su vida, y su mundo* (The Person: Its Essence, Its Life, and Its World; 1950). The influence of Existentialism—felt in Argentina as elsewhere in Latin America—is reflected in the writings of Carlos Astrada (b. 1894), author of *La revolución existencialista* (The Existentialist Revolution; 1952), and Vicente Fatone (b. 1903), author of *La existencia humana y sus filósofos* (Human Existence and Its Philosophers; 1953).

Mario Bunge (b. 1919) is an Argentine philosopher and theoretical physicist who has very close ties with the United States, where he has taught at various universities. Indeed, his most important works have all been published in English in the United States: *The Philosophy of Space-Time* (1955), *Causality: The Place of the Causal Principle in Modern Science* (second edition, 1963), *Metascientific Queries* (1959), *Intuition and Science* (1962), and *The Myth of Simplicity: Problems of Scientific Philosophy* (1963). In the work of Mario Bunge, we find a departure from the humanistic-metaphysical approach that has hitherto characterized Latin American philosophy;

he even adopts a "metascientific" approach to the problem of ethics.

In Peru, there is an active philosophic movement whose leading representative is Mariano Iberico (b. 1892), author of an important treatise on metaphysics: *La aparición: Ensayos sobre el ser y el aparecer* (Appearance: Essays on Being and Seeming; 1950), and a work on the meaning of metaphor (*Estudio sobre la metáfora*, 1965).

Mexico lost two of its leading philosophers—José Vasconcelos and Samuel Ramos—in the same month of the same year: June, 1959. Vasconcelos' last philosophical work was *Todología: filosofía de la coordinación* (1952), for which he coined the neologism *todología*, "allology," from the Spanish word *todo*, meaning "all." Herein he attempted the difficult task of reconciling his philosophical doctrines with his religious faith. The last volume of Vasconcelos' memoirs—closing the series that began in 1936 with *Ulises criollo* (translation, *A Mexican Ulysses*, 1963)—was published posthumously in 1959 under the title *La flama*, especially fitting for one whose spirit was ever aflame for some cause that he considered right or against some force that he regarded as wrong. He was a fighting philosopher. Samuel Ramos' *El perfil del hombre y de la cultura en México* (1938) was at long last translated into English in 1962 (*Profile of Man and Culture in Mexico*).

In the realm of the essay, the collected critical essays of Pedro Henríquez Ureña (1884–1946) were published in 1960, under the title *Obra crítica*, with an admirable introduction by Jorge Luis Borges. Especially significant for the understanding of Latin American culture are his *Seis ensayos en busca de nuestra expresión* (Six Essays in Search of Our Expression), originally published in 1928.* Another writer from the Caribbean, the poet and essayist José Balseiro (b. 1900), born in Puerto Rico, has published two volumes of essays on Latin American themes, which he calls *Expresión de Hispanoamérica* (1960 and 1963), covering such topics as the Spanish language

* Excerpts translated into English will be found in *Readings in Latin-American Civilization*, ed. Benjamin Keen (Boston, 1955).

in Puerto Rico, "Unamuno and America," and "Notes on the *Martín Fierro.*"

The late Mariano Picón-Salas (1901–65), one of the leading liberal intellectuals of Venezuela, who served his country as ambassador to Brazil and Mexico, was the author of a brilliant interpretation of Hispanic American culture from the Conquest to independence (*De la Conquista a la Independencia,* 1944; second edition, 1950; translation, *A Cultural History of Spanish America,* 1964). This was based on a series of lectures given at various universities in the United States. Picón-Salas dealt with the cultural confrontation of America and Europe in *Europa-América: Preguntas a la esfinge de la cultura* (1947), and contributed to the understanding of his own country in *Comprensión de Venezuela* (1950). His countryman Arturo Uslar-Pietri (b. 1905), has a similar range of interests, as manifested in his study of men and letters in Venezuela (*Letras y hombres de Venezuela,* 1948), and of values in human society (*Valores humanos,* 1955). But he also achieved a solid reputation as a writer of history and of historical fiction. His novel *Las lanzas rojas* (1930), which deals with the Venezuelan struggle for independence, has been translated into English (*The Red Lances,* 1963).

The Colombian Germán Arciniegas (b. 1900) is an essayist and historian whose work is well known in the United States. His *Biografía del Caribe* (1945) was translated into English as *Caribbean: Sea of the New World* (1946). Other translations include *The State of Latin America* (1952) and *Amerigo and the New World: The Life and Times of Vespucci* (1955). He cultivated the biographical essay in two companion volumes titled *América mágica* (1959), the first subtitled *Los hombres y los meses* (Men and Months), the second *Las mujeres y las horas* (Women and the Hours). History, biography, and legend are interwoven in these vivid portraits of celebrated men and women of the Americas.

Since the death of Alfonso Reyes, the chief living essayist of Spanish America is undoubtedly Jorge Luis Borges of Argentina, who is equally important as a poet and writer of fiction.

A supreme stylist, Borges is one of the most original writers in the Spanish language today, with a unique combination of wit, fantasy, realism, and satire. Strangely, it was not until 1962, when he himself was sixty-three, that Borges began to be widely known and appreciated in the United States. In that year, two English translations of his essays and short fiction appeared: one entitled *Ficciones* (keeping the Spanish title), the other—containing ten essays and eight "parables" in addition to short stories—entitled *Labyrinths*. Borges often leads the reader through labyrinths of erudition and fantasy, and in so doing he manages to be both profound and entertaining.

In Peru, the essay was cultivated with distinction by José Gálvez (1885–1960) and by Luis Fabio Xammar (1911–47), both of whom were also well-known poets. Gálvez—a senator and a prominent public figure—wrote on the emergence of a national Peruvian literature (*Posibilidad de una genuina literatura nacional*), on the vanishing charm of his native city (*Una Lima que se va*), and on the sociocultural problems of Hispanic America (*Problemas hispanoamericanos*). In 1962, a committee of prominent intellectuals, headed by Víctor Andrés Belaúnde, undertook the publication of the complete works of the eminent essayist and historian José de la Riva-Agüero (1885–1944), in eighteen volumes. Riva-Agüero's pioneer study of the "human geography" of Peru, *Paisajes peruanos* (Peruvian Landscapes), originally written in 1912–15 and published fragmentarily, was finally published in its entirety in 1955, with a long and excellent introduction by the historian Raúl Porras Barrenechea (1897–1960), at one time ambassador to Spain and later minister of foreign affairs. The leading literary critic in Peru is Estuardo Núñez (b. 1908).

The new generation in Peru was represented by Sebastián Salazar Bondy (1924–65)—poet, playwright, essayist, writer of fiction—who in 1964 brought out a small book that made a large stir: *Lima la horrible* (Lima the Horrible). This was a strong, almost violent attack on the long-cherished concept of "romantic" Lima—nourished by such writers as Ricardo Palma and José Gálvez—with its viceroyal past, its grilled balconies, its beautiful women with veiled faces (*las tapadas*), its glamorous society. Salazar Bondy denounced what he regarded as sham and pretense, the false front of a society closing its eyes to the needs and problems of the present. In applying the "shock treatment" to Peruvian society, he revived the tactics used by González Prada in the previous century.

As a matter of fact, the writers of fiction among the new generation had not waited for this signal in order to begin their exploration and exposé of urban conditions and social tensions—the sprawling slums, the restless, delinquent youth, and the ferment of changing values and insistent vindications. While writers such as José María Arguedas (b. 1913) and Carlos E. Zavaleta (b. 1928) had concerned themselves primarily with the plight of the Indian in the *sierra* (highland), another group of novelists began, in the 1960's to concentrate on the urban scene. Oswaldo Reinoso's novel of urban youth in Lima, *Los inocentes,* and *La ciudad y los perros* (translation, *The Time of the Hero,* 1966), by Mario Vargas Llosa, both published in 1962, marked a turning point in this direction, which has also been followed by Julio Ramón Ribeyro (b. 1929) and Enrique Congrains (b. 1932). Arguedas himself, not to be outdone by the younger writers, published in 1965 his most powerful novel to date, *Todas las sangres* (All the Races), a profound and masterly synthesis, in terms of character and conflict, of the problems of Peruvian society.

Of the novelists mentioned in the preceding chapter, two have died—Alcides Arguedas of Bolivia, in 1948, and Mariano Azuela of Mexico, in 1952. Two of Azuela's novels, *The Flies* and *The Bosses,* were published together in an English translation in 1956. In the 1940's, some Mexican novelists—perhaps as a reaction to the obsession with the Revolution of 1910–20 —began to look to the remote past, to the Indian civilizations before the Conquest and to the early colonial period. Representative of this trend are the novel by Ermilo Abreu Gómez, *Quetzalcóatl: Sueño y vigilia* (Quetzalcóatl: Dream and Vigil; 1947), and several historical novels by Francisco Monterde dealing with the Aztecs, notably *Moctezuma II: Señor de Anáhuac* (1947).

The most important Mexican novelist of the present time is Agustín Yáñez (b. 1904), whose *Al filo del agua* (1947), translated as *The Edge of the Storm* (1963), has been called "the most ambitious Mexican novel of the contemporary period" (Fernando Alegría). Among other novels by Yáñez are *La creación* (Creation; 1959), *La tierra pródiga* (The Prodigal Land; 1960), and *Las tierras flacas* (The Barren Lands; 1962). The "new modernism" is represented by Carlos Fuentes (b. 1929), whose *La región más transparente* (1958; translation, *Where the Air Is Clear,* 1960) utilizes many of the devices developed by such writers as Joyce, Kafka, and Faulkner. This work marks a definite break with the social realism that dominated the Mexican novel for so many decades.

The most important novelist of Central America is the Guatemalan Miguel Angel Asturias (b. 1899), whose reputation was established with the political novel *El Señor Presidente* (1948; translated, with the same title, 1964), an impassioned portrayal of the evils of dictatorship. This was followed in 1949 by *Hombres de maíz,* the theme of which has been stated by the author: "It is based on the struggle sustained between the native of the countryside, who believes that the corn should be planted only for sustenance, and the enterprising *criollo,* who cultivates for profit, burning forests of precious woods and impoverishing the land in order to get rich." The roots of this novel reach far back in the Maya past, its myths and its symbols. In his more recent novels, Asturias deals with contemporary political and socio-economic conflicts arising from foreign domination of local industry.

The Cuban writer of French extraction Alejo Carpentier (b. 1904) is best known for his novels, though he has also written poetry and an excellent history of music in Cuba. He lived for many years in Venezuela, returning to Cuba after Castro's revolution of 1959. Three of his novels have been translated into English: *El reino de este mundo* (*The Kingdom of This World,* 1949), about life in Haiti, *Los pasos perdidos* (*The Lost*

Steps, 1956), an adventure in the Amazonian jungle, and *El siglo de las luces* (1962; translation, *Explosion in a Cathedral,* 1963), on the French Revolution in the Caribbean.

The bitter and bloody political conflicts in Colombia provide the background of violence for a powerful novel, *El Cristo de espaldas* (Christ Turns His Back; 1952), by Eduardo Caballero Calderón (b. 1910). The Ecuadorian Alfredo Pareja Diezcanseco (b. 1908) has written a history of Ecuador and several works on art, but is probably best known for his novels dealing with the contemporary history of his native land, specifically the period since 1925. This historical series culminated in the three-volume work collectively titled *Los nuevos años* (The New Years; 1956–64). The leading Puerto Rican novelist, Enrique Laguerre (b. 1906), deals with the social problems of his native island in *La resaca* (The Undertow; 1949).

In Argentina, Eduardo Mallea affirmed his position as the leading novelist with such works as *Los enemigos del alma* (The Enemies of the Soul; 1950), *La torre* (The Tower; 1951), *La sala de espera* (The Waiting Room; 1953), and *La razón humana* (Human Reason; 1960). Ernesto Sábato (b. 1909) is one of the most brilliant and controversial of contemporary Argentine writers—critic, essayist, novelist, and theatrical director. His best-known novels are *El túnel* (The Tunnel) and *Sobre héroes y tumbas* (On Heroes and Tombs), both published in 1961. The most notable new talent in the Argentine novel is Beatriz Guido (b. 1924), whose theme, family life in Argentina, is charged with political and social overtones. Her novel *La casa del ángel* (1954; translation, *The House of the Angel,* 1956), which established her reputation, was followed by *Fin de fiesta* (End of the Feast; 1956), *El incendio y las visperas* (The Fire and the Days Before; 1964; translation, *End of a Day,* 1966), and *La mano en la trampa* (The Hand in the Trap; 1961), a volume of short stories. Several of her novels and stories have been filmed by her husband, Leopoldo Torre-Nilsson (b. 1924), the leading film director of Latin America. Among the films thus made are *End of Innocence, Summerskin,* and *The Terrace.*

The tradition of realism in the Chilean novel is represented by Mariano Latorre (1886–1955), Fernando Santiván (b. 1886), and Rafael Maluenda (b. 1885). The modern trend in Chile may be said to have begun with *Hijo de ladrón* (Thief's Son; 1951), by Manuel Rojas (b. 1896), whose *Obras completas* (novels, stories, essays, poems), were published in 1961. Juan Marín (1901–63)—doctor of medicine, diplomat, traveler—wrote short stories and novels, including *Paralelo 53 sur* (53rd Parallel South) and *Viento negro* (Black Wind). The collected works of the novelist and short-story writer Marta Brunet (b. 1901) were published in 1963.

In the mid-1960's, Pablo Neruda of Chile was still the most famous of living Spanish American poets, although his fame has an admixture of notoriety because of his militant Communism. Since 1946, he has published *Tercera residencia* (1947), *Canto general* (1950), *Odas elementales* (1954), *Extravagario* (1958), *Navegaciones y regresos* (1959), and *Canción de gesta* (1960). *Elementary Odes* (translated by Carlos Lozano) and *Selected Poems of Pablo Neruda* (translated by Ben Bellit) both appeared in 1961. Jorge Carrera Andrade of Ecuador published his collected verse of the period 1940–50 in a volume titled *Lugar de origen* (Place of Origin; 1951), which confirmed his high place in Spanish American poetry. In Mexico, Octavio Paz (b. 1914) has greatly increased his reputation with the publication of such volumes as *Libertad bajo palabra* (Liberty Under Oath; 1949), *Semillas para un himno* (Seeds for a Hymn; 1952), *Piedra de sol* (The Sun Stone; 1958), and *La estación violenta* (The Violent Season; 1958). His poetry reflects the cosmopolitanism of a professional diplomat who has served in many posts, including several in the Far East; at the same time, the character and destiny of Mexico are basic themes in most of his work, both in verse and prose. His volumes of essays include *Las peras del olmo* (The Pears of the Elm) and *El laberinto de la soledad* (translation, *The Labyrinth of Solitude,* 1962). A selection of his poems translated by Muriel Rukeyser was published in 1963.

Among the older Cuban poets, Mariano Brull (1891–1956)

was the first to take up Dadaism, producing such untranslatable verbal extravaganzas as:

> *Filiflama alabe cunre*
> *ala olalúnea alifera*
> *alveóla jitanjáfora*
> *liris salumba salífera*

The trajectory of his lyrical exuberance can be traced from *La casa del silencio* (The House of Silence; 1916) to *Tiempo en pena* (Time Grieving; 1950). Eugenio Florit (b. 1903) chose to follow in the path of the great Spanish poet Juan Ramón Jiménez (who died in Puerto Rico); his intimate and melancholy lyricism is revealed in *Poema mío* (1947), containing his verse from 1920 to 1944, and especially in *Asonante final y otros poemas* (Final Assonance and Other Poems, 1956). Emilio Ballagas (1908–54) continued in the Afro-Cuban tradition of Nicolás Guillén—the so-called *poesía negra;* his *Obras poéticas* (Collected Poems) were published in 1955 with a controversial introduction by another Cuban poet, Cinto Vitier (b. 1921), who today is probably the most notable of his generation. Vitier's collection of poems, *Escrito y cantado* (Written and Sung), was published in 1959. José Lezama Lima (b. 1912), founded the avant-garde review *Orígenes* in 1944, and thereafter followed a surrealist trend in his poetry—for example, in the volume titled *Analecta del reloj* (Analect of the Clock; 1953). He has been called (by Anderson Imbert) "the most original figure to appear in Cuban literature since 1937."

Among Venezuelan poets of the present day are León de Greiff (b. 1895), Rafael Maya (b. 1897), and Germán Pardo García (b. 1902). De Greiff, once the leader of the avant-garde, reveals an affinity with Mallarmé in his combination of an esoteric vocabulary, a recondite imagery, and a controlled formalism. Maya is traditional, seeking order and clarity amid desolation and disorder, tending toward introspection in *Navegación nocturna* (Nocturnal Navigation; 1959). The prolific Pardo García (he has published more than twenty volumes) expresses the "romantic agony" of contemporary life in such books as *Lucero sin orillas* (The Shoreless Sea; 1952) and *Hay piedras como lágrimas* (There Are Stones Like Tears; 1957).

Over the past twenty years, the Argentine poet Alberto Girri (b. 1919) has definitely established his reputation as a major figure, with a series of twelve volumes ranging from *Playa sola* (Lonely Beach; 1946) to *El ojo* (The Eye; 1964). He is profound, sometimes difficult, always sincere and unsentimental, with an extraordinary sense of imagery, of association, and of the necessary word in the right place. In 1964, he was awarded a Guggenheim Fellowship for the study of contemporary poetry in the United States, of which he has made many fine translations (an anthology, *Poesía americana contemporánea,* was published in 1956). His *Poemas elegidos* (Selected Poems) appeared in 1965. Girri is also a writer of short stories and a critical essayist of distinction.

The Latin American theater as a whole is little known outside its respective countries, although some of the leading playwrights, particularly those of Mexico and Argentina, are beginning to receive recognition in the United States and elsewhere. In Argentina, the playwright with the most solidly established reputation (he is also known as a writer of short stories) is Samuel Eichelbaum (b. 1894). Although some of his plays are concerned with political and social problems of Argentine life, Eichelbaum is not a realist in the literal sense of aiming to depict "a slice of life." In his own words: "The highest responsibility of the author resides in the liberty that is inherent in artistic creation, in its independence with respect to any preconceived notion of reality or of truth." Whether he is writing somber dramas of the subconscious, such as *Divorcio nupcial* (Nuptial Divorce) and *Vergüenza de querer* (The Shame of Loving), or comedies, such as *Las aguas del mundo* (The Waters of the Earth; 1959), he is essentially concerned with the realization of character "in the world imagined by the dramatist."

Conrado Nalé Roxlo (b. 1898), author of several volumes of

poetry and of humorous stories, achieved an immediate success with his first play, *La cola de la sirena* (The Tail of the Mermaid), in 1941, followed by three others that were equally successful: *El pacto de Cristina* (Christine's Pact; 1945), *Una viuda difícil* (A Difficult Widow; 1944), and *Judith y las rosas* (Judith and the Roses; 1956). Poetry and humor mingle with realism in his plays. In *La cola de la sirena,* a wealthy and blasé young man in search of adventure falls in love with a mermaid whom he has fished out of the sea; when she undergoes an operation that transforms her into a normal woman, he is disillusioned and abandons her.

Among Argentine playwrights of a more recent generation, Omar Del Carlo (b. 1918) has transmuted the myth of Persephone into the contemporary setting of Buenos Aires in *Proserpina y el extranjero* (Persephone and the Stranger); Carlos Gorostiza (b. 1920) is concerned mainly with social problems in his two-act drama *El puente* (translation, *The Bridge,* 1961) and with the history of the Argentine frontier in *El último perro* (The Last Dog).

The most prominent contemporary playwright of Mexico is Rodolfo Usigli (b. 1905), who has written almost every type of play, from political farce to historical drama. His *Corona de sombra* (Crown of Shadow; 1947) deals with the tragedy of the Emperor Maximilian of Mexico and his wife Carlotta. In *El niño y la niebla* (The Child and the Mist; 1951), he employs recent Mexican history: the assassination of Carranza in 1920. His three-act drama *Another Springtime* was translated into English by Wayne Wolf (1961). Other well-known Mexican playwrights are Francisco Monterde (b. 1894), Salvador Novo (b. 1904), Carlos Solórzano, and Mauricio Magdaleno (b. 1906), who has specialized in plays dealing with the Mexican Revolution (Teatro Revolucionario Mexicano). Two women playwrights of Mexico merit attention: Elena Garro (b. 1918), author of *Un hogar sólido* (A Solid Household; 1958), which contains several plays, and Josefina Hernández (b. 1928), who became known by her play *Los sordomudos* (The Deaf-mutes;

1953), a study of social and moral disintegration in a Mexican provincial family of the middle class.

The theater in Chile has taken great forward strides during the past decade or so. Among the older playwrights are Eduardo Barrios (b. 1884), who has written chiefly social comedies, including the extremely successful *Papá y mamá;* and Nathanael Yáñez Silva (b. 1884), whose numerous works span the period 1904–43. Notable among the more recent playwrights are Egon Wolff (b. 1926) and Luis Alberto Heiremans (b. 1928). Wolff's play *La niña madre* (The Girl Mother), in three acts, was translated into English as *A Touch of Blue* and produced by the Yale University Theatre Group in 1961. In addition to writing some twelve plays since 1951, Heiremans has translated or adapted plays from English and French; his three-act play *El palomar* (The Dovecot) was translated into German and produced in Munich as *Das Taubenhaus* (1962).

In musical composition, the trend known as "folkloristic nationalism" had run its course as a major creative movement by 1950. Most of the important composers identified with this trend had died: Eduardo Fabini of Uruguay in 1950, Pedro Humberto Allende of Chile and Heitor Villa-Lobos of Brazil both in the same year, 1959. Of the prominent composers of the newer generation, only Camargo Guarnieri of Brazil has persisted along the line of folkloristic nationalism. It is true that composers who began their careers in the 1940's could scarcely avoid the influence of musical nationalism in their early compositions. Such was the case with Blas Galindo (b. 1910) of Mexico, Antonio Estévez (b. 1916) of Venezuela, Roque Cordero (b. 1917) of Panama, and Alberto Ginastera of Argentina. Most composers, however, have avoided the cul-de-sac of nationalism by turning toward classical forms and combining them with the new international techniques of the twentieth century, such as serialism or twelve-tone writing. Cordero did this very impressively in his *Second Symphony* (1956) and in the works that followed that important composition, such as the *Concerto for Violin and Orchestra* (1962).

Ginastera has joined the forefront of contemporary composition with a series of remarkable works written since 1955, notably the *Variaciones concertantes* for chamber orchestra (1955), the *Second String Quartet* (1958), the *Cantata for Magic America* (1960, for soprano and percussion), the *Concerto for Piano and Orchestra* (1961), the *Concerto for Violin and Orchestra* (1963)—commissioned by the New York Philharmonic Orchestra—and the grand opera *Don Rodrigo* (1964), commissioned by the municipality of Buenos Aires and produced at the Teatro Colón on July 24, 1964. The United States première of *Don Rodrigo* took place in New York on February 22, 1966. The libretto, by the Spanish playwright Alejandro Casona, deals with the downfall of the last Visigothic king of Spain, defeated by the Moors, A.D. 711. But the plot is legendary rather than historical; the music is largely twelve-tone and follows a highly organized tripartite formal structure based on traditional musical forms, such as the suite, the rondo, the canon, and the aria.

For composers born after 1920, nationalism has ceased to be an issue, except in some musically retarded countries still struggling to overcome their anachronistic situation. After the end of World War II, new international currents—and others not so new (such as Schoenberg's method of composing with twelve tones)—began to have an effect in wider sectors of Latin America. This change of attitude is revealed in the work of such composers as Héctor Tosar of Uruguay and Roberto Caamaño of Argentina (both born in 1923), and Gustavo Becerra of Chile (b. 1925). Of the three, Tosar has remained the most traditional (*Sinfonía concertante,* for piano and orchestra, 1957; *Te Deum,* for soli, chorus, and orchestra, 1963), while Becerra has veered toward Webern (*String Quartet No. 6,* 1960). Caamaño adheres to a sophisticated neoclassicism in his *Five Pieces for String Quartet,* opus 21, and *Quintet for Piano and Strings,* opus 25 (1964).

Carlos Chávez of Mexico, once considered a leading representative of nationalism, has become a champion of internationalism—or, as he prefers to call it, "universalism." To be sure, there was always an abstract, non-national aspect in the music of Chávez, and in the later works he emphasized and developed this tendency (his third through seventh symphonies; *Concerto for Violin and Orchestra*, 1948–50; *Invention for Piano*, 1958). When Chávez was invited to deliver the Charles Eliot Norton Lectures at Harvard in 1960–61, he described his professional philosophy with his customary articulateness (the lectures were published under the title *Musical Thought* in 1961).

For many years, the modern trend in Cuban music was dominated by the personality of José Ardévol (b. 1911), a composer of Spanish origin who settled in Havana in 1930 and founded the Grupo de Renovación Musical with a number of his pupils and followers. One of his compositions, for wind instruments, piano, and percussion, is titled *Homenaje a tres plátanos fritos* (Homage to Three Fried Bananas); perhaps this was a gibe at the folkloristic nationalism that he considered obsolete. But neither Ardévol nor any of his followers (most of whom shifted readily to Castro's camp after the revolution of 1959) succeeded in giving modern Cuban musical composition a prestige comparable to that achieved by Roldán and García Caturla. The most talented among the younger Cuban composers—Julián Orbón and Aurelio de la Vega—repudiated the Castro regime and came to the United States. Although they are almost exactly the same age (both were born in 1925), they are very different in temperament and tradition. Orbón is very much influenced by his Spanish background, as witness his *Tres cantigas del rey,* for soprano, string quartet, harpsichord, and percussion, based on medieval Spanish texts. De la Vega is definitely modern, using atonal and serial techniques, as well as electronic media (*Coordinates for Magnetic Tape,* 1963). De la Vega became a naturalized citizen of the United States in 1966.

Musical talent has not been lacking in Latin America—both in performance and in composition—but the educational opportunities have not always permitted the full development of this talent. An important step toward rectifying this situation was taken with the creation in 1962 of the Latin American

Center for Advanced Musical Studies, located in Buenos Aires, sponsored by the Instituto Torcuato Di Tella, and directed by Alberto Ginastera. The author of these lines was privileged to serve as Visiting Lecturer at this Center in 1964 and thereby was thrown into daily contact with the eleven young composers selected, on a fellowship basis, to attend the first two-year course. They came from Mexico, Ecuador, Colombia, Peru, Bolivia, Brazil, and Argentina; they had an opportunity to study with such eminent composers as Aaron Copland, Olivier Messiaen, Ricardo Malipiero, Luigi Dallapiccolla, and of course Ginastera himself. If their work and their creative spirit are typical, the future of musical composition in Latin America is assured.

In artistic creation, however, one must not expect history to repeat itself or to follow an unchanging line of development. Because of the great prestige given musical nationalism by Villa-Lobos, there was a tendency in Brazil to prolong that trend long after its aesthetic validity had become questionable. The chief champion of this nationalism-at-all-costs has been Camargo Guarnieri, who publicly denounced international modernism as antipatriotic and who has influenced his pupils to cling to the nationalist line. The overwhelming personality of Villa-Lobos, added to the intransigent attitude of Guarnieri, created a difficult situation for the younger Brazilian composers. A movement against folkloristic nationalism was started in Brazil in 1939 under the leadership of a twelve-tone composer of German origin, Hans Joachim Koellreutter (b. 1911), who founded the group called Música Viva. But the two most talented pupils of Koellreutter, César Guerra Peixe (b. 1914) and Claudio Santoro (b. 1919), soon abandoned atonalism and defected to the ranks of nationalism. Subsequently, however, Santoro abandoned folklorism and with his *Eighth Symphony* (1964) established an indisputable claim as Brazil's leading symphonist.

In the field of modern architecture, Mexico and Brazil have taken the lead, although interesting developments are also to be found in other countries, notably Venezuela and Colombia.

Mexican architects have concentrated largely on filling the need for schools, hospitals, factories, housing developments, and office buildings (Mexico City now has many skyscrapers, in spite of the lack of a solid foundation for such buildings). Among the most successful large-scale housing projects for workers, sponsored by the government, are the units known as "President Miguel Alemán" and "President Benito Juárez." José Villagrán García (b. 1901) and Juan O'Gorman (b. 1905) are among the leaders of the modern architectural movement in Mexico. But some idea of the extent of this movement may be conveyed by the fact that more than a hundred architects and artists collaborated in building the University City for the National University of Mexico, which is undoubtedly the most impressive single product of modern Mexican architecture, if its many units are considered as a whole. From the Olympic Stadium (1951–52), decorated by Diego Rivera, to the magnificent Central Library (1951–53), designed by Juan O'Gorman, Gustavo Saavedra, and Juan Martínez de Velasco, the Ciudad Universitaria commands admiration for the boldness and beauty of its structures, in which architectural and decorative elements are completely integrated.

The Spanish-born architect Félix Candela (b. 1910), who migrated to Mexico in 1930, has specialized in reinforced concrete structures, particularly in the form of shells. His first important project was a concrete shell for the Cosmic Ray Pavilion of the University of Mexico, designed in 1950. He has designed and built almost every kind of structure, from churches to warehouses, using shells and cantilevered shelters that soar out into space, experimenting with hyperbolic paraboloids, elliptical domes, and undulating folds, as in the restaurant at Xochimilco that he completed in 1958.

Private houses of modern design, but sometimes drawing upon traditional Mexican elements—as in those designed by Luis Barragán (b. 1902)—have been built in the residential sections of Mexico City by such architects as Francisco Artigas (b. 1916), Juan Sordo Madaleno (b. 1916), and Enrique de la Mora (b. 1907). De la Mora is also noted for the most striking modern church in Mexico, that of La Purísima in Monterrey (1947).

In Brazil, the leading architects are Oscar Niemeyer (b. 1907), Lúcio Costa (b. 1902), and Affonso Eduardo Reidy (1902–64). Niemeyer first attracted attention with a group of strikingly original buildings at Pampulha (Belo Horizonte), including the extraordinary Church of St. Francis, with its paraboloid shell vaults and its painted tile murals by Portinari. At the same time, he built his own house in Rio de Janeiro, on a hill overlooking the sea; Henry-Russell Hitchcock has remarked that "as an expression of lyrical response to landscape it is unique in the modern world." Using his favorite curvilinear forms, Niemeyer continued to design remarkable buildings, public and private, throughout Brazil, including the Montreal Office Building in São Paulo, the Public Library in Belo Horizonte, and the Youth Center in Diamantina.

But Niemeyer's world-wide fame came as a result of his designs for Brasília, the new capital of Brazil, built where nothing had stood before (about 900 miles northwest of Rio de Janeiro). With this new capital, the Brazilian government hoped to emphasize the development of the vast unpopulated areas of the interior. Niemeyer was appointed chief architect of Brasília, and Lúcio Costa was responsible for the plan of the city. Work was begun in 1956 and the new capital was inaugurated in 1960; but it was still far from finished four years later. By that time, nevertheless, the main official buildings had been completed: the Presidential Palace and Chapel, the Congress Building with its tall twin towers, the Supreme Court building, and the Ministries. The city was planned with three main zones: monumental, residential, and commercial. The government buildings are grouped in an area called Praça dos Tres Poderes (Place of the Three Powers), symbolizing the three branches of government: executive, legislative, judicial. Nearby are the amazingly original Cathedral (unfinished in 1965), the most revolutionary ecclesiastical structure of modern times, and the National Theater, in the unusual form of a low, truncated pyramid. The English architect David Crease has described Brasília as "probably the largest single building enterprise since the time of the Pharaohs, and possibly the largest ever in a free society."

In recent years, there has been tremendous architectural development in Caracas, the capital of Venezuela. Large-scale housing developments, apartment houses, and office buildings have been designed by a number of architects with definitely modern and original ideas, of whom we may mention Moisés Benacerraf (b. 1924), Guido Bermúdez (b. 1925), and especially Carlos Raúl Villanueva (b. 1900), who designed the extremely impressive University City of Caracas, particularly the auditorium and covered plaza (1952–53) and the Olympic Stadium (1950–51).

In Argentina, there has been little scope for modern architecture, but some interesting houses and public buildings have been designed by the most original contemporary architect of that country, Amancio Williams (b. 1913), notably his own house at Mar del Plata (1943), with a bridgelike curved slab that supports the whole house. His daringly original and scientifically scrupulous project for an auditorium for the presentation of music and "plastic spectacle" looks ahead to the twenty-first century—hence it has remained only a project thus far.

On the whole, architecture in Latin America holds its own with the best anywhere in the world, and in some cases, it excels in boldness and originality of conception and execution. University cities such as those of Mexico and Caracas cannot be matched elsewhere, and Brasília stands as a unique urban achievement in the modern world.

Since 1946, painting and the graphic arts in Latin America have surged forward to become very much a part of the mainstream of contemporary art. Nationalism has been replaced by internationalism. This does not mean that artists have lost the sense of a national or American identity, but rather that most of them have, in the main, repudiated nationalism for its localism, its nativism, and its overt exploitation of local color. Only a few of them—such as Eduardo Kingman Riofrío (b. 1913) and Oswaldo Guayasamín (b. 1919) of Ecuador—

continue to paint indigenous subjects under the influence of the Mexican muralists. Others, notably Alejandro Obregón (b. 1921) of Colombia, Fernando de Szyszlo (b. 1925) of Peru, and Rodolfo Abularach (b. 1933) of Guatemala, have found various ways of expressing a national identity (on the spiritual-cultural level) through forms and techniques that are entirely contemporary. Obregón is a figurative painter influenced by cubism and expressionism, whose visual vocabulary derives in large measure from recollections of his birthplace, the seaport of Barranquilla. Though he paints natural forms, both animate and inanimate, including condors and volcanoes, he transforms the subjects into a vibrant pictorial composition dominated by quasi-abstract qualities, as in "Cattle Drowning in the Magdalena" or "Carniverous Flowers." Fernando de Szyszlo, working within the domain of abstract expressionism, has drawn upon pre-Columbian ceramics and textiles, as well as upon Incan mythology, for his powerful symbolic paintings, such as "Black Sun," "Yawar Fiesta," and the "Cajamarca" series inspired by the Quechua elegy on the death of the Inca Atahualpa. Rodolfo Abularach has used decorative and symbolic designs and images from ancient Maya temples and steles in his very personal and beautifully executed abstractions (oils and drawings).

Throughout Latin America, there were those among the older artists who led the movement away from overt nationalism and pictorial realism: Carlos Mérida and Rufino Tamayo in Mexico (Mérida was born in Guatemala, in 1893, but has lived and worked in Mexico); Emilio Pettoruti in Argentina; Amelia Peláez (b. 1897) and Wifredo Lam (b. 1902) in Cuba; Ricardo Grau (b. 1908) in Peru; Tarsila do Amaral in Brazil. At the same time, there were certain major figures who adhered to nationalism and naturalism, and who nevertheless remain important because of their exceptional talent and impressive production. Several Brazilian painters fall into this category, notably Emiliano Di Cavalcanti (b. 1897), Alberto da Veiga Guignard (1896–1962), Alfredo Volpi (b. 1896), and above all Cândido Portinari (1903–62). Of these, Portinari was equally important for his murals—at the Ministry of Education in Rio de Janeiro, the Library of Congress in Washington, and the United Nations Building in New York—and for his easel paintings, which include a large number of excellent portraits and many powerful canvases depicting the misery of the underprivileged. Portinari had a strong sense of social responsibility mixed with a deep compassion for human suffering. He has left, in his thousands of paintings, an immense and all-embracing pictorial record of Brazil, its history, its legends, its economy, its varied human types.

After cubism, surrealism and abstract expressionism were the two artistic trends that had the widest impact in Latin America. Roberto Matta Echauren (b. 1912) was one of the first to become identified with surrealism, when he went to Paris in 1934; he later stayed in New York, from 1938 to 1948, and then, after a period of six years in Rome, settled in Paris and became a French citizen. His connection with his native land is therefore tenuous; but perhaps traces of his Latin American origin can be found in the telluric images and symbols of such metaphysical abstractions as "The Unthinkable" or "Under the Flames of Delusion," or his mural for the Unesco Building in Paris. In at least one of his paintings, "Birth of America," Matta offers evidence that the symbolism of America remains present in his mind. Very similar is the situation of another Chilean painter, Enrique Zañartu, who was born in Paris (in 1921) and has lived there since 1949. Prior to that, he worked with Stanley William Hayter in New York. Although he is an abstract expressionist identified with the New School of Paris, French critics have discerned in his work images derived from memories of the snow-capped Andes, the bright-hued lakes of southern Chile, and the arid coastal region of the north. A third Chilean abstract painter, Nemesio Antúñez (b. 1918), has been influenced by Matta and also by Hayter, with whom he worked both in New York and Paris. Returning to Chile in 1953, he organized the Taller 99 (a modern art studio) and in 1962 was appointed director of the Museum of Contemporary Art in Santiago. He has worked with oils, water colors, and engravings, nearly always basing his abstractions on a profound affinity with nature, as in "Andean River," "Heart of the Cordillera," and "Vertical Volcano"; or on man-made objects, as in "The Red Tablecloth," with its undulating checkered patterns.

Other leading exponents of abstract expressionism include Manabu Mabe (b. 1924) in Brazil, Clorindo Testa (b. 1923), Miguel Ocampo (b. 1922), and Mario Pucciarelli (b. 1928) in Argentina, Armando Morales (b. 1927) in Nicaragua, Alberto Dávila (b. 1912) in Peru, and María Luisa Pacheco (b. 1919) in Bolivia. Two important painters, Sarah Grilo (b. 1920) and José Antonio Fernández Muro (b. 1920), both of Argentina, have taken elements from both abstract expressionism and constructivism, while evolving toward personal styles of great freedom and flexibility, including the use of graffiti (Grilo) and embossed rubbings—*frottage*—chiefly from manhole covers (Fernández Muro).

There is an important group of neofigurative painters (La Nueva Figuración) in Argentina, including Ernesto Deira (b. 1928), Jorge de la Vega (b. 1930), Rómulo Maccio (b. 1931), Luis Felipe Noé (b. 1933), and Antonio Segui (b. 1934). Often using mixed media, they use expressionistic distortion, stressing the monstrous and the grotesque, the subconscious fears and anxieties of modern man. Typical of this trend is Maccio's canvas "To Live: Without a Guarantee" (1963), with a nuclear blast exploding in the cranium of a man, the lower half of whose face is a gruesome, inhuman mask.

At the other end of the spectrum are the constructivists, who put their faith in the purest of abstract forms and in the geometrical depiction of space. Again, this group is especially important in Argentina, where it is known as Pintura Generativa (Generative Painting). Its representatives include Miguel Angel Vidal (b. 1928), Ary Brizzi (b. 1930), Eduardo MacEntyre (b. 1929), and Carlos Silva (b. 1930). Constructivism in Venezuela is represented by Alejandro Otero (b. 1921) and Jesús Soto (b. 1923). Otero passed through figurative and quasifigurative phases before turning to geometric abstraction in the early 1950's. His series of "Colorrhythms," begun in 1955, are executed in Duco with an airbrush on rectangular wooden panels; color forms and spatial forms create a dynamic interplay of rhythms, emphasized by vertical parallels of strong colors. Otero has also worked with aluminum constructions, as in his mosaic and aluminum murals for the Public Amphitheater in Caracas. Soto has used plexiglas sheets mounted on masonite and has also experimented with multidimensional space—in the "Vibrations" series (1962–63)—by using suspended wire shapes in front of brightly colored wood or masonite panels. More recently, he has been including "found objects" in his paintings. In Brazil, Waldemar Cordeiro (b. 1925) represents the constructivist trend, and adherents are also found in other parts of Latin America.

Not all artists, of course, can be classified under one of these groups or tendencies. Ivan Serpa (b. 1923) of Brazil, for example, has cultivated various styles, including both abstract expressionism and constructivism. In Colombia, Eduardo Ramírez Villamizar (b. 1922), began as an expressionist but around 1950 veered toward geometrical abstraction, and later began to work with reliefs in plaster or wood. This phase led to the mural relief in bronze that he executed for the Bank of the Republic in Cúcuta (1962).

Certain artists have consistently followed their own individual course, regardless of changing trends and styles. Such is the case of the great Argentine painter Raquel Forner (b. 1902), who has absorbed elements of expressionism, surrealism, and informalism and dominated them all by her powerful personal style. She has created her own pictorial world, surrealist in its setting and imagery, but emotionally and symbolically related to the terror and tension of the modern world: monstrous figures, elaborate allegories, and fantastic landscapes are imbued with compassion and a sense of tragedy. This is particularly true of her painting in the 1940's and 1950's ("The March," 1954; "Apocalypsis," 1955; "Evasion," 1958). Subsequently, she began to concentrate on a single theme throughout a series of paintings, as in the "Astronaut" series of the early 1960's and the series titled "The Voyage with No Return" (1965), inspired by the death of her husband, the sculptor Alfredo Bigatti. While these later paintings may be described as neofigurative, they are essentially a development and enrichment of her earlier work, rather than the adoption of a new style. Raquel Forner is also a master engraver: her colored prints from the "Astronaut" series attest to this.

In Mexico, José Luis Cuevas (b. 1933) has developed his own type of neofigurative art, chiefly in the form of black-and-white ink drawings depicting "a homogenized race of goblins, sometimes humorous in inflection, sometimes sinister, but always bloblike, with large heads stuck in their torsos and preternaturally spindly legs" (Parker Tyler). An artist in the line of Goya and Orozco—and a master draughtsman—Cuevas uses these hallucinatory figures to reveal a truth that at times may be both repulsive and compelling.

Orozco, Tamayo, and Cuevas may be regarded as the precursors of the neofigurative movement of the 1960's in Mexico known as Nueva Presencia, whose members have also called themselves "Los Interioristas" (The Insiders). In their manifesto, issued in 1961, they said: "We strive for an art that communicates in the clearest and most direct way possible our commitment to man." Co-authors of the manifesto were Arnold Belkin and Francisco Icaza (both born in 1931, the former in Canada). Other members of the group include Francisco Corzas (b. 1936), Emilio Ortiz (b. 1936), Leonel Góngora (b. 1933), Artemio Sepúlveda (b. 1936), and José Muñóz (b. 1929).

There are many ways of communicating in art, and one of the most effective during the 1960's has proved to be pop art, which spread from the United States to Europe and (more slowly) to Latin America. Pop art can scarcely be classified solely under painting, for it includes three-dimensional "assemblages" and the use of "found objects." The leading exponent of this trend in Mexico is Alberto Gironella (b. 1929), who makes use of collages as well as three-dimensional assemblages. In Argentina, Carlos Squirru (b. 1934), who studied in the United States, has worked along similar lines. There are strong social and psychological implications in the work of both men.

So-called op art has its chief Latin American exponent in the Argentine Julio Le Parc (b. 1928). He went to Paris in the 1950's, and in 1960 formed there, together with other Argentine and French artists, the Groupe de Recherche d'Art Visuel. The aim of this group is to do away with "passive contemplation on the part of the spectator," by involving the latter in a dynamic visual experience through combinations of color, light, mass, and motion. It also repudiates all "extra-visual" appeal, be it anecdotal, descriptive, symbolic, or representational. In 1964, the Group organized a large exhibition of its work, which was shown with extraordinary success in many countries, including Argentina. Another member of the original Group is the Argentine sculptor Gyula Kosice (b. 1924), whose abstract constructions include gyrating hemispheres and forms based on the tensions of parabolic curves.

In the realm of sculpture, two Argentine artists of the older generation stand out: Pablo Curatela Manes (1891–1962) and Alfredo Bigatti (1898–1964). Bigatti started as a pupil of Bourdelle but veered toward modernism under the influence of Meštrovic. Curatela Manes also studied with Bourdelle, but his close friendship with the painter Juan Gris was more decisive in guiding him toward new forms of spatial expression. From the strongly dynamic "Rugby" of 1926 to the abstract works of his final years in Paris, Curatela Manes was a creative innovator, always true to his own individuality. Alicia Penalba (b. 1918) was a pupil of Zadkine but later came under the influence of Arp and Brancusi. Living in Paris since 1948, she has developed a distinctively personal style, often using totemlike structures, as in "Magic Forest." Another Argentine sculptress, Noemí Gerstein (b. 1910), also worked with Zadkine in Paris. After passing from naturalism to cubism, she eventually concentrated on a totally abstract style of free spatial constructions using tubular strips of metal.

International recognition has also been achieved by Marina Núñez del Prado (b. 1910) of Bolivia, who works in the tradition of Arp and Brancusi, using materials found in her native country: basalt, white onyx, granite, guayacan wood. With these she achieves spectacular effects of form and color, as in the dreamlike torso of "The White Venus" (1960), in white onyx, or "The Black Venus" (1958), in basalt. She has been called "the sculptress of rolling curves and volumes symbolizing the Bolivian Indian" (Archipenko).

In Colombia, Edgar Negret (b. 1920) has worked with a wide diversity of materials, including plaster, stone, fine wire, aluminum plates, and polychromed iron, to achieve highly imaginative abstractions. In Peru, Joaquín Roca Rey (b. 1923) is a versatile sculptor who has worked with both representational and abstract forms, somewhat influenced by Henry Moore, using a variety of materials: wood, bronze, iron, stainless steel, and plaster. Roberto González Goyri (b. 1924) of Guatemala has done both painting and sculpture, but is best known for the latter. He has executed monumental bas-reliefs for several government buildings for Guatemala City. In 1964 he received the first prize for sculpture in a competition for artists from Central America.

In the field of art history, Angel Guido (1896–1960) of Argentina, an architect by profession, introduced the principles of Wölfflin and Worringer to Latin America. His most important work, *Redescubrimiento de América en el arte* (1944), deals with "the rediscovery of America" (in a cultural-aesthetic sense) through the study of its art, from the colonial period to the present. Among other Argentine art historians, Mario J. Buschiazzo (b. 1902) has concentrated on architecture of the colonial period; Julio E. Payró (b. 1899) and Jorge Romero Brest (b. 1905) have written mostly about modern art, chiefly painting. Romero Brest is head of the art section of the Instituto Torcuato Di Tella in Buenos Aires, which organizes important national and international exhibitions. In Mexico, the leading art historian is Justino Fernández, director of the Institute for Aesthetic Research of the National University of Mexico, and author of numerous books, including studies of Orozco and Tamayo. Two painters, Jean Charlot (b. 1898) and Miguel Covarrubias, have written important books about art in Mexico. José Gómez Sicre (b. 1916) of Cuba, chief of the Division of Visual Arts of the Pan American Union, has written a book on Cuban painting and has been extremely active in making Latin American art better known in the United States.

In the twenty years that have elapsed since Pedro Henríquez Ureña wrote the *Historia de la cultura en la América Hispánica,* the cultural accomplishments of Latin America have received increasing attention and recognition throughout the world, particularly in architecture, painting, graphic arts, sculpture, and music. The work of Oscar Niemeyer, Carlos Raúl Villanueva, Félix Candela, and Amancio Williams is known wherever new developments in contemporary architecture are studied. The painters and graphic artists of Latin America are prominently represented in the galleries and museums of New York, Paris, Rome, and other international art centers. Exhibitions devoted to Latin American art have steadily grown in number and size. An example is the exhibition "Art of Latin America Since Independence"; organized in 1966 by Yale University and the University of Texas, it consisted of some four hundred items. In music, Alberto Ginastera has taken his place among the foremost of contemporary composers, while many younger composers are mastering the new techniques of electronic and aleatoric music. Never has cultural interchange between the United States and Latin America been so intense and so fruitful as at the present time, nor manifested on so many different levels of endeavor, from the aesthetic to the scientific.

Today, Latin America finds itself at a critical juncture, with many of its traditional values demolished or strongly threatened by social, political, and economic pressures. There is clamor for change everywhere, clearly reflected in the new realistic literature and in the restless activity of the masses. The middle classes are surging forward, and there is much talk of the "new men" who will lead the Latin American nations to new levels of prosperity and achievement. Nearly all agree that there are wrongs to redress in Latin America, but there is sharp disagreement on the means to remedy these wrongs. Yet even those who favor evolution rather than revolution concede that evolution must now proceed so rapidly, if disaster is to be avoided, that it becomes, in effect, a revolutionary movement in one form or another. A climate of reform prevails, impelled by a sense of urgency. Whatever the outcome, the rich cultural heritage of Latin America, and the historic role of its intellectuals as men of action, give promise that the humanities will be among the main sources of renewed vitality and social progress.

Bibliography

Selected Works in English

I. GENERAL

A. Literary and Cultural History

ALEXANDER, HARTLEY B. *Latin American Mythology.* New York, 1965.

ANDERSON IMBERT, ENRIQUE. *Spanish American Literature: A History.* Translated by JOHN V. FALCONIERI. Detroit, 1963.

ARIAS-LARRETA, ABRAHAM. *Indo-American Literature.* 2 vols. Vol. I: *Pre-Columbian Literature.* Vol. II: *From Columbus to Bolívar.* New York, 1964.

BELAÚNDE, VICTOR ANDRÉS. *Hispanic American Culture.* Houston, Tex., 1931

COSÍO VILLEGAS, DANIEL. *American Extremes.* Translated by AMÉRICA PAREDES. Austin, Tex., 1964.

CRAWFORD, WILLIAM REX. *A Century of Latin American Thought.* Cambridge, Mass., 1961.

FOSTER, GEORGE M. *Culture and Conquest: America's Spanish Heritage.* Chicago, 1960.

GRIFFIN, CHARLES C. (ed.). *Concerning Latin American Culture.* New York, 1940.

HANKE, LEWIS. *Bartolomé de las Casas—Bookman, Scholar, and Propagandist.* Philadelphia, 1952.

HENRÍQUEZ UREÑA, PEDRO. *Literary Currents in Hispanic America.* Cambridge, Mass., 1945.

HESPELT, E. HERMAN (ed.). *An Outline History of Spanish American Literature.* New York, 1941.

Intellectual Trends in Latin America: Papers Read at a Conference . . . sponsored by the Institute of Latin-American Studies, University of Texas. Austin, Tex., 1945.

LANNING, JOHN TATE. *Academic Culture in the Spanish Colonies.* New York, 1940.

LEONARD, IRVING A. *Books of the Brave: Being an Account of Books and of Men in the Spanish Conquest and Settlement of the Sixteenth-Century New World.* Cambridge, Mass., 1949.

PICÓN-SALAS, MARIANO. *A Cultural History of Spanish America: From Conquest to Independence.* Berkeley, Calif., 1964.

REYES, ALFONSO. *The Position of America and Other Essays.* New York, 1950.

SÁNCHEZ REULET, ANÍBAL. *Contemporary Latin American Philosophy.* Albuquerque, N.M., 1954.

TORRES-RIOSECO, ARTURO. *Aspects of Spanish-American Literature.* Berkeley, Calif., 1963.

————. *New World Literature: Tradition and Revolt in Latin America.* Berkeley, Calif., 1949.

WHITAKER, ARTHUR P. (ed.). *Latin America and the Enlightenment.* Ithaca, N.Y., 1961.

WILGUS, A. CURTIS. *The Caribbean: Its Culture.* Gainesville, Fla., 1955.

ZEA, LEOPOLDO. *The Latin-American Mind.* Berkeley, Calif., 1963.

B. *Literature in Translation (Anthologies)*

ARCINIEGAS, GERMÁN (ed.). *The Green Continent: A Comprehensive View of Latin America by Its Leading Writers.* Translated by HARRIET DE ONÍS *et al.* New York, 1944.

BLACKWELL, ALICE S. *Some Spanish American Poets.* 2d ed. Philadelphia, 1937.

COESTER, ALFRED. *An Anthology of the Modernista Movement in Spanish America.* Boston, 1924.

CRAIG, G. DUNDAS (ed.). *The Modernist Trend in Spanish-American Poetry.* Berkeley, Calif., 1934.

FITTS, DUDLEY (ed.). *Anthology of Contemporary Latin-American Poetry.* Norfolk, Conn., 1962.

HAYS, HENRY R. *Twelve Spanish American Poets.* New Haven, Conn., 1943.

JOHNSON, MILDRED E. (ed. and trans.). *Swan, Cygnets, and Owl: An Anthology of Modernist Poetry in Spanish America.* Columbia, Mo., 1956.

JONES, WILLIS K. *Spanish-American Literature Before 1888.* New York, 1965.

———. *Spanish-American Literature Since 1888.* New York, 1965.

LOWENFELS, LILLIAN, and NAN BRAYMER (eds. and trans.). *Modern Poetry from Spain and Latin America.* New York, 1964.

ONÍS, HARRIET DE (ed. and trans.). *The Golden Land: An Anthology of Latin American Folklore in Literature.* Rev. ed. New York, 1961.

POORE, DUDLEY, and ANGEL FLORES (eds.). *Fiesta in November: Stories from Latin America.* Boston, 1942.

WALSH, THOMAS (ed.). *Hispanic Anthology: Poems Translated from the Spanish by English and North American Poets.* New York and London, 1920.

C. Political History and Social Sciences

ADAMS, ROBERT N. *Contemporary Cultures in Latin America.* San Francisco, 1966.

BERNSTEIN, HARRY. *Modern and Contemporary Latin America.* Philadelphia, 1952.

CROW, JOHN A. *Spanish American Life.* New York, 1963.

DAVIS, HAROLD E. *The Americas in History.* New York, 1953.

———. *Social Science Trends in Latin America.* Washington, D.C., 1950.

DOZER, DONALD M. *Latin America: An Interpretive History.* New York, 1962.

FITZGIBBON, RUSSELL H. (ed.). *The Constitutions of the Americas.* Chicago, 1948.

HANKE, LEWIS. *The Spanish Struggle for Justice in the Conquest of America.* Philadelphia, 1949.

HARING, CLARENCE H. *The Spanish Empire in America.* New York, 1947.

HERRING, HUBERT C. *A History of Latin America from the Beginnings to the Present.* 2d rev. ed. New York, 1961.

JAMES, PRESTON E. *An Introduction to Latin America.* New York, 1964.

MADARIAGA, SALVADOR DE. *The Fall of the Spanish American Empire.* New York, 1963.

————. *The Rise of the Spanish American Empire.* New York, 1965.

MECHAM, J. LLOYD. *Church and State in Latin America.* Chapel Hill, N.C., 1934.

MOSES, BERNARD. *South America on the Eve of Emancipation.* New York, 1965.

RECASÉNS SICHES, LUIS, *et al. Latin-American Legal Philosophy.* Translated by GORDON IRELAND *et al.* Cambridge, Mass., 1948.

SILVERT, K. H. *Reaction and Revolution in Latin America.* New York, 1961.

TANNENBAUM, FRANK. *Slave and Citizen: The Negro in the Americas.* New York, 1947.

————. *Ten Keys to Latin America.* New York, 1962.

WILGUS, A. CURTIS (ed.). *Colonial Hispanic America.* New York, 1963.

————. *History and Historians of Hispanic America.* New York, 1965.

D. Plastic and Graphic Arts

CALI, FRANÇOIS. *Spanish Arts of Latin America.* New York, 1961.

CATLIN, STANTON L., and TERENCE GRIEDER. *Art of Latin America Since Independence.* New Haven, Conn., 1966.

DAMAZ, PAUL F. *Art in Latin American Architecture.* New York, 1963.

EMMERICH, ANDRÉ. *Sweat of the Sun and Tears of the Moon: Gold and Silver in Pre-Columbian Art.* Seattle, 1965.

HITCHCOCK, HENRY-RUSSELL. *Latin American Architecture Since 1945.* New York, 1955.

KELEMEN, PÁL. *Baroque and Rococo in Latin America.* New York, 1951.

————. *Medieval American Art.* 2 vols. New York, 1943.

KIRSTEIN, LINCOLN. *The Latin American Collection of the Museum of Modern Art.* New York, 1943.

KUBLER, GEORGE, and MARTÍN SORIA. *Art and Architecture in Spain and Portugal and Their American Dominions: 1500 to 1800.* Baltimore, 1959.

ROBERTSON, DONALD. *Pre-Columbian Architecture.* New York, 1963.

SMITH, ROBERT C., and ELIZABETH WILDER. *A Guide to the Art of Latin America.* Washington, D.C., 1948.

WHYTE, BERTHA K. *Seven Treasure Cities of Latin America.* New York, 1964.

WILDER, ELIZABETH (ed.). *Studies in Latin American Art: Proceedings of a Conference Held in the Museum of Modern Art, New York, 28–31 May 1945.* Washington, D.C., 1949.

E. Music and Dance

CHASE, GILBERT. *A Guide to the Music of Latin America.* Washington, D.C., 1962.

————. "Latin America," in *A History of Song,* ed. DENIS STEVENS. London and New York, 1960.

————. *The Music of Spain.* 2d rev. ed. New York, 1958. (Chapter 17: "Hispanic Music in the Americas.")

DURÁN, GUSTAVO. *Recordings of Latin American Songs and Dances.* 2d ed., revised and enlarged by GILBERT CHASE. Washington, D.C., 1950. (An annotated selective list of popular and folk-popular music.)

HAGUE, ELEANOR. *Latin American Music, Past and Present.* Santa Ana, Calif., 1934.

LANGE, FRANCISCO CURT (ed.). *Latin-American Art Music for*

the Piano by Twelve Contemporary Composers. New York, 1942.

LEKIS, LISA. *Folk Dance of Latin America.* Gainesville, Fla., 1958.

SLONIMSKY, NICOLAS. *Music of Latin America.* New York, 1945.

II. ARGENTINA

A. Literary History and Criticism

ANDERSON, THEODORE. *Carlos María Ocantos: Argentine Novelist.* New Haven, Conn., 1934.

BARRENECHEA, ANA MARÍA. *Borges the Labyrinth Maker.* Translated by ROBERT LIMA. New York, 1965.

CUTHBERTSON, STUART. *The Poetry of José Mármol.* Boulder, Colo., 1935.

HOLE, MYRA C. *Bartolomé Mitre: A Poet in Action.* New York, 1947.

LICHTBLAU, MYRON. *The Argentine Novel in the Nineteenth Century.* New York, 1959.

POLT, JOHN H. B. *The Writings of Eduardo Mallea.* Berkeley, Calif., 1959.

RICHARDSON, RUTH. *Florencio Sánchez and the Argentine Theatre.* New York, 1923.

TINKER, EDWARD LAROQUE. *Life and Literature of the Pampas.* Gainesville, Fla., 1961.

B. Literature in Translation

BIERSTADT, EDWARD H. (ed.). *Three Plays of the Argentine.* New York, 1929.

BORGES, JORGE LUIS. *Dreamtigers.* Translated from *El hacedor* (The Maker) by MILDRED BOYER and HAROLD MORLAND. Austin, Tex., 1964.

————. *Ficciones.* Edited, and with an Introduction, by ANTHONY KERRIGAN. New York, 1962.

————. *Labyrinths: Selected Stories and Other Writings.* Edited by DONALD A. YATES and JAMES E. IRBY. New York, 1962.

FRANK, WALDO (ed.). *Tales from the Argentine.* Translated by ANITA BRENNER. New York, 1930.

GÁLVEZ, MANUEL. *Holy Wednesday.* Translated by WARRE B. WELLS. New York, 1934.

————. *Nacha Regules.* Translated by L. ONGLEY. New York, 1922.

GUIDO, BEATRIZ. *The House of the Angel.* Translated by JOAN C. MACLEAN. New York, 1957.

————. *End of a Day (El incendio y las visperas).* Translated by A. D. POWERS. New York, 1966.

GÜIRALDES, RICARDO. *Don Segundo Sombra: Shadow on the Pampas.* Translated by HARRIET DE ONÍS. New York, 1965.

HERNÁNDEZ, JOSÉ. *The Gaucho: Martín Fierro.* Translated by WALTER OWEN. New York, 1936.

————. *Martín Fierro: The Argentine Gaucho Epic.* Translated into English prose, with an Introduction and notes, by HENRY A. HOLMES. New York, 1923.

LEGUIZAMÓN, MARTINIANO P. *Calandria: A Drama of Gaucho Life.* New York, 1932.

MALLEA, EDUARDO. *The Bay of Silence.* Translated by STUART E. GRUMMON. New York, 1944.

MÁRMOL, JOSÉ. *Amalia: A Romance of the Argentine.* New York, 1919.

ROJAS, RICARDO. *The Invisible Christ.* New York, 1931.

SÁNCHEZ, FLORENCIO. *Representative Plays.* Translated by WILLIS K. JONES. Washington, D.C., 1961.

SARMIENTO, DOMINGO F. *Travels.* A selection from *Viajes,* translated by INÉS MUÑOZ. Washington, D.C., 1963.

C. History and Biography

BUNKLEY, GEORGE I. *The Life of Sarmiento.* Princeton, N.J., 1952.

JEFFREY, WILLIAM H. *Mitre and Argentina.* New York, 1952.

LEVENE, RICARDO. *A History of Argentina.* Edited and translated by WILLIAM S. ROBERTSON. Chapel Hill, N.C., 1937.

PENDLE, GEORGE. *Argentina.* 2d ed. London and New York, 1961.

ROJAS, RICARDO. *San Martín, Knight of the Andes.* New York, 1945.

ROMERO, JOSÉ LUIS. *A History of Argentine Political Thought.* Stanford, Calif., 1963.

SARMIENTO, DOMINGO F. *Life in the Argentine Republic in the Days of the Tyrants; or, Civilization and Barbarism (Facundo).* Translated by MRS. HORACE MANN. New York, 1961.

SCOBIE, JAMES R. *Argentina: A City and a Nation.* New York, 1964.

WHITAKER, ARTHUR P. *Argentina.* Englewood Cliffs, N.J., 1964.

WHITE, JOHN W. *Argentina: The Life Story of a Nation.* New York, 1942.

III. BOLIVIA

A. History and Description

ALEXANDER, ROBERT J. *The Bolivian National Revolution.* New Brunswick, N.J., 1958.

ARNADE, CHARLES W. *The Emergence of the Republic of Bolivia.* Gainesville, Fla., 1957.

ASTURIAS, MIGUEL ANGEL. *Bolivia: An Undiscovered Land.* London, 1961.

HANKE, LEWIS. *The Imperial City of Potosí.* The Hague, 1956.

LEONARD, OLEN E. *Bolivia: Land, People, and Institutions.* Washington, D.C., 1952.

OSBORNE, HAROLD. *Bolivia: A Land Divided.* 3d ed. New York, 1964.

OSTRIA GUTIÉRREZ, ALBERTO. *The Tragedy of Bolivia: A People Crucified.* New York, 1958.

B. Literature and Art

BELLAMY, H. D., and P. ALLAN. *The Great Idol of Tiahuanaco.* New York, 1959.

COSTA DU NELS, ADOLFO. *Bewitched Lands (Tierras hechizadas).* Translated by STUART E. GRUMMON. New York, 1944.

LEAVITT, STURGIS E. *A Tentative Bibliography of Bolivian Literature.* Cambridge, Mass., 1933.

STEVENSON, ROBERT. *The Music of Peru: Aboriginal and Vice-royal Periods.* Washington, D.C., 1960. (Includes a chapter on "Alto Perú," that is, Bolivia.)

WETHEY, HAROLD E. "Mestizo Architecture in Bolivia," *The Art Quarterly* (Winter, 1951), pp. 283–308.

IV. BRAZIL

A. Literary and Cultural History

AZEVEDO, FERNANDO DE. *Brazilian Culture: An Introduction to the Study of Culture in Brazil.* Translated by W. REX CRAWFORD. New York, 1950.

BANDEIRA, MANUEL. *A Brief History of Brazilian Literature.* Translated by R. E. DIMMICK. New York, 1964.

BOXER, CHARLES R. *The Golden Age of Brazil, 1695–1750.* Berkeley, Calif., 1962.

COSTA, JOÃO CRUZ. *A History of Ideas in Brazil: The Evolution of Philosophy in Brazil and the Evolution of National History.* Translated by SUZETTE MACEDO. Berkeley, Calif., 1964.

ELLISON, FREDERICK P. *Brazil's New Novel—Four Northeastern Masters: José Lins do Rêgo, Jorge Amado, Graciliano Ramos, Rachel de Queiroz.* Berkeley, Calif., 1954.

FREYRE, GILBERTO. *New World in the Tropics: The Culture of Modern Brazil.* New York, 1959.

HILL, LAWRENCE F. (ed.). *Brazil: Chapters by Manoel Cardozo and Others.* Berkeley, Calif., 1947. (Includes chapters on art, music, and literature.)

MACHADO, JOSÉ BETTENCOURT. *Machado of Brazil: The Life and Times of Machado de Assis.* New York, 1953.

PUTNAM, SAMUEL. *Marvellous Journey: A Survey of Four Centuries of Brazilian Writing.* New York, 1948.

SAYERS, RAYMOND S. *The Negro in Brazilian Literature.* New York, 1956.

VERÍSSIMO, ERICO. *Brazilian Literature: An Outline.* New York, 1945.

B. *Literature in Translation*

ALENCAR, JOSÉ MARTINIANO DE. *Iracema, the Honeylips: A Legend of Brazil.* Translated by N. BIDELL. Rio de Janeiro, n.d.

AMADO, JORGE. "Sea of the Dead: Yemanjá, Mistress of the Seas and the Sails," trans. DUDLEY POORE, in *Fiesta in November,* Boston, 1942.

———. *The Two Deaths of Quincas Wateryell.* Translated by BARBARA SHELBY. New York, 1965.

———. *The Violent Land (Terras do Sim Fim).* Translated by SAMUEL PUTNAM. New York, 1945.

ANDRADE, CARLOS DRUMMOND DE. *In the Middle of the Road.* Edited and translated by JOHN NIST. Tucson, Ariz., 1965. (Sixty-three selected poems.)

ANDRADE, MARIO DE. *Fräulein (Amar, Verbo Intransitivo).* Translated by MARGARET R. HOLLINGSWORTH. New York, 1933.

ARANHA, JOSÉ PEREIRA DA GRAÇA. *Canaan.* Translated by MARIANO J. LORENTE. Boston, 1920.

ASSIS, JOAQUIM MARIA MACHADO DE. *Dom Casmurro.* Translated by HELEN CALDWELL. New York, 1953.

———. *Epitaph of a Small Winner: Posthumous Memoirs of Brás Cubas (Memórias Postumas de Brás Cubas).* Translated by WILLIAM L. GROSSMAN. New York, 1952.

———. *Esau and Jacob.* Translated by HELEN CALDWELL. Berkeley, Calif., 1965.

———. *Philosopher or Dog? (Quincas Borba).* Translated by CLOTILDE WILSON. New York, 1954.

AZEVEDO, ALOÍSIO TANCREDO GONÇALVES DE. *A Brazilian Tenement (O Cortiço).* Translated by HARRY W. BROWN. New York, 1926.

CRULS, GASTÃO LUÍS. *The Mysterious Amazonia.* Translated by J. T. W. SADLER. Rio de Janeiro, 1944.

GOLDBERG, ISAAC (trans.). *Brazilian Tales.* Boston, 1921.

LIMA, JORGE DE. *Poems.* Translated by MELISSA S. HULL. Rio de Janeiro, 1952.

NIST, JOHN (ed. and trans.). *Modern Brazilian Poetry: An Anthology.* Bloomington, Ind., 1962.

RAMOS, GRACILIANO. *Anguish (Angústia).* Translated by L. C. KAPLAN. New York, 1946.

RÊGO, JOSÉ LINS DO. *Plantation Boy (Menino de Engenho).* New York, 1966.

SETÚBAL, PAULO DE OLIVEIRA. *Domitila: The Romance of an Emperor's Mistress (A Marquesa de Santos).* Translated by MARGARET RICHARDSON. New York, 1930.

TAUNAY, ALFREDO MARIA ADRIANO D'ESCRAGNOLLE. *Inocencia.* Translated by HENRIQUETA CHAMBERLAIN. New York, 1945.

VERÍSSIMO, ERICO. *Consider the Lilies of the Field (Olhai os Lírios do Campo).* Translated by JEAN N. KARNOFF. New York, 1947.

———. *Crossroads (Caminhos Cruzados).* Translated by L. C. KAPLAN. New York, 1943.

———. *Mexico (México: História Duma Viagem).* Translated by L. L. BARRETT. New York, 1960.

———. *Night (Noite).* Translated by L. L. BARRETT. New York, 1956.

———. *The Rest Is Silence (O Resto é Silencio).* Translated L. C. KAPLAN. New York, 1946.

———. *Time and the Wind (O Tempo e o Vento).* Translated by L. L. BARRETT. New York, 1951.

C. History and Social Science

BAKLANOFF, ERIC N. (ed.). *New Perspectives of Brazil.* Nashville, Tenn., 1966.

BURNS, BRADFORD E. (ed.). *A Documentary History of Brazil.* New York, 1966.

COSTA, LUIZ EDMUNDO DA. *Rio in the Time of the Viceroys.*

Translated, with an Epilogue, by DOROTHEA H. MOMSEN. Rio de Janeiro, 1936.

CUNHA, EUCLIDES DA. *Rebellion in the Backlands (Os Sertões).* Translated by SAMUEL PUTNAM. Chicago, 1944.

CUNNINGHAME GRAHAM, ROBERT B. *A Brazilian Mystic: Being the Life and Miracles of Antônio Conselheiro.* New York, 1926.

FREYRE, GILBERTO. *The Mansions and the Shanties: The Making of Modern Brazil (Sobrados e Mucambos).* Translated by HARRIET DE ONÍS. New York, 1963.

———. *The Masters and the Slaves (Casa Grande e Senzala).* Translated by SAMUEL PUTNAM. 2d ed. New York, 1956.

HARING, CLARENCE H. *Empire in Brazil: A New World Experiment with Monarchy.* Cambridge, Mass., 1958.

MOOG, CLODOMIR VIANNA. *Bandeirantes and Pioneers.* Translated by HARRIET DE ONÍS. New York, 1963.

LIVERMORE, H. V., and W. J. ENTWHISTLE (eds.). *Portugal and Brazil: An Introduction.* Oxford, Eng., 1953.

PIERSON, DONALD. *Negroes in Brazil: A Study of Race Contact in Bahia.* Chicago, 1942.

RAMOS, ARTHUR. *The Negro in Brazil.* Translated by RICHARD PATTEE. Washington, D.C., 1939.

SMITH, T. LYNN. *Brazil: People and Institutions.* 3d ed. Baton Rouge, La., 1963.

WAGLEY, CHARLES. *An Introduction to Brazil.* New York, 1965.

E. *Music and Art*

BARDI, P. M. *The Arts in Brazil.* Milan, 1956.

———. *Tropical Gardens of Burle-Marx.* New York, 1963.

CASTEDO, LEOPOLDO. *The Baroque Prevalence in Brazilian Art.* New York, 1964.

CUNHA, LUIZ DE ALMEIDA. *Brazil.* Translated by WILLIAM C. MEIN. (Pan American Union Art in Latin America Today Series.) Washington, D.C., 1960.

FRANCK, KLAUS (ed.). *The Works of Affonso Eduardo Reidy.* Introduction by S. GIEDION. New York, 1960.

GÓMEZ SICRE, JOSÉ. *Four Artists of the Americas.* Translated by GEORGE E. COMPTON. Washington, D.C., 1957. (Includes Roberto Burle-Marx of Brazil.)

GOODWIN, PHILIP L. *Brazil Builds: Architecture New and Old, 1652–1942.* New York, 1943.

KENT, ROCKWELL. *Cândido Portinari: His Life and Art.* Chicago, 1940.

LUPER, ALBERT T. *The Music of Brazil.* (Pan American Union Music Series, No. 9.) Washington, D.C., 1943.

MARIZ, VASCO. *Heitor Villa-Lobos.* Translated by GILBERT CHASE. Gainesville, Fla., 1963.

MINDLIN, HENRIQUE E. *Modern Architecture in Brazil.* New York, 1956.

PAPADAKI, STAMO. *Oscar Niemeyer.* (The Masters of World Architecture Series.) New York, 1960.

V. CENTRAL AMERICA

A. History and Description

BIESANZ, JOHN and MAVIS. *People of Panama.* New York, 1955.

BRIGHMAN, WILLIAM T. *Guatemala: Land of the Quetzal.* (First published in 1887.) Edited by WILLIAM POPENOE. Gainesville, Fla., 1964.

COLVIN, GERARD. *Central America.* New York, 1962.

HUXLEY, ALDOUS. *Beyond the Mexique Bay.* New York, 1960.

KELSEY, VERA, and LILLY DE JONGH OSBORNE. *Four Keys to Guatemala.* New York, 1961.

OAKES, MAUD. *The Two Crosses of Todos Santos.* New York, 1951.

PARKER, FRANKLIN D. *The Central American Republics.* London, 1964.

RODRÍGUEZ, MARIO. *Central America.* Englewood Cliffs, N.J., 1965.

WHETTEN, NATHAN L. *Guatemala: The Land and the People.* New Haven, Conn., 1961.

B. Literature

ASTURIAS, MIGUEL ANGEL. *El Señor Presidente.* New York. 1964.

DARÍO, RUBÉN. *Selected Poems.* Translated by LYSANDER KEMP. Austin, Tex., 1965.

FOGELQUIST, DONALD. *Rubén Darío in Search of Inspiration.* New York, 1963.

Popol Vuh: The Sacred Book of the Ancient Quiché Maya. English translation by DELIA GOETZ and SYLVANUS G. MORLEY (from the Spanish translation of ADRIÁN RECINOS). Norman, Okla., 1957.

WATLAND, C. D. *Poet-Errant: A Biography of Rubén Darío.* New York, 1965.

C. Art and Archaeology

BLOM, FRANS, and OLIVER LA FARGE. *Tribes and Temples.* 2 vols. New Orleans, 1926–27.

BODE, BARBARA. *The Dance of the Conquest of Guatemala.* New Orleans, 1961.

DOCKSTADER, FREDERICK J. *Indian Art in Middle America.* New York, 1964.

OSBORNE, LILLY DE JONGH. *Indian Crafts of Guatemala and El Salvador.* Norman, Okla., 1965.

SPINDEN, HERBERT J. *Maya Art and Civilization.* New York, 1960.

STEPHENS, JOHN L. *Incidents of Travel in Central America, Chiapas, and Yucatán,* ed. RICHARD L. PREDMORE. New Brunswick, N.J., 1956.

THOMPSON, J. ERIC. *The Rise and Fall of Maya Civilization.* Norman, Okla., 1954.

VON HAGEN, VICTOR. *Maya Explorer: John Lloyd Stephens and the Lost Cities of Central America.* Norman, Okla., 1949.
———. *World of the Maya.* New York, 1960.

WAUCHOPE, ROBERT. *They Found the Buried Cities: Exploration and Excavation in the American Tropics.* Chicago, 1965.

VI. CHILE

A. History and Social Science

BUTLAND, GILBERT J. *Chile: An Outline of Its Geography, Economics, and Politics.* London and New York, 1953.

GALDAMES, LUIS. *A History of Chile.* Translated by ISAAC J. COX. New York, 1964.

GIL, FEDERICO G. *Genesis and Modernization of Political Parties in Chile.* Gainesville, Fla., 1962.

SILVERT, K. H. *Chile Yesterday and Today.* New York, 1965.

SUBERCASEAUX, BENJAMÍN. *Chile: A Geographic Extravaganza.* New York, 1943.

B. Literary Criticism

ARCE DE VÁZQUEZ, MARGOT. *Gabriela Mistral: The Poet and Her Work.* Translated by HELENE MASSIO ANDERSON. New York, 1964.

CASTILLO, HOMERO, and RAÚL SILVA CASTRO. *Bibliography of the Chilean Novel.* Charlottesville, Va., 1961.

FEIN, JOHN M. *Modernismo in Chilean Literature: The Second Period.* Durham, N.C., 1964.

HOLMES, HENRY A. *Vicente Huidobro and Creationism.* New York, 1933.

C. Literature in Translation

BLEST GANA, ALBERTO. *Martin Rivas.* Translated by G. A. UMPHREY. Boston, 1936.

HUIDOBRO, VICENTE. *Mirror of a Mage (Cagliostro).* Translated by WARRE B. WELLS. Boston, 1931.

———. *Portrait of a Paladin.* Translated by WARRE B. WELLS. New York, 1932.

MISTRAL, GABRIELA. *Selected Poems.* Translated by LANGSTON HUGHES. Bloomington, Ind., 1957.

NERUDA, PABLO. *Elementary Odes*. A bilingual edition with English translations by CARLOS LOZANO. New York, 1961.

———. *Selected Poems of Pablo Neruda*. Translated by BEN BELLIT. New York, 1961.

VII. COLOMBIA

A. History and Social Science

FALS-BORDA, ORLANDO. *Peasant Society in the Colombian Andes*. Gainesville, Fla., 1955.

GALBRAITH, W. O. *Colombia: A General Survey*. London and New York, 1953.

HENAO, JESÚS M., and GERARDO ARRUBLA. *History of Colombia*. Edited and translated by J. FRED RIPPY. Chapel Hill, N.C., 1938.

HOLT, PAT M. *Colombia Today and Tomorrow*. New York, 1964.

MARTZ, JOHN D. *Colombia: A Contemporary Political Survey*. Chapel Hill, N.C., 1962.

PARKS, E. TAYLOR. *Colombia and the United States, 1765–1934*. Durham, N.C., 1935.

RUSSELL, WILLIAM R. *The Bolivar Countries: Colombia, Ecuador, Venezuela*. New York, 1949.

WEST, ROBERT C. *The Pacific Lowlands: A Negroid Area of the American Tropics*. Baton Rouge, La., 1957.

B. Literature and Art

CARLI, ENZO. *Pre-Conquest Goldsmiths' Work of Colombia*. London, 1957.

DUFFEY, FRANK W. *The Early Cuadro de Costumbres in Colombia*. Chapel Hill, N.C., 1956.

ISAACS, JORGE. *María: A South American Romance*. Translated by THOMAS A. JANVIER. New York, 1925.

LEAVITT, STURGIS E. *A Tentative Bibliography of Colombian Literature*. Cambridge, Mass., 1934.

RIVERA, JOSÉ EUSTASIO. *The Vortex (La vorágine).* Translated by EARLE K. JAMES. New York, 1935.

TRABA, MARTA. *Colombia.* (Pan American Union Art in Latin America Today Series.) Washington, D.C., 1959.

VIII. CUBA

A. General

CHAPMAN, CHARLES E. *A History of the Cuban Republic.* New York, 1936.

DRAPER, THEODORE. *Castroism: Theory and Practice.* New York, 1965.

——. *Castro's Revolution: Myths and Realities.* New York, 1962.

GRAY, RICHARD B. *José Martí: Cuban Patriot.* Gainesville, Fla., 1962.

HUBERMAN, LEO. *Cuba: Anatomy of a Revolution.* New York, 1961.

MacGAFFEY, WYATH. *Cuba: Its People, Its Society, Its Culture.* New York, 1962.

MAÑACH, JORGE. *Martí, Apostle of Freedom.* Translated by COLEY TAYLOR. New York, 1950.

NELSON, LOWRY. *Rural Cuba.* Minneapolis, 1950.

ORTIZ, FERNANDO. *Cuban Counterpoint: Tobacco and Sugar.* Translated by HARRIET DE ONÍS. New York, 1947.

PFLAUM, IRVING P. *Tragic Island: How Communism Came to Cuba.* Englewood Cliffs, N.J., 1961.

WRIGHT, IRENE A. *The Early History of Cuba, 1492–1586.* New York, 1916.

B. Literature, Music, and Art

CARPENTIER, ALEJO. *Explosion in a Cathedral (El siglo de las luces).* Boston, 1963.

——. *The Kingdom of This World (El reino de este mundo).* New York, 1949.

——. *The Lost Steps (Los pasos perdidos).* New York, 1953.

FORD, J. D. M. *A Bibliography of Cuban Belles-Lettres.* Cambridge, Mass., 1933.

GÓMEZ SICRE, JOSÉ. *Cuban Painting of Today (Pintura cubana de hoy).* Bilingual text, with English translation by H. T. RIDDLE. Havana, 1944.

————. *Four Artists of the Americas.* Translated by GEORGE E. COMPTON. Washington, D.C., 1957. (Includes Amelia Peláez of Cuba.)

GRENET, EMILIO (ed.). *Popular Cuban Music: Eighty Revised and Corrected Compositions, Together with an Essay on the Evolution of Music in Cuba.* Havana, 1939.

STIMSON, FREDERICK S. *Cuba's Romantic Poet: The Story of Plácido.* Chapel Hill, N.C., 1964.

WILLIAMS, EDWIN B. *The Life and Dramatic Works of Gertrude Gómez de Avellaneda.* Philadelphia, 1924.

IX. DOMINICAN REPUBLIC

A. History and Description

BOSCH, JUAN. *The Unfinished Experiment: Democracy in the Dominican Republic (Crisis de la democracia de América en la República Dominicana).* New York, 1965.

COOPER, PAGE. *Sambumbia: A Discovery of the Dominican Republic, the Modern Hispaniola.* New York, 1947.

FAGG, JOHN E. *Cuba, Haiti, and the Dominican Republic.* Englewood Cliffs, N.J., 1965.

HICKS, ALBERT C. *Blood in the Streets: The Life and Rule of Trujillo.* New York, 1946.

RODMAN, SELDEN. *Quisqueya: A History of the Dominican Republic.* Seattle, 1964.

WALKER, STANLEY. *Journey Toward the Sunlight: A Story of the Dominican Republic and Its People.* New York, 1947.

B. Literature, Music, and Art

ANDRADE, MANUEL JOSÉ. *Folklore of the Dominican Republic.* New York, 1930.

COOPERSMITH, JACOB. *Music and Musicians of the Dominican Republic*. Washington, D.C., 1949.

GALVÁN, MANUEL DE JESÚS. *The Cross and the Sword*. Translation of *Enriquillo* by ROBERT GRAVES. Foreword by MAX HENRÍQUEZ UREÑA. Bloomington, Ind., 1954.

KRIEGER, HERBERT W. *Aboriginal Indian Pottery of the Dominican Republic*. Washington, D.C., 1931.

X. ECUADOR

A. History and Description

BLANKSTEN, GEORGE I. *Ecuador: Constitutions and Caudillos*. Berkeley, Calif., 1951.

BLOMBERG, ROLF (ed.). *Ecuador: Andean Mosaic*. Stockholm, 1952.

EICHLER, ARTURO. *Ecuador: Snow Peaks and Jungles*. New York, 1955.

FRANKLIN, ALBERT B. *Ecuador: Portrait of a People*. Garden City, N.Y., 1943.

LINKE, LILO. *Ecuador: Country of Contrasts*. 3d ed. London and New York, 1960.

RUSSELL, WILLIAM R. *The Bolivar Countries: Colombia, Ecuador, Venezuela*. New York, 1949.

VON HAGEN, VICTOR W. *Ecuador and the Galapagos Islands*. Norman, Okla., 1949.

B. Literature

GIL GILBERT, ENRIQUE. *Our Daily Bread (Nuestro pan)*. Translated by DUDLEY POORE. New York, 1943.

RIVERA, GUILLERMO. *A Tentative Bibliography of the Belles-Lettres of Ecuador*. Cambridge, Mass., 1934.

XI. MEXICO

A. Pre-Hispanic Culture and Civilization

BERNAL, IGNACIO. *Mexico Before Cortez: Art, History, Legend*. Translation of *Tenochtitlan en una isla* by WILLIS BARNSTONE. New York, 1963.

————. ed. *Mexican Wall Paintings of the Maya and Aztec Periods*. New York, 1964.

BRINTON, DANIEL G. *Ancient Nahuatl Poetry: Sacred Songs of the Ancient Mexicans*. Philadelphia, 1890.

CASO, ALFONSO. *The People of the Sun*. Norman, Okla., 1958.

CLARK, JAMES C. (trans.). *Codex Mendoza*. 3 vols. London, 1938.

CORNYN, JOHN H. (trans.). *The Song of Quetzalcoatl*. Translated from the Aztec. Yellow Springs, Ohio, 1931.

DURÁN, DIEGO. *The Aztecs: The History of the Indies of New Spain*. Translated, with notes, by DORIS HEYDEN and FERNANDO HORCASITAS. Introduction by IGNACIO BERNAL. New York, 1964.

KINGSBOROUGH, LORD (EDWARD KING). *Antiquities of Mexico*. 9 vols. London, 1930–48.

MAUDSLEY, A. P. (ed.). *The Maya and Their Neighbors*. New York, 1940.

MOTOLINÍA, TORIBIO DE. *History of the Indians of New Spain*. Translated by ELIZABETH ANDROS FORSTER. Berkeley, Calif., 1950.

————. *Motolinia's History of the Indians of New Spain*. Translated and annotated, with a bio-bibliographical study of the author, by FRANCIS BORGIA STECK. Washington, D.C., 1951.

PETERSON, FREDERICK A. *Ancient Mexico: An Introduction to the Pre-Hispanic Cultures*. New York, 1959.

REED, ALMA. *The Ancient Past of Mexico*. New York, 1964.

ROBERTSON, DONALD. *Mexican Manuscript Painting of the Early Colonial Period*. New Haven, Conn., 1959.

SAHAGÚN, BERNARDINO DE. *General History of the Things of New Spain*. (The *Florentine Codex*.) Translated from the Aztec, with notes and illustrations, by ARTHUR J. O. ANDERSON and CHARLES E. DIBBLE. 10 vols. Santa Fe, N.M., 1950–61.

————. *A History of Ancient Mexico (Historia general de las cosas de Nueva España)*. Translated by FANNY BANDELIER. Nashville, Tenn., 1932. (Books I–IV.)

SPINDEN, HERBERT J. *Ancient Civilizations of Mexico and Central America.* New York, 1928.

THOMPSON, J. ERIC. *Mexico Before Cortez.* New York, 1933.

VAILLANT, GEORGE C. and SUZANNAH B. *The Aztecs of Mexico.* Rev. ed. New York, 1962.

VON HAGEN, VICTOR W. *The Aztec: Man and Tribe.* New York, 1962.

WESTHEIM, PAUL. *Art of Ancient Mexico.* Translated by U. BERNARD. New York. 1963.

————. *Sculpture of Ancient Mexico.* New York, 1963.

ZORITA (ZURITA), ALONSO DE. *Life and Labor in Ancient Mexico: The Brief and Summary Relation of the Lords of New Spain.* Translated by BENJAMIN KEEN. New Brunswick, N.J., 1963.

B. Political and Cultural History

BANCROFT, HERBERT H. *The Conquest of Mexico.* 3 vols. New York, 1883.

BENÍTEZ, FERNANDO. *The Century After Cortez (Los primeros mexicanos: La vida criolla en el siglo XVI).* Translated by JOAN MACLEAN. Chicago, 1965.

BRADEN, C. S. *Religious Aspects of the Conquest of Mexico.* Durham, N.C., 1930.

BRANDENBURG, FRANK R. *Making of Modern Mexico.* New York, 1964.

CALCOTT, WILFRED H. *Liberalism in Mexico, 1857–1929.* Hamden, Conn., 1965.

CERWIN, HERBERT. *Bernal Díaz: Historian of the Conquest.* Norman, Okla., 1963.

CLINE, HOWARD F. *Mexico: From Revolution to Evolution.* New York, 1962.

CORTÉS, HERNÁN. *Letters of Cortés.* Translated and edited by F. A. MACNUTT. 2 vols. New York and London, 1908.

CUMBERLAND, CHARLES C. *Mexican Revolution: Genesis Under Madero.* Austin, Tex., 1952.

DÍAZ DEL CASTILLO, BERNAL. *The Conquest of New Spain.* Translated by J. M. COHEN. Baltimore, 1963.

————. *The Discovery and Conquest of Mexico*. Introduction by IRVING LEONARD. New York, 1965.

————. *The True History of the Conquest of New Spain*. Translated by A. P. MAUDSLEY. 5 vols. London. 1908–16.

GIBSON, CHARLES. *The Aztecs Under Spanish Rule: A History of the Indians of the Valley of Mexico, 1519–1810*. Stanford, Calif., 1964.

KNELLER, GEORGE F. *The Education of the Mexican Nation*. New York, 1951.

LEÓN-PORTILLA, MIGUEL (ed.). *Broken Spears: The Aztec Account of the Conquest of Mexico*. Translated by LYSANDER KEMP. Boston, 1962.

PARKES, HENRY B. *History of Mexico*. Rev. ed. New York, 1960.

PRESCOTT, WILLIAM H. *The Conquest of Mexico*. Edited by T. A. JOYCE and illustrated by KEITH HENDERSON. 2 vols. New York, 1922. (Also available in a Modern Library edition, together with *The Conquest of Peru*.)

RAMOS, SAMUEL. *Profile of Man and Culture in Mexico*. Translated by PETER G. EARLE. Austin, Tex., 1962.

ROMANELL, PATRICK. *Making of the Mexican Mind*. Lincoln, Neb., 1952.

TANNENBAUM, FRANK. *Mexico: The Struggle for Peace and Bread*. New York, 1950.

TIMMONS, WILBERT H. *Morelos of Mexico: Priest, Soldier, Statesman*. El Paso, Tex., 1963.

VASCONCELOS, JOSÉ, and MANUEL GAMIO. *Aspects of Mexican Civilization*. Chicago, 1926.

WILGUS, A. CURTIS (ed.). *The Caribbean: Mexico Today*. Gainesville, Fla., 1964.

C. Literary History and Criticism

BRUSHWOOD, J. S. *The Romantic Novel in Mexico*. Columbia, Mo., 1954.

LEONARD, IRVING A. *Baroque Times in Old Mexico*. Ann Arbor, Mich., 1959.

————. *Don Carlos de Sigüenza y Góngora—A Mexican Savant of the Seventeenth Century*. Berkeley, Calif., 1929.

MARTÍNEZ, JOSÉ LUIS (ed.). *The Modern Mexican Essay.* Translated by H. W. HILBORN. Toronto, 1965.

READ, J. LLOYD. *The Mexican Historical Novel, 1826–1910.* New York, 1939.

SPELL, JEFFERSON R. *The Life and Works of José Fernández de Lizardi.* Philadelphia, 1931.

WALKER, NELL. *The Life and Works of Manuel Gutiérrez Nájera.* Columbia, Mo., 1927.

WELLMAN, ESTHER T. *Amado Nervo: Mexico's Religious Poet.* New York, 1936.

D. Literature in Translation

AZUELA, MARIANO. *Marcela: A Mexican Love Story (Mala yerba).* Translated by ANITA BRENNER. New York, 1932.

———. *Two Novels of Mexico: The Flies, The Bosses (Las moscas* and *Los caciques).* Translated by LESLEY B. SIMPSON. Berkeley, Calif., 1956.

———. *The Underdogs (Los de abajo).* Translated by E. MUNGUÍA. New York, 1929.

FERNÁNDEZ DE LIZARDI, JOSÉ JOAQUÍN. *The Itching Parrot (El periquillo sarniento).* Translated, and with an Introduction, by KATHERINE ANNE PORTER. Garden City, N.Y., 1942.

FUENTES, CARLOS. *Aura.* Translated by LYSANDER KEMP. New York, 1965.

———. *The Death of Artemio Cruz.* New York, 1964.

———. *The Good Conscience (Las buenas conciencias).* Translated by SAM HILEMAN. New York, 1961.

———. *Where the Air Is Clear (La región más transparente).* Translated by SAM HILEMAN. New York, 1960.

GUZMÁN, MARTÍN LUIS. *The Eagle and the Serpent (El aguila y la serpiente).* Translated by HARRIET DE ONÍS. New York, 1930.

———. *Memoirs of Pancho Villa.* Translated by V. TAYLOR. Austin, Tex., 1965.

LÓPEZ Y FUENTES, GREGORIO. *El Indio.* Translated by ANITA BRENNER. Indianapolis, 1937.

MAGDALENO, MAURICIO. *Sunburst (El resplendor)*. Translated by ANITA BRENNER. New York, 1944.

MENÉNDEZ, MIGUEL ANGEL. *Nayar*. Translated by ANGEL FLORES. New York, 1942.

NERVO, AMADO. *Confessions of a Modern Poet*. Translated by DOROTHY KRESS. Boston, 1935.

———. *Plenitude*. Translated by W. F. RICE. Los Angeles, 1928.

———. *Plenitude*. Translated by A. TEJA ZABRE. Mexico, 1938.

PAZ, OCTAVIO (ed.). *Anthology of Mexican Poetry*. Translated by SAMUEL BECKETT. Indianapolis, 1958.

———. *The Labyrinth of Solitude: Life and Thought in Mexico*. Translated by LYSANDER KEMP. New York, 1962.

———. *Selected Poems of Octavio Paz*. A bilingual edition, with English translations by MURIEL RUKEYSER. Bloomington, Ind., 1963.

TORRES BODET, JAIME. *Selected Poems*. A bilingual edition, with English translations by SONJA KARSEN. Bloomington, Ind., 1964.

VASCONCELOS, JOSÉ. *A Mexican Ulysses (Ulises criollo)*. Translated and abridged by W. REX CRAWFORD. Bloomington, Ind., 1963.

YAÑEZ, AGUSTÍN. *The Edge of the Storm (Al filo del agua)*. Translated by ETHEL BRINTON. Austin, Tex., 1963.

E. Description and Interpretation

CALDERÓN DE LA BARCA, FRANCES ERSKINE INGLIS. *Life in Mexico During a Residence of Two Years in That Country*. (First published in 1843.) New York, 1931.

COVARRUBIAS, MIGUEL. *Mexico South: The Isthmus of Tehuantepec*. New York, 1946.

GRUENING, ERNEST. *Mexico and Its Heritage*. New York, 1928.

HERRING, HUBERT C., and KATHERINE TERRILL (eds.). *The Genius of Mexico*. New York, 1931.

HERRING, HUBERT C., and HERBERT WEINSTOCK (eds.). *Renascent Mexico*. New York, 1935.

HOYNINGEN-HUENE, GEORGE. *Mexican Heritage*. Photographs by HOYNINGEN-HUENE, with text by ALFONSO REYES. New York, 1946.

REYES, ALFONSO. *Mexico in a Nutshell and Other Essays.* Translated by CHARLES RAMSDELL. Berkeley, Calif., 1964.

F. Anthropology and Sociology

BRENNER, ANITA. *Idols Behind Altars*. New York, 1929.

LEWIS, OSCAR. *The Children of Sánchez: Autobiography of a Mexican Family*. New York, 1961.

———. *Tepoztlán, Village in Mexico*. New York, 1960.

PARSONS, ELSIE C. *Mitla, Town of Souls*. Chicago, 1936.

REDFIELD, ROBERT. *Tepoztlán, a Mexican Village: A Study of Folk Life*. Chicago, 1930.

———. *Folk Culture of Yucatán*. Chicago, 1941.

WHETTEN, NATHAN L. *Rural Mexico*. Chicago, 1948.

WOLF, ERIC. *Sons of the Shaking Earth*. Chicago, 1959.

G. Plastic and Graphic Arts

BORN, ESTHER. *New Architecture in Mexico*. With supplementary articles on contemporary painting and sculpture by JUSTINO FERNÁNDEZ. New York, 1937.

CASTRO LEAL, ANTONIO, *et al. Twenty Centuries of Mexican Art*. Mexico, 1940.

CETTO, MAX L. *Modern Architecture in Mexico*. New York, 1961.

CHARLOT, JEAN. *Mexican Art and the Academy of San Carlos*. Austin, Tex., 1962.

———. *The Mexican Mural Renaissance, 1920–1925*. New Haven, Conn., 1962.

COVARRUBIAS, MIGUEL. *Indian Art in Mexico and Central America*. Mexico, 1940.

DICKERSON, ALBERT I. (ed.). *The Orozco Frescoes at Dartmouth*. Hanover, N.H., 1934.

EDWARDS, EMILY. *Frescoes by Diego Rivera in Cuernavaca*. Mexico, 1932.

————. *Modern Mexican Frescoes*. Mexico, 1934.

EVANS, ERNESTINE. *The Frescoes of Diego Rivera*. New York, 1929.

FABER, COLIN. *Candela, Master of Shells*. New York, 1963.

HALE, GARDNER. *Fresco Painting*. With a Preface by JOSÉ CLEMENTE OROZCO. New York, 1933.

HELM, MACKINLEY. *Man of Fire: José Clemente Orozco*. New York, 1953.

————. *Modern Mexican Painters*. New York, 1941.

KUBLER, GEORGE. *Mexican Architecture of the Sixteenth century*. 2 vols. New Haven, Conn., 1948.

MYERS, BERNARD. *Mexican Painting in Our Time*. New York, 1956.

MYERS, I. E. *Mexico's Modern Architecture*. In cooperation with the National Institute of Fine Arts of Mexico. New York, 1952.

OROZCO, JOSÉ CLEMENTE. *Autobiography*. Translated by ROBERT C. STEPHENSON. Austin, Tex., 1962.

PAINE, FRANCES F. *Diego Rivera*. With notes by JERE ABBOTT. New York, 1931.

PIERROT, GEORGE F., and EDGAR P. RICHARDSON. *The Diego Rivera Frescoes*. Detroit, 1934.

REED, ALMA M. *José Clemente Orozco*. New York, 1956.

————. *The Mexican Muralists*. New York, 1960.

RIVERA, DIEGO. *The Frescoes of Diego Rivera*. Nineteen color reproductions, and with explanatory notes by JERE ABBOTT. New York, 1933.

————, and BERTRAM D. WOLFE. *Portrait of America*. New York, 1934.

————. *Portrait of Mexico*. New York, 1937.

SCHMECKEBIER, LAURENCE E. *Modern Mexican Art*. Minneapolis, 1939.

SHIPWAY, VERA C. and WARREN. *The Mexican House, Old and New*. New York, 1961.

STEWART, VIRGINIA. *Contemporary Mexican Artists*. Palo Alto, Calif., 1951.

WOLFE, BERTRAM D. *The Fabulous Life of Diego Rivera*. New York, 1963.

H. Music, Dance, and Folklore

CHÁVEZ, CARLOS. *My Musical Thought*. Cambridge, Mass., 1961.

COPLAND, AARON. *Our New Music*. New York, 1941. (Includes "Composer from Mexico: Carlos Chávez.")

MARTÍ, SAMUEL, and GERTRUDE PROKOSCH KURATH. *Dances of Anáhuac: The Choreography and Music of Precortesian Dances*. Chicago, 1964.

MENDOZA, VICENTE. *Mexican Folksongs: Selected and Harmonized*. New York, 1948.

SIMMONS, MERLE E. *The Mexican Corrido as a Source for Interpretive Study of Modern Mexico (1870–1950)*. Bloomington, Ind., 1957.

STEVENSON, ROBERT. *The Music of Mexico*. New York, 1952.

TOOR, FRANCES. *A Treasury of Mexican Folkways: The Customs, Myths, Folklore, Traditions, Beliefs, Fiestas, Dances, and Songs of the Mexican People*. New York, 1947. (Includes 100 drawings by Carlos Mérida.)

WEINSTOCK, HERBERT. *Carlos Chávez*. Washington, D.C., 1944.

———. *Mexican Music: Notes for Concerts Arranged by Carlos Chávez as Part of the Exhibition: Twenty Centuries of Mexican Art, at the Museum of Modern Art*. New York, 1940.

XII. PARAGUAY

A. Cultural Background

CUNNINGHAME GRAHAM, ROBERT B. *A Vanished Arcadia: Being Some Account of the Jesuits in Paraguay, 1607 to 1767*. New York and London, 1924.

ELLIOTT, ARTHUR E. *Paraguay: Its Cultural Heritage, Social Conditions, and Educational Problems*. New York, 1931.

RAPHAEL, MAXWELL I. *A Tentative Bibliography of Paraguayan Literature*. Cambridge, Mass., 1934.

B. History and Biography

CUNNINGHAME GRAHAM, ROBERT B. *Portrait of a Dictator: Francisco Solano López (1865–1870)*. London, 1933.

PENDLE, GEORGE. *Paraguay: A Riverside Nation.* 2d ed. London and New York, 1956.

RAINE, PHILIP. *Paraguay.* New Brunswick, N.J., 1956.

SERVICE, ELMAN R. *Spanish-Guarani Relations in Early Colonial Paraguay.* Ann Arbor, Mich., 1954.

WARREN, HARRIS G. *Paraguay: An Informal History.* Norman, Okla., 1949.

XIII. PERU

A. Archaeology and Indigenous Cultures

BENNETT, WENDELL C., and JUNIUS BIRD. *Andean Culture History.* 2d rev. ed. New York, 1964.

BINGHAM, HIRAM. *Lost City of the Incas: The Story of Machu Picchu and Its Builders.* New York, 1948.

BRUNDAGE, BURR C. *Empire of the Inca.* Norman, Okla., 1963.

BUSHNELL, GEOFFREY H. S. *Peru.* Rev. ed. New York, 1963.

CIEZA DE LEÓN, PEDRO DE. *The Incas.* Translated by HARRIET DE ONÍS. Edited by VICTOR W. VON HAGEN. Norman, Okla., 1959.

DOERING, HEINRICH U. *The Art of Ancient Peru.* New York, 1952.

GARCILASO DE LA VEGA, EL INCA. *The Incas: The Royal Commentaries of the Inca Garcilaso de la Vega.* Translated by MARÍA JOLAS from the critical, annotated French edition of ALAIN GHEERBRAUT. New York, 1961.

———. *Royal Commentaries of the Inca and the General History of Peru.* Translated by H. V. LIVERMORE. Austin, Tex., 1965.

D'HARCOURT, RAOUL, *et al. Textiles of Ancient Peru and Their Techniques.* Translated by S. BROWN. Seattle, 1965.

MASON, J. ALDEN. *The Ancient Civilizations of Peru.* Baltimore, 1957.

MEAD, CHARLES W. *The Incas of Peru.* New York, 1924.

MEANS, PHILIP A. *Ancient Civilizations of the Andes.* New York and London, 1936.

MÚJICA GALLO, MIGUEL. *The Gold of Peru*. With an Introduction by RAÚL PORRAS BARRENECHEA. Recklinghausen, West Germany, 1959.

SARMIENTO DE GAMBOA, PEDRO. *History of the Incas*. Edited and translated by SIR CLEMENTS R. MARKHAM. Cambridge, Eng., 1907.

VALCÁRCEL, LUIS E. *Ancient Peruvian Art: Sculpture*. Lima, 1937.

VON HAGEN, VICTOR W. *Realm of the Incas*. New York, 1961.

B. History and Social Science

ADAMS, RICHARD N. *A Community in the Andes: Problems and Progress in Muquiyauyo*. Seattle, 1959.

KANTOR, HARRY. *The Ideology and Program of the Peruvian Aprista Movement*. Berkeley, Calif., 1953.

MEANS, PHILIP A. *Fall of the Inca Empire and the Spanish Rule in Peru, 1530–1780*. New York, 1932.

PIZARRO, PEDRO. *Relation of the Discovery and Conquest of the Kingdoms of Peru*. Edited and translated by PHILIP A. MEANS. 2 vols. New York, 1921.

PRESCOTT, WILLIAM H. *History of the Conquest of Peru*. London, 1847. (A Modern Library edition is available.)

STEIN, WILLIAM W. *Hualcan: Life in the Highlands of Peru*. Ithaca, N.Y., 1961.

C. Literature in Translation

ALEGRÍA, CIRO. *The Golden Serpent (La serpiente de oro)*. Translated by HARRIET DE ONÍS. New York, 1943.

———. *Broad and Alien Is the World (El mundo es ancho y ajeno)*. Translated by HARRIET DE ONÍS. New York, 1941.

"CONCOLORCORVO." *El Lazarillo: A Guide for Inexperienced Travellers Between Buenos Aires and Lima*. Translated by WALTER D. KLINE. Bloomington, Ind., 1965.

GARCÍA CALDERÓN, VENTURA. *The Lottery Ticket*. Translated by RICHARD PHIBBS. London, 1945.

————. *The White Llama (La venganza del condor).* Translated by RICHARD PHIBBS. London, 1938.

MATTO DE TURNER, CLORINDA. *Birds Without a Nest: A Story of Indian Life and Priestly Oppression in Peru (Aves sin nido).* Translated by C. J. THYME. London, 1904.

Ollanta: An Ancient Inca Drama. Bilingual edition: Quechua text, with English translation by CLEMENTS R. MARKHAM. London, 1871.

PALMA, RICARDO. *Knights of the Cape.* (Selections from *Tradiciones peruanas.*) Translated by HARRIET DE ONÍS. New York, 1945.

SANTOS CHOCANO, JOSÉ. *Spirit of the Andes.* Translated by EDNA W. UNDERWOOD. Portland, Ore., 1935.

D. Music and Art

ACHA, JUAN W. *Peru.* (Pan American Union Art in Latin America Today Series.) Washington, D.C., 1961.

COSSÍO DEL POMAR, FELIPE. *Peruvian Colonial Art: The Cuzco School of Painting.* Translated by G. ARBAIZA. New York, 1965.

MUSEUM OF FINE ARTS. *Twenty-five Centuries of Peruvian Art.* Boston, 1965.

SITWELL, SACHEVERELL. *Golden Wall and Mirador.* New York, 1961.

STEVENSON, ROBERT. *The Music of Peru: Aboriginal and Viceroyal Periods.* Washington, D.C., 1960.

WETHEY, HAROLD E. *Colonial Architecture and Sculpture in Peru.* Cambridge, Mass., 1949.

XIV. PUERTO RICO

AITKEN, THOMAS, JR. *Poet in the Fortress: The Story of Luis Muñoz Marín.* New York, 1964.

HANSON, EARL P. *Puerto Rico: Land of Wonders.* New York, 1960.

LEWIS, GORDON N. *Puerto Rico*. New York, 1963.

MIDDLEDICK, R. A. *The History of Porto Rico*. New York, 1903.

PAGE, HOMER. *Puerto Rico: The Quiet Revolution*. New York, 1963.

RAND, CHRISTOPHER. *The Puerto Ricans*. New York, 1958.

RIVERA, GUILLERMO. *A Tentative Bibliography of the Belles-Lettres of Porto Rico*. Cambridge, Mass., 1931.

XV. URUGUAY

A. General

FITZGIBBON, RUSSELL A. *Uruguay: Portrait of a Democracy*. New Brunswick, N.J., 1954.

HUDSON, W. H. *The Purple Land*. New York, 1927.

PENDLE, GEORGE. *Uruguay: South America's First Welfare State*. 3d ed. New York, 1963.

STREET, JOHN. *Artigas and the Emancipation of Uruguay*. Cambridge, Eng., 1959.

TAYLOR, PHILIP B. *Government and Politics of Uruguay*. New Orleans, 1960.

B. Literature

COESTER, ALFRED L. *A Tentative Bibliography of the Belles-Lettres of Uruguay*. Cambridge, Mass., 1931.

PEREDA, ENRIQUE. *Rodó's Main Sources*. San Juan, P.R., 1948.

RODÓ, ENRIQUE. *Ariel*. Translated by F. J. STIMSON, with an introductory essay by the author. Boston, 1922.

———. *The Motives of Proteus (Motivos de Proteo)*. With a brief essay on Rodó by HAVELOCK ELLIS. New York, 1928.

QUIROGA, HORACIO. *South American Jungle Tales (Cuentos de la selva)*. Translated by ARTHUR LIVINGSTON. New York, 1922.

TINKER, EDWARD LAROQUE. *The Cult of the Gaucho and the Creation of a Literature*. Worcester, Mass., 1947.

———. *Life and Literature of the Pampas*. Gainesville, Fla., 1961.

XVI. VENEZUELA

A. General

ALEXANDER, ROBERT J. *The Venezuelan Democratic Revolution: A Profile of the Regime of Rómulo Bettancourt.* New Brunswick, N.J., 1964.

LIEUWEN, EDWIN. *Venezuela.* 2d ed. London and New York, 1965.

MARSLAND, WILLIAM D. and AMY L. *Venezuela Through Its History.* New York, 1954.

MORÓN, GUILLERMO. *A History of Venezuela.* Edited and translated by JOHN STREET. New York, 1964.

WATTERS, MARY. *A History of the Church in Venezuela, 1810–1930.* Chapel Hill, N.C., 1933.

B. Literature and Music

BLANCO-FOMBONA, RUFINO. *The Man of Gold.* Translated by ISAAC GOLDBERG. New York, 1920.

GALLEGOS, RÓMULO. *Doña Barbara.* Translated by ROBERT MALLOY. New York, 1931.

MILINOWSKI, MARTA. *Teresa Carreño, "By the Grace of God."* New Haven and London, 1940.

RADCLIFF, DILLWYN F. *Venezuelan Prose Fiction.* New York, 1933.

USLAR-PIETRI, ARTURO. *The Red Lances (Las lanzas rojas).* New York, 1963.

Biographical Index

The Spanish letters *ch*, *ll*, and *rr* are indexed in accordance with English alphabetization.

Brazilian and Portuguese compound names, except those that are hyphenated and those few governed by custom (e.g., Santos Dumont), are entered under the last surname.